W9-BXD-185

CULTURAL CITIZENSHIP

ISSUES in CULTURAL and MEDIA STUDIES

Series editor: Stuart Allen

Published titles:

CULTURAL CITIZENSHIP
Cosmopolitan Questions

Nick Stevenson

OPEN UNIVERSITY PRESS

Open University Press
McGraw-Hill Education
McGraw-Hill House
Shoppenhangers Road
Maidenhead
Berkshire
England
SL6 2QL

email: enquiries@openup.co.uk
world wide web: www.openup.co.uk

First published 2003

Copyright © Nick Stevenson 2003

All rights reserved. Except for the quotation of short passages for the purpose of criticism and review, no part of this publication may be reproduced, stored in a retrieval system, or transmitted, in any form or by any means, electronic, mechanical, photocopying, recording or otherwise, without the prior written permission of the publisher or a licence from the Copyright Licensing Agency Limited. Details of such licences (for reprographic reproduction) may be obtained from the Copyright Licensing Agency Ltd of 90 Tottenham Court Road, London, W1T 4LP.

A catalogue record of this book is available from the British Library

ISBN 0 335 20878 9 (pb)   0 335 20879 7 (hb)

Library of Congress Cataloging-in-Publication Data
CIP data applied for

Typeset by RefineCatch Limited, Bungay, Suffolk
Printed in the UK by Bell & Bain Ltd, Glasgow

For Raymond Williams

[The] belief that human beings can live in radically different ways, by radically different values, in radically different kinds of social order. It is always the pressure not to believe this, by what is in the end a parachialism in time.

Raymond Williams

CONTENTS

SERIES EDITOR'S FOREWORD

'Citizenship,' in the words of Martha Gellhorn, one of the last century's greatest war correspondents, 'is a tough occupation.' She believed that as citizens we are obliged to make our own informed opinion, and to stand by it. 'The evils of the time change,' she observed, 'but are never in short supply and would go unchallenged unless there were conscientious people to say: not if I can help it.' Dissent, based on morality and reason, is at the heart of what it means to be a citizen, in her view. And while the challenge of citizenship may be getting more difficult all of the time, there is nevertheless always room for optimism. 'There has to be a better way to run the world,' she insisted, 'and we better see that we get it.'

Precisely what is meant by the word 'citizenship', especially with regard to certain avowed rights, obligations or responsibilities associated with it, is historically-specific and will vary dramatically from one national context to the next. In any given society this process of definition is never secured once and for all, of course, but rather is subject to the contradictions of power, especially as they are experienced, negotiated and resisted as part of everyday life. It is by exploring a range of pressing questions at this level, the very materiality of our lived engagement with citizenship, that Nick Stevenson's *Cultural Citizenship* seeks to intervene in current debates. 'Cultural citzenship', he argues, is a newly emerging interdisciplinary concept that is concerned with issues of recognition and respect, of responsibility and pleasure, and with visibility and marginality. It encompasses politics with a capital and a small 'p', such that viewing a soap opera can be regarded as being just as political as voting in an election. At the same time, Stevenson contends, the concept of cultural citizenship is also concerned to search for a new ethics that can help guide us through these turbulent and contested times.

Cultural Citizenship brings together perspectives from political theory, social theory and cultural studies. The book's distinctiveness lies in its commitment to providing a critical examination of culture and citizenship that cuts across these disciplinary boundaries. In the case of multiculturalism, for example, Stevenson argues that it has been political theorists who have sought to investigate the normative significance of living in an increasingly pluralistic society. How does the polity in modern societies respond to a diversity of claims for recognition, from the physically-challenged to different ethnic minorities? Still, he suggests, it has been social theory that has perhaps most clearly sought to explain how these claims are linked to globalisation, new communication technologies, and the displacement of peoples from their host nation. Moreover, social theorists are more likely to be concerned with how the citizenship claims which emerge in this context are the result of ideological struggle, demands by social movements and questions of power and influence. Turning to cultural studies, Stevenson points out that important work has been undertaken to recover the subjugated knowledges of the displaced and marginalised. In this respect, then, multiculturalism goes beyond the struggle for political rights, entailing new forms of recognition for a wide range of cultural practices. *Cultural Citizenship*, in its critical assessment of the connections that can be discerned across these three areas of enquiry, invites new ways of thinking about citizenship for a new century.

The *Issues in Cultural and Media Studies* series aims to facilitate a diverse range of critical investigations into pressing questions considered to be central to current thinking and research. In light of the remarkable speed at which the conceptual agendas of cultural and media studies are changing, the authors are committed to contributing to what is an ongoing process of re-evaluation and critique. Each of the books is intended to provide a lively, innovative and comprehensive introduction to a specific topical issue from a fresh perspective. The reader is offered a thorough grounding in the most salient debates indicative of the book's subject, as well as important insights into how new modes of enquiry may be established for future explorations. Taken as a whole, then, the series is designed to cover the core components of cultural and media studies courses in an imaginatively distinctive and engaging manner.

Stuart Allan

ACKNOWLEDGEMENTS

I would like to thank Stuart Allan and Justin Vaughan for their help and considerable patience while they have been waiting for me to finish this book. I would also like to thank Maurice Roche, Kate Nash, Bryan Turner, Ruth Lister and Gerard Delanty for writing such good books on citizenship and for suggesting that it might be a topic that interested me. This work has been the product of the devising of a new course for the students at the School of Sociology and Social Policy on citizenship, and I should like to thank Julia O'Connell Davison (with whom I teach the course) for making it a pleasure rather than a chore.

This book would also have been very different if it had not been for the comments and conversations of Michael Kenny, Anthony Elliott, Steven Yearley, Joke Hermes, Nigel Clark, Jagdish Patel, Anthony Giddens, Paul Ransome, Claire Annesley, David Hesmondhaugh, Peter Jackson, Robert Unwin and David Moore. If they look closely enough I'm sure they will be able to detect their presence in the text. I should also like to thank the Sheffield Political Theory Reading Group (which included Michael Kenny, Andrew Gamble and Mathew Festenstein among others) for the wine and for listening to an amateur political theorist. I should also like to thank the recently formed Sociology of Culture Reading Group at Nottingham (run by Alan Aldridge) for providing a stimulating place to exchange ideas.

Finally, the biggest thank you of all must go to Lucy James, who has read the text in its entirety (more than once) and has made many valuable suggestions and corrections. Both Lucy and our daughter Eve Anna James have served to remind me that questions of citizenship are never far from the more intimate details of our daily lives. Whether sorting the rubbish, watching television or changing a nappy, we are never outside of political concerns.

INTRODUCTION

This book has been written at a time when there has been a considerable revival of interest in the academic study of citizenship. There have been intense debates as to whether citizenship is in decline or whether it is in the process of being renewed in a new form appropriate for a global age. The study of citizenship has also been redefined by new questions arising from the growing significance of the media and popular culture, new social movements, feminism, globalization, the erosion of the environment and multiculturalism. Citizenship can no longer be exclusively defined by questions of class, but needs to be broadened to take on additional areas of study and concern. My contribution to this ongoing debate is to suggest ways in which 'cultural' questions might be linked to these dimensions. Whether we define citizenship through questions of rights, notions of obligation and duty, membership of overlapping communities or normalization, questions of culture are not far away. I show that the reasons for this are largely due to the fact that we can now be said to live in an informational and technological society unlike any other. Most of the assumptions and examples contained within this book come from the overdeveloped societies of North America and Europe. This work is not a view from nowhere but is located in questioning what kinds of citizenship are now appropriate for these societies, given a certain level of social, economic and, indeed, cultural development. More personally, the book evokes a time when I discovered through punk music that culture, difference and justice were linked in ways I had not previously appreciated. The argument offered here seeks to demonstrate the ways in which politics and culture are becoming increasingly interconnected within modern societies.

This book can also be read as an interdisciplinary guide to a range of concerns that have been raised by sociology, political theory and cultural studies. The work is a genuine hybrid. No doubt individual sociologists, political theorists and practitioners and theorists within cultural studies will find much to agree and disagree with in this respect. However, the book's success or failure will be determined by the extent to which I manage to persuade others of the importance of moving beyond their own disciplines in the study of citizenship. There is much to be learned from interdisciplinary studies within these and other areas. That this case still needs to be made highlights the unnecessary conservatism that remains at the heart of many academic debates.

In the first chapter I feel my way into some of the debates that have sought to link the study of citizenship and culture. The backdrop to the book, as I have mentioned, is the transformation to a new information-based society, and the continued relevance of questions of citizenship. Here I argue that ideas and perspectives from liberal and republican traditions of citizenship remain relevant. In particular, I demonstrate that a critical notion of civil society is central for cultural understandings of citizenship. From here, I also consider processes of normalization, globalization and individualization, before seeking to criticize communitarian understandings of citizenship. The aim of this first chapter is to promote the idea that cultural citizenship refers to the possibility of communication and dialogue within a cultural society. This is the dominant theme of the book, and recurs throughout the main chapters.

Chapter 2 develops a cosmopolitan understanding of citizenship at different levels that links global conceptions of citizenship with the development of the self, multiculturalism and the need for city-based citizenship. The idea of cosmopolitanism, which is perhaps the second main theme of the book, concerns the need to develop new democratic institutions that stretch beyond the borders of the nation, and to deconstruct the boundaries and oppositions that prevent the politicization of everyday life.

A concern with boundaries can also be found in Chapter 3, which begins by reconsidering the assumed oppositions between culture and nature. Ecological citizenship requires both new forms of public space and the political reconnection of questions of culture and nature if it is to raise many of the questions modern societies are currently seeking to avoid. Here I seek to argue for an ecological citizenship that has moved beyond individualized escape attempts and communalism to connect responsibility and pleasure in interesting ways.

Chapter 4, on mediated citizenship, similarly argues that ideas of nationhood have overly dominated our thinking. The rise of transnational media organizations, the mediated struggle for human rights, speed cultures, the Internet, gendered ideas of popular culture and compassion fatigue are just some of the reasons why we might readjust our assumptions in this regard. In this respect, the mediated dimensions of citizenship should now be considered central to the struggles for justice and recognition within a global arena.

Chapter 5 looks more closely at the impact of consumerism, consumption and cultural policy, before linking these concerns to those of citizenship. Here the dominant theme is the recovery of a common cultural citizenship that might be adequate for modern cosmopolitan societies. In this respect, I continue to find many of the ideas of Raymond Williams relevant to my study. It is, then, perhaps fitting that this book is dedicated to his 'living' memory.

I hope that this book will persuade those who are not familiar with the concept of citizenship of its continued relevance in the modern world. Here I have in mind some of my more sceptical students and academic critics. For others who are familiar with the citizenship literature, I hope to suggest that there is much to be learnt by studying its practice and conception through more cultural frameworks.

1 | CULTURAL CITIZENSHIP

Recent debates within cultural studies and citizenship studies might suggest that culture and citizenship have little in common. The term 'culture' is usually associated with a mix of public and private institutions, including museums, libraries, schools, cinemas and the media, while more specifically being connected with the dialogic production of meaning and aesthetics through a variety of practices. Citizenship, on the other hand, is more often thought to be about membership, belonging, rights and obligations. In institutional terms the terrain of citizenship is usually marked out by abstract legal definitions as to who is to be included and excluded from the political community. Yet whether we are talking about the risk society, network capitalism or the concerns of social movements, ideas of symbolic challenge and exclusion remain central.

The power to name, construct meaning and exert control over the flow of information within contemporary societies is one of today's central structural divisions. Power is not solely based upon material dimensions, but also involves the capacity to throw into question established codes and to rework frameworks of common understanding. This means that the locus of cultural citizenship will have to occupy positions both inside and outside the formal structures of administrative power. To talk of cultural citizenship means that we take questions of rights and responsibilities far beyond the technocratic agendas of mainstream politics and media. That is to say, we seek to form an appreciation of the ways in which 'ordinary' understandings become constructed, of issues of interpretative conflict and semiotic plurality more generally. In other words, how do questions of entitlement and duty relate to the diversity of culture evident within everyday life, and what is the relationship between an increasingly 'symbolic' society and the practice of politics? What modes of exclusion become apparent within an information society?

These concerns point to an age where our definitions of citizenship and society more generally are being transformed. Which community we owe our loyalties to, what foods are safe to eat, how important is the nation as opposed to more global concerns and how I might decide upon my sexuality all increasingly involve cultural questions. How we address these issues will depend upon shifting discourses and narratives that have become available to us in a variety of social contexts. As Castells (1997: 359) puts it, the 'sites of this power are people's minds'. Indeed, one of the central issues the book will seek to address is how we might provide fertile ground for what I shall call the cosmopolitan imagination. Many in the social sciences have neglected the idea of the imagination. Castoriadis (1997) has argued that all societies are dependent upon the creation of webs of meaning that are carried by society's institutions and individuals. Society, then, is always a self-creation that depends upon norms, values and languages that help to give diverse societies a sense of unity. The 'imaginary' is a social and historical creation, and serves to remind us that society must always create symbolic forms beyond the purely functional.

Cosmopolitanism is a way of viewing the world that among other things dispenses with national exclusivity, dichotomous forms of gendered and racial thinking and rigid separations between culture and nature. Such a sensibility would be open to the new spaces of political and ethical engagement that seeks to appreciate the ways in which humanity is mixed into intercultural ways of life. Arguably, cosmopolitan thinking is concerned with the transgression of boundaries and markers, and the development of an inclusive cultural democracy and citizenship. Yet cosmopolitanism is not only concerned with intermixing and the ethical relations between the self and the other, but seeks an institutional and political grounding in the context of shared global problems. A concern for cosmopolitan dimensions will inevitably seek to develop an understanding of the discourses, codes and narratives that make such political understandings a possibility. As Lawrence Grossberg (1992: 64) has argued, 'no democratic political struggle can be effectively organized without the power of the popular'. However, before moving on to such questions it is important to try to understand how issues of culture and citizenship became caught up with each other. Here I will argue that we need to consider the development of questions of cultural citizenship within the contours of a shared information society. The emergence of such a society requires not only that we rethink our notions of culture and citizenship, but also that we seek to develop a new understanding of contemporary social transformations.

T. H. Marshall and Raymond Williams: a cultural citizenship?

The idea of citizenship evokes a political tradition that is concerned to debate the involvement of individuals in shaping the laws and decisions of society. It has, however, only been in modern times that this has come to include people outside of a narrow class of educated property owners. While 'citizenship' has come to mean something different in, say, Iran, Chile and Britain, here I want to concentrate upon the meanings that have become connected to the term in North America and Europe. More recently, it has been the understandings that have become connected to the late T. H. Marshall's (1992) book *Citizenship and Social Class* that have had the greatest impact on ongoing debates.

T. H. Marshall (1992), as is well known, was concerned with the historical development of civil, political and social rights in the British national context. Marshall drew attention to the contradiction between the formations of capitalism and class, and the principle of equality enshrined within the granting of basic rights. Such a view of citizenship was hardly surprising given that Marshall was writing in the 1940s and 1950s, when identity and social conflicts were dominated by class. The setting up of the welfare state, the possibility of full male employment, the nuclear family, the dominance of the nation-state and the separation between an elite literary culture and a popular mass culture all inform his dimensions of citizenship. Marshall perceived that the principle of civil and political rights had been granted in the eighteenth and nineteenth centuries, whereas the twentieth century had seen the acceptance of the idea of social rights.

As many of Marshall's critics have pointed out, however, questions of civil and political rights are far from settled, and social rights were threatened once the post-war compromise between capital and labour came under attack (Roche 1994). Further, Turner (1994) argues that the postmodernization of culture and the globalization of politics have rendered much of the literature in respect of citizenship inadequate. The attack on traditional divisions between high and low culture poses serious questions in terms of the common or national cultures that might be transmitted by public institutions. The diversification and fragmentation of public tastes and lifestyles have undermined a previously assumed 'cultural' consensus. Further, the development of transnational spheres of governance, instantaneous news and global networks among new social movements has questioned the assumed connection between citizenship and the nation-state. These processes undermine, or at least call into question, the correspondence that citizenship has traditionally drawn between belonging and the nation-state. Marshall's analysis – while still influential – fails to locate the state within a complex web of international flows and relations, while assuming that the 'political' works within stable national cultures. The context of increasing cultural diversity and globalization brings to the fore questions of cultural, as well as civil, political and social, rights.

More recently, Jan Pakulski (1997) has argued that 'cultural' citizenship should be viewed in terms of satisfying demands for full inclusion into the social community. Such claims should be seen in the context of the waning of the welfare state and class identities, and the formation of new social and cultural movements focusing on the rights of groups from children to the disabled. Cultural rights, in this sense, herald 'a new breed of claims for unhindered representation, recognition without marginalisation, acceptance and integration without normalising distortion' (Pakulski 1997: 80). These rights go beyond rights for welfare protection, political representation or civil justice, and focus on the right to propagate a cultural identity or lifestyle. These claims, however, are likely to be as problematic as the implementation of social rights. Pakulski suggests that there is already a perceived backlash against 'politically correct' programmes and unease about bureaucratic attempts to regulate the cultural sphere. These questions aside, Pakulski (1997) argues that any attempt to rethink models of citizenship would have to problematize questions of culture in ways that are not evident in Marshall's initial formulation of citizenship (see also Turner 1994).

However, while criticisms of Marshall's neglect of culture are well represented within the citizenship literature, there have been other attempts to link cultural and political questions more systematically to an analysis of modern society. While we might point here to the early Frankfurt School and others, I think Raymond Williams outlined a more germane level of enquiry.

In this context, Williams provides an interesting contrast with Marshall, given their shared context of post-war British society. What Williams (1965) termed the 'long revolution' was an attempt to link economic, social and political issues to cultural questions. Here he problematized the development of standardized cultural products, a paternalistic state and a capitalist economic system that had stalled the possibility of a more participatory and genuinely diverse popular culture. Arguing in the context of British society in the 1960s, Williams suggested an alternative democratic framework, where a radically decentralized communications system would be open to the 'challenge and view' of a republic of voices (Williams 1962: 134). The idea was to represent the voices of ordinary people, artists and radical critics so that they might engage with a wider public on issues of common concern. As Ruth Lister (1997) has argued, liberal ideas of citizenship such as Marshall's tend to emphasize the institutional development of rights. This view, as Williams (1989a) clearly understood, needs to be supplemented with a republican emphasis upon popular participation. A society of actively engaged citizens requires both the protection offered by rights and opportunities to participate. Williams, along with other members of the New Left, sought to move towards a society that saw the development of more substantial economic rights (through participation within the workplace), the establishment of a genuinely democratic polity and a diverse civic and popular culture.

Williams (1965) called the long revolution the historical possibility of realizing the creative and learning potential of the people. This would witness the creation of the material conditions for an enlightened, educated and participatory democracy through a socialist transformation of society. Such a society would create the conditions for free, open and authentic expression. Williams offered an 'ideal type' of free communication when he wrote:

> A good society depends upon the free availability of facts and opinions, and on the growth of vision and consciousness – the articulation of what men have actually seen and known and felt. Any restriction of the freedom of individual contribution is actually a restriction of the resources of society.
>
> (Williams 1962: 124–5)

The dialectic of the long revolution is constituted through the contradiction between the maintenance of capitalism and the communicative 'potential' of ordinary people. That is, capitalism has facilitated the development of new technologies, broadened access to the education system and provided new means through which 'the people' could communicate with one another. However, the growth of a synthetic popular culture and the continued existence of class divisions and cultural elitism has prevented the possibility of the development of what Williams (1989b) termed a 'culture in common'.[1]

Unlike Marshall, then, Williams takes the organization of cultural production and the generation of a diversity of meanings to be central to the definition of modern society. The ways in which we communicate with one another and share cultural experiences cannot be considered a peripheral question in Williams's analysis. In this respect, he merges anthropological and artistic definitions of culture. For Williams, 'culture' signifies the dual meaning of a 'way of life' and the aesthetic creativity of artistic practices:

> A culture has two aspects: the known meanings and directions, which its members are trained to; the new observations and meanings, which are offered and tested. We use the culture in these two senses; to mean a whole way of life – the common meanings; to mean arts and learning – the special process of discovery and creative effort.
>
> (Williams 1988: 4)

Hence, while Marshall argues that the inclusive fabric of society mainly depends upon the provision of rights, Williams argues for the importance of society's communicative channels giving a voice to those excluded from the main centres of cultural and political power.[2] In short, Williams provides a model of cultural democracy that links questions of society, meaning and aesthetics in ways that are absent from Marshall's more legalistic framework. The common circulation of different artistic and political perspectives that are open to a range of popular criticism is key to the idea of the long revolution.

The long revolution is centrally concerned with the capacity of citizens to learn. While both Marshall and Williams perceive capitalism as the main obstacle to an inclusive society, it is Williams who more decisively links these questions to cultural concerns. For Marshall, to belong is to have access to rights. While for Williams this is important, it must be supplemented with the opportunities to shape the common culture. Inclusivity, then, is not just a matter of law, economics and politics, but is centrally defined by a cultural dimension.

Yet despite his many insights, Williams remains caught up with an analysis of culture and society that placed the labour movement at its centre, viewed the development of popular culture from a specifically literary perspective and is insufficiently concerned with questions of obligation (Stevenson 2002). The model outlined by Williams is premised on the idea that a socialist trans-formation of society would be accompanied by the displacement of commercial forms of culture by more literary and artistic alternatives. The problem here is perhaps similar to that with Marshall, in that we have now moved into a society that is quite different from the one within which Williams formulated his ideas. Yet what remains important is the way he links questions of democracy and social justice to a cultural arena.

As I have indicated, the perspectives of Marshall and Williams cannot be resurrected to resolve analytically the dilemmas of the present. Both were writing in the context of a society whose central conflicts were defined by 'industrialism'. By this I mean that both Marshall and Williams argued that society could be understood through a central conflict, and that this could be progressively transcended by a collectively constructed alternative social order. For Marshall it was the principle of equality upheld by civil, political and social rights as opposed to the dominant structure of a class society, and for Williams it was the communicative human nature of the people as opposed to the social power of state and capital. My argument is that society can no longer be defined through a master metaphor that reveals the 'essential nature' of other social relations. Further, notions of social and cultural progress need to be radically rethought. Before I outline what I take to be the new dimensions of a theory of culture and citizenship, we need to spend some time understanding this new society.

Cultural citizenship in the information age

What are the key components of an information society, and how does it differ from an industrial society? Further, in what ways does 'culture' play an increasingly defining role in helping to shape such a society? An information society offers a form of social transformation as profound as the industrial revolution. This, as we shall see throughout this book, has profound implications for the working of citizenship. While this will come later, here I want to demonstrate the main contours of this new society. This can be substantiated through six main arguments.

The first, as I have indicated, is that modern society cannot be defined through a central conflict. Sociology and political analysis more generally have tended to look to a single dynamic to explain the evolution of modern life (Giddens 1990). For example, we have already seen through Williams and Marshall just how popular such arguments were in seeking to explain the dynamics of industrial society. Such views are no longer sustainable (if they ever were) within an information society that has become increasingly organized through diverse networks. Hence, we might say that what structures are to industrial society, networks are to post-industrial society. Whereas structures imply that society has a centre that organizes or determines all the other social relations, the idea of networks implies a vision of dynamic circuits that have no defining centre. Networks are spread across space and time and are increasingly utilized to organize the places and spaces where we work, live, think and love.

We might view economies, media, social movements and transportations all as networks that are organized vertically rather than horizontally (Urry 2000a). If, as Melucci (1996a) comments, 'the system has no centre', then we will have to abandon metaphors that depend upon the 'overthrow' of the existing order, or the ideas of 'capturing power' or indeed of 'revolutionary programmes'. Modern society cannot be made to fit a unitary law that defines its essence. Radical forms of politics will have to rethink both concepts and strategies if they are to remain relevant to the modern world. As Laclau and Mouffe (1985) observed, society is constituted through a multiplicity of antagonisms in a discursive field that has no fixity.

The second argument is that information rather than labour power has become the key resource within modern society. In this new economy it is the application of knowledge and technology in customized production that best ensures economic success. The technological level of the enterprise is a much better guide to its competitiveness than older indices like labour costs (Castells 1996). The rapid development of informational technology in the 1970s in Silicon Valley in the USA enabled capital to restructure itself after the impacts of a worldwide recession. 'Informationalism' has allowed organizations to achieve increasing flexibility in terms of more knowledge-dependent and less hierarchical structures. New technology has enabled large structures to coordinate their activities worldwide, while building in reflexive inputs both to respond quickly to the current state of the market and to benefit from economies of scale (Castells and Hall 1994). Hence, whereas industrialism was oriented towards economic growth, informationalism is more concerned with the development of knowledge and the creation of networks. The digitalization of knowledge bases allows information to be processed and stored across huge distances. Thus capitalism depends less upon the state and more upon the ability of a common informational system to transmit knowledge across distanciated networks (Castells 1996).

The dominance of the flows of capital as opposed to the locality of labour has heightened processes of social exclusion. The new informational economy is characterized through simultaneous processes of economic development and underdevelopment. The 'black holes' of the informational economy include people who are socially and culturally outside of communication with mainstream society. While informationalism has led to increased employment within the higher tiers of management, there has also been a substantial reduction in low-skilled employment and heightened exclusion of the Earth's poorer regions from the flows of global capital. These excluded zones (which cannot be mapped on to any simple North/South divide) have responded to such processes by operating 'perverse' forms of inclusion. This has fostered the expansion of illegal and criminal economies within inner-city ghettos and the planet's most marginalized economies.

The informational economy also has definite cultural effects. Television in particular and the media in general have become central and defining institutions in modern society. Castells illustrates this by pointing to the fact that television currently frames the language and types of symbolic exchange that help to define society. The centrality of modern communications in contemporary culture therefore delivers not a mass culture, but what Castells calls a culture of 'real virtuality'. A media environment has now surpassed the idea of a mass culture, and messages are explicitly customized to the symbolic languages of the intended audience. The future will be governed not so much by a homogenous, mass produced culture repressing human diversity, but by a diversified popular culture where competitive advantage comes through product differentiation and audience segmentation. For Castells (1996), 'we are not living in a global village, but in customized cottages globally produced and locally distributed.'

The third major social change is the impact of globalization on modern economies, politics and cultures. A number of theorists have pointed to the emergence of a global cosmopolitan culture as significant in terms of questions related to citizenship. As Giddens (1994) argues, globalization should not be simply conceptualized as capitalization, as it includes such features as the technological ability of satellite communication to recontextualize imagery and information across time and space. Contemporary societies have witnessed the development of time–space distanciation that was not evident in pre-modern societies. By this Giddens means that within the pre-modern period time and space were always strongly located in terms of physical place. The turning of night into day or the passing of the seasons served to act as localized markers of time and space. With the invention of clock time we could say that time has become separated from space, and that time and space have become empty phenomena. The pulling apart of time and space can be visualized in calendars, railway timetables and maps. These devices enable time and space to be coordinated without any reference to notions of place – they are abstract means of ordering social activity. These processes can also be connected to what Giddens calls the disembedding of social systems.

Modernity, according to Giddens, is a post-traditional social order, where the 'emptying out' of time and space allows for the stretching of social relations. While global does not mean universal, international media organizations are none the less able to transport images and representations across time and space and on to the television sets of the globe's citizens. For Giddens, the relocation of information from localized contexts that is evident within modern communication networks is made possible via the uncoupling of time and space, and disembedding mechanisms such as technical media. These devices involve the separation of social relations 'from local contexts of interaction and their restructuring across indefinite spans of time–space' (Giddens 1990: 21).

These institutional transformations arguably make possible the increasingly global scope of much contemporary entertainment and news. More crucially, such processes produce cultural diasporas, in that communities of taste, habit and belief become detached from national contexts. The self-definition of community was until recently thought to be the primary responsibility of the nation-state. However, the legislative force of the state and ideas of community have become progressively decoupled. These cultural transformations, along with the implosion of expert cultures into everyday life, have helped to promote a world of culturally accomplished 'clever people' (Giddens 1994: 94). By this Giddens means that the populace of Western societies are used to eating foreign foods, challenging the professional power of their doctors and being informed about global events. He notes that the world in an information society is better informed than it ever has been.

Modern culture has both democratized 'expert cultures' and made widely available a surface familiarity with other ways of life that are distant in time and space. As Urry (1995) notes, mass communications, along with other cultural processes such as the internationalization of tourism, have helped to produce a certain openness to the rich patterns of geographical and historical cultures the globe has to offer. Yet Castells (1996) argues that reactions to globalization represent a more predominant trend than Giddens seems to allow for. For Castells (1997: 69), 'people all over the world resent loss of control over their lives, over their environment, over their jobs, over their economies, over their governments, over their countries, and, ultimately, over the fate of the Earth.' The task of any oppositional movement must be to connect local experiences to a more global agenda.

The fourth transformation is the breakdown of belief in the ideas of progress and certainty and their replacement by risk, doubt and uncertainty. Beck (1992) makes an initial distinction between ideas of risk assessment that accompanied modernity and pre-industrial notions of fate. Risks that are defined as fate place them beyond human control. The plagues, famines and natural disasters that characterized the pre-industrial world were under this rubric to be endured by humanity. Conversely, along with industrial society came notions of risk, in that they were explicitly based upon calculable decisions made within the context of a technological civilization. This set up a calculus of risks involving legal definitions, insurance companies and protection against the hazards of the industrial society. The welfare state was a way of insuring against the risks of industrialism associated with illness, old age and unemployment. However, since the middle of the twentieth century, industrial society has been confronted with questions of uninsurable risk. The potential destruction of the planet in a nuclear and chemical age has meant that humans are now living with risks they cannot be insured against. Who is to say how safe our food is after BSE? How do we know there will not be another Chernobyl? What are the long-term consequences of global warming? Can we be sure that networked capitalism will not lead to global financial collapse?

Beck argues that the development of scientific rationality and economic progress have produced a range of ecological risks, from the pollution of the seas to the poisoning of the population. These risks can no longer be dismissed as the side-effects of industrialism. Instead, they have become central to the definition of society at the start of the twenty-first century. The risk society evolves through two phases: the first is where the evident dangers of self-destruction are dealt with through the legal and political institutions of industrial society. These might include reliance upon scientific experts, the belief that new laws and political policies can effectively deal with pollution and the idea that ecological questions are secondary to notions of economic distribution. In the contemporary risk society none of these features and claims can be sustained. The emergence of a post-traditional society has seen the axes of the family, gender, occupation and belief in science and economic progress become radically undermined.

The fifth aspect of the information society is the idea of reflexivity, which seriously challenges the sociological pessimism and optimism of industrial society. Beck (1997) has consistently sought to argue that the 'age of side-effects' or the 'breakup of industrial society' does not necessarily lead in one direction rather than another. Giving up faith in industrial progress does not guarantee that we will ask the 'right' questions and that modernity will not continue to propagate a 'dark side'. Eighteenth- and nineteenth-century Europe and North America saw the development of democracy and universal principles, as well as the persistence and development of the oppression of women, nationalism, racism and other features, which culminated in the concentration camps. That is, 'reflexive' modernization may lead not to a reflection upon modernization and its consequences, but to forms of counter-modernization. Whereas 'reflexive' modernization dissolves the boundaries of class, gender and nation, counter-modernity seeks to renaturalize these questions by recreating boundaries and repressing critical questions. Counter-modernity represents the partial repression of doubt, ambiguity and ethical complexity. However, this is not the same thing as tradition, as counter-modernity is a reactive response to the radical questioning of tradition.

In this respect, Giddens (1991) has argued that we are all increasingly involved in reflexively producing our own identities. That is, we are all responsible for monitoring our own autobiographies. Increasingly we live in a world of complex choices where the lifestyles we lead are increasingly through choice rather than tradition. Reflexivity is evident where 'social practices are constantly examined and reformed in the light of incoming information about those very practices, thus constitutively altering their character' (Giddens 1990: 38). These processes help to foster a new society where the self is lived as a reflexive project. The choices we make, however, have few guarantees attached to them and foster a sense of our personal and collective futures as being unwritten.

The paradox of reflexivity is that the more we seek to shape our biographies, the more aware we become of the risks that are involved. For example, the more I start to think about my diet the more 'conscious' I become of the sheer number of risk assessments that have to be made in respect of the food that I eat. It is perhaps these dimensions that explain the attraction of what Melucci (1989) has called 'integralism'. This is the allure of fundamentalist solutions to problems of reflexivity. Melucci (1989: 181) comments:

Under the influence of integralism, people become intolerant. They search for the master key which unlocks every door of reality, and consequently they become incapable of distinguishing among the different levels of reality. They long for unity. They turn their backs on complexity. They become incapable of recognizing differences, and in personal and political terms they become bigoted and judgemental.

Sixth, and finally, we have shifted from a society based upon production to a genuinely consumer society. This is a society where everyday life has become saturated with images, signs and icons. As Baudrillard (1998) has argued, it is increasingly the signs and meanings of objects that are consumed, rather than the desire to fill pre-existing biological needs. It is the associated images and signs of youth and coolness that evoke our desires for products. For Baudrillard there is little point in arguing that the symbolic associations of certain products are an expression of inauthentic or false needs. The ideological effect of newspapers, magazines, advertisements and the cinema lies in the ways in which cultural distinctions are articulated and how consumers are addressed as autonomous subjects. What is interesting about my desire for a new pair of Levi's is not that it is repressing my real needs, but the ways in which such feelings become linked to a sense of myself as desirable, youthful, sexual and different. Consumer societies progressively seek to simulate, create and invent cultural connotations and emotions associating them with consumer products. This creates a society in which 'you have to try everything, for consumerist man is haunted by the fear of "missing" something, some form of enjoyment or other' (Baudrillard 1998: 80).

Such a view also has implications for the operation of citizenship. The simulation of signs and images within a consumer society both overloads modernity with information and changes the dimensions of culture and the economy. Through the development of modern information systems in respect of cable, the Internet, the proliferation of lifestyle magazines and newspapers and 24-hour news, we live our lives in the context of information blizzards. Further, the consumption of signs means that politics and economics are now subject to the need to stimulate new sensations and pleasures. The continued growth of the capitalist economy is dependent upon individual consumers having their tastes galvanized by the social production of fun, freedom and new lifestyle demands. This is not to reduce consumption to economic imperatives, but to suggest that the stimulation of fresh desires has now become a central part of the cultural economy. The need to keep ahead of competitors in the design and niche marketing of goods means that it is product innovation and flexible specialization that create competitive advantage (Harvey 1989). Further, the development of financial services and consumer credit and the quickening rate of design turnover has created a society where the pleasures of consumption are more highly valued than the duties of citizenship (Bourdieu 1984). As we shall see, the commodification of everyday life has had a diversity of effects on contemporary cultures and citizenships.

The culturation of citizenship

While these six transformations are in need of qualification, they have all broadly impacted upon the terrain I call cultural citizenship. These interrelated changes all point to the increasing importance of knowledge and culture in shaping the definition of modern society. From the importance of 'culture' in determining the competitiveness of the modern economy, to the increasingly symbolic nature of political protests, we are currently living within a cultural society unlike any other. Yet these questions leave open the question as to what we mean by 'culture'. If by 'culture' we mean the specific activities of artists or the simple description of the values and beliefs of different groups then these claims would not make much sense. Further, how we think about culture has implications for the ways in which we think about citizenship. For example, if cultures are assumed to be homogenous and national in definition then it would make sense to prioritize the tie between the nation-state and claims to citizenship. Yet if we explore different, less 'organic' and more fluid and con-tested metaphors then our understanding of the tie between culture and society would need to be rethought.

If cultures are considered to be travelling, hybrid patterns that are always being intermixed, then this would make questions of globalization more rather than less important. Under this definition we would have to conceive of the tie between nations and cultures as just one of the ways in which culture becomes organized in a society that has no connecting centre. We would also need to reject the Romantic idea that 'culture' stands opposed to society, or indeed that it can be used as a form of critique against society. Culture is not the special domain of aesthetic values that can be used to criticize the instrumental workings of late capitalism. We may wish to criticize the specific ways in which 'cultures' are organized by the capitalist economy, but this should not be because they corrupt culture's presumed authenticity. We might also recognize that certain aesthetic experiences are marginalized within a profit-orientated economic system, but this is different from arguing that the market undermines culture's presumed purity. Neither can we assume that cultures can be unproblematically attached to social groups or nations. There is no authentically working-class, white or English culture to oppose against outsiders. In this sense, we are all hybrids now. Cultures are not hermetically sealed in the way such examples imagine.

In thinking about the complex circuits of culture in modern society, I believe that we need to start with a 'symbolic' definition of culture. As J. B. Thompson (1990: 132) writes:

> culture is the patterns of meanings embodied in symbolic forms, including actions, utterances and meaningful objects of various kinds, by virtue of which individuals communicate with one another and share their experiences, conceptions and beliefs.

To follow this through, cultures are systems of representation that carry meanings that are not determined by material dimensions. All this means is that in the interpretation of an event it is the meanings that become attached to the 'event' that are crucial for understanding its significance. The other point here is that symbolic cultures are mobile rather than static. Despite the claims of cultural nationalists, cultures are not rooted to the spot, but are inevitably open-ended and capable of travelling through time and space. Within this process cultures are communicated and shared, but we cannot be certain that meanings will be interpreted in the same way from one person to the next. Culture is as much about difference as it is about sameness. The meanings generated by 'global events' will depend upon the different concepts, stocks of knowledge and frameworks that become attached to these events and the ways in which these are contested, understood, circulated and distributed among peoples across the planet. Hence, just as societies have no determining centre, the same can be said of cultures.

In these terms, culture operates in what Ulf Hannerz has called the 'global ecumene'. By this he means that cultures move in a diversity of networks that have developed a variety of linkages. Hannerz (2000: 62) writes:

> There are more ethnic diasporas than ever before, dispersed kinship groups, multinational business corporations and transnational occupational communities, as well as movements, youth cultures, and other expressive lifestyles with a self-consciously border-crossing orientation: not to speak of media, from the *International Herald Tribune* to CNN and whatever is on the Internet. Each of them engaged in its own particular way in the management of culture.

This is of course different from saying that we cannot still talk of cultures of power that continue to dominate the flows and translations of literatures, visual images and perspectives. Melucci (1996a) has argued that within the 'cultural' society inequality is as much about access to resources as it is about the ability to exert control over powerful symbolic codes. The control of the powerful over dominant discourses and frameworks of understanding is one of the key structural divisions within the world today. In this context, Melucci argues that we redefine 'exploitation' in cultural terms. Cultural domination is tied not to a lack of information, but to the 'exclusion from the power of naming' (Melucci 1996b: 182). In a global information age we can very easily detect core centres of cultural power that are able to control the distribution of symbols, languages and ideas for the consumption of the rest of the world. The possibility of resisting these dominant codes remains at the level of ideological interruption or indeed at the level of withdrawal from communication altogether.

These reflections also bring us back to questions of citizenship. How are our definitions changing in this respect? During the past decade, questions of citizenship have come increasingly to the fore. This has been widely recognized as being connected to the growing crisis of the welfare state in Western democratic nations, the demise of 'actually existed socialism', the critical questioning of liberalism and social democracy and the development of informational capitalism. There is renewed interest across a range of academic specialisms in the study of citizenship. The question of membership and belonging in terms of our common rights and duties has arguably been heightened in an age where the liquidity of capital and the demise of communism have brought into question older Left/Right binarisms (Giddens 1994). Yet to conceive of citizenship in these terms is at once both important and overly narrow. While it matters greatly whether we need to rethink our ideas in respect of social democracy and liberalism, we also need to address the 'cultural dimension' of citizenship (Stevenson 2001). The emergence of new social movements and critical questions that can be related to 'identity' politics has been crucial in this respect. Social movements in respect of race and ethnicity, gender and sexuality, disability and others have all sought to interrupt the construction of dominant cultures. These movements look to challenge widely held stereotypes that once permeated the symbolic cultures of civil society.

The deconstruction of ideas that have been associated with the 'normal' citizen has attempted to widen the 'inclusive' fabric of the community, while creating space for difference and otherness. Questions of 'cultural' citizenship therefore seek to rework images, assumptions and representations that are seen to be exclusive as well as marginalizing. At heart, then, these dimensions ask: how might we build an inclusive society? Crucial in this respect is how we imagine and construct public space.

Civil society, culture and public space

Questions of inclusion and exclusion, as we have seen, are at the heart of notions of cultural citizenship. In particular, how to achieve widespread participation in issues of genuinely communal concern is at the heart of our discussion. For Raymond Williams (1962) this was the possibility of achieving a genuinely participative and educative democracy. These points are usually addressed through discussion of the need to develop an inclusive civil society. Cultural inclusion, taking our lead from Marshall and Williams, should be concerned with both having access to certain rights and the opportunity to have your voice heard, in the knowledge that you will be given the ear of the community.

Cultural citizenship concerns the development of a communications-based society. Cohen and Arato (1992) argue that democracy is maintained through formal institutions and procedures, and through the maintenance of civil society. Here rights of communication and dialogue have a necessary priority over all other social and economic rights. Whereas Marxism criticized capitalist societies for instituting mere bourgeois rights, and liberalism has sought to remain agnostic in respect of the lifestyle choices of its citizens, a politics based upon a communicative civil society takes us in a different direction. Civil society should 'institutionalize' the everyday practice of democratic communication. Similarly, Michael Walzer (1992: 89) has identified civil society as a 'space of uncoerced human association and also the set of relational networks – formed for the sake of family, faith, interest and ideology'.

Notably, the revival of interest in civil society came from dissident Eastern European intellectuals who sought to construct domains of civic association and engagement not controlled by the state. The argument here was that a free and democratic society would necessarily be underpinned by a variety of associations that had gained at least relative forms of independence from the state. These concerns also found resonance within the West, given the growing concern that privatized lifestyles encouraged by neo-liberalism were undermining a wider culture of democratic engagement (Keane 1989). While many have noted that ideas of civil society have long and complex histories, it is difficult to see how definitions of citizenship and democracy that wish to retain a participatory basis can ignore the concept (Kumar 1993). Jean Leca (1992: 21) writes:

> citizenship only exists if there is a social space between the public and private spheres. If society is conceived as the confrontation between particular interests or as the product of the political activity of the state, the possibility of citizenship is excluded.

In terms of contemporary thinkers, it has been Habermas (1989) who has taken these questions most seriously. If we are breaking with the idea that social totality will become transformed through an international movement of workers that will instigate a more just and democratic society, then how we choose to communicate with each other becomes ever more important. The idea that social problems cannot be swept away through wholesale transformations fostered by revolutionaries, technologies or indeed governments reintroduces the idea of morality and ethics. For Habermas (1990) the idea of discourse ethics is based upon the notion that the rightness or the justness of the norms we uphold can only be secured by our ability to give good reasons. In turn, these norms are considered valid if they gain the consent of others within a shared community. The moral principles that we uphold must be more than the prejudices of the particular group to which we happen to belong. Such collectively held norms can only be considered valid if they are judged impartially. In this sense, our ethical claims can be said to be deontological, in that their rightness cannot be secured by social conventions or appeals to tradition (Habermas 1990). The achievement of a universal ethical stance, therefore, requires that participants in practical discourse transcend their own egoistic position in order to negotiate with the horizons of other cultures and perspectives. A norm can only be considered valid if all those it would potentially affect would freely accept it. These remarks, as should be clear, represent a radical reworking of the universalistic thinking of Kant, and a forcible rejection of relativistic standpoints.

In making these claims, however, Habermas is clear that we need to separate moral questions from ethical reflections that are related to the good life. This is especially necessary in modern multicultural societies that juxtapose and mix different cultural traditions and orientations. For example, we are unlikely to be able to reach universal agreement on questions such as to which particular communities we owe loyalty. We might have obligations to a particular region, football team, nation, religious group or family. These networks of identity-sustaining connection are likely to inform collective and individual forms of self-understanding. Habermas argues that such questions are best described as ethical rather than moral, and are largely driven by the issue of 'what is right for me'. On the other hand, moral concerns are more properly associated with whether or not particular maxims are appropriate for the whole community. Whereas participants in processes of self-clarification inevitably remain tied to their communities and identities, moral questions require that we break and distance ourselves from our immediate ties to consider questions of universal rightness and justice (Habermas 1990). In this view justice would always need to come before our particular communal attachments.

Habermas's (1996) most recent writing on the public sphere has sought to define more precisely its dynamic and spatially complex nature. Habermas links the cognitive capacity of the self and the institutional mechanisms of society in the promotion of a critical pluralistic culture. The distinction between ethics (questions of what is right for me) and morality (questions of what is right for the community) means that the public sphere is continually involved in a process of deciding what can reasonably be decided by the community and what cannot. The ease, or otherwise, with which such questions can be decided presupposes a participatory democratic culture that is able to couple the increasing individualism evident in ethical decisions and dilemmas with a need for a moral discourse at the level of the community. The primary task of the public sphere, therefore, is the detection and identification of public problems that need to be fed into the procedures of government and the state.

The public sphere in the modern media age operates as a 'signalling device' highlighting matters of public importance that have to be decided upon by the structures of representative democracy. Public opinion, in this respect, is not the result of opinion polls (although these are a contributing factor) but proceeds from a period of proper focused debate. Referring back to more familiar themes that can be associated with Habermas's notion of the public sphere, he argues that agreement can only emerge after a period of what he calls 'exhaustive controversy' (Habermas 1996: 362). However, Habermas is clear that such widespread discussions only become converted into communicative power once they pass through the institutional matrix of democratic will formation. Public opinion has been activated once the various interactive agencies of state and civil society have become focused on a particular problem. An informed public culture, in this respect, is built upon the complex interaction of a number of different public realms and arenas. Habermas (1996: 374) writes:

> the public sphere is differentiated into levels according to the density of communication, organizational complexity, and range – from the episodic publics found in taverns, coffee houses, or on the streets; through the *occasional* or 'arranged' publics of particular presentations and events, such as theatre performances, rock concerts, party assemblies, or church congresses; up to the *abstract* public sphere of isolated readers, listeners, and viewers scattered across large geographic areas, or even around the globe, and brought together only through the mass media.

The relationship between systemic sources of social power and civil society is crucial in determining public opinion. Habermas argues that the professionalization of opinion management, through an array of spin doctors, pollsters and spokespeople for powerful vested interests, unequally distributes the opportunities for exerting a powerful influence on public opinion. The 'managers' of public opinion, however, have to work within certain constraints, in that once an interpretation or perception appears within the public arena it is open to questions of public scrutiny and legitimacy.

The domain of civil society is much more than a well scripted public relations exercise, but crucially involves the direct intervention of ethical communities, feminist campaigners, green networks, religious denominations, trade unions, ethnic organizations and parents' groups. A society-wide conversation is dependent upon the emergence of an 'energetic civil society' that is able to force issues and perspectives on to a public agenda. A robust civil society ensures that the communicative basis of society never becomes completely colonized by agencies of money and power. Civil society, then, under certain circumstances, is able to convert itself into communicative power through the channels of public communication and the activation of public normative sentiment. For the public sphere to be socially just, it must both prevent the manipulation of the public by forces with vested interests in social control and pull together an otherwise fragmented public. A widespread, publicly inclusive conversation would shatter attempts at 'information processing strategies' and replace them with genuinely communicative interests and passions. A communicative civil society would produce a cultural citizenship where the public were capable of *learning* from one another's viewpoints.

The creation of a robust civil society is, however, constantly threatened by the colonizing capacity of money and power. According to Benjamin Barber (2001) there are at least three dangers to the creation of an engaged civil society. The first is the bureaucratic mechanisms of government that seek to manage and limit public criticism. These can emerge through hegemonic strategies of 'incorporation' and exclusion, censorship and the division of oppositional sentiments. The second is the belief that markets promote democratization. Markets tend to promote individualistic goals and choices, limiting our capacity to deliberate upon the common good. Finally, civil society is threatened by a yearning for undifferentiated and homogeneous communities. Whereas markets foster individual yearnings, they unintentionally promote unsatisfied desires for communal solidarity. This promotes a basic ambivalence where 'the thinner the market's social nexus, the thicker and more bloody the response to it' (Barber 2001: 272). Hence, whereas Barber does not press this point, any analysis of a genuinely *civil* society would need to investigate the construction of cultural identity. The problem here is that Habermas rarely takes these questions as seriously as he might.

More recently, Habermas (2001) has argued that in an age where the state is continually permeated by global flows of money and power, only the development of a genuinely global civil society and public sphere will foster the development of cosmopolitan solidarity. The impact of economic globalization has shifted the locus of control from the state's regulation of territory to the imperatives of speed capitalism. These developments (among others) have shaken the idea of the nation being the basis for civic solidarity. As 'money replaces power', national governments become dragged into a position where they are compelled to deregulate existing social legislation to prevent the flight of capital (Habermas 2001: 78). Globalization, then, simultaneously forces governments to open themselves to a diversity of cultural life, while shrinking the capacity of the state to govern. Such a situation requires the development of new forms of civic solidarity that are no longer based upon the nation. A genuinely cosmopolitan civil society could not be rooted in a particular collective identity, but would need to find its support from the moral universalism of human rights perspectives. This would require, as the philosopher Martha C. Nussbaum (1996: 17) has commented, that we 'put right before country and universal reason before the symbols of national belonging'.

The political and cultural question becomes how to promote genuinely cosmopolitan definitions, practices and understandings of public space. That is, an institutional definition of civil society (usually made up of relatively independent organizations likes churches, trade unions, schools and the media) does not go far enough.

Arguably, Habermas's analysis of civil society stops short of an investigation into the ways in which civil society has become historically and culturally constructed. While he correctly emphasizes the normative importance of human rights for fostering civic solidarity, he understates the cultural dimensions of what he calls a 'cosmopolitan consciousness' (Habermas 2001: 112). For example, Jeffrey Alexander (1992) argues that civil society is not merely an institutional realm, but is constructed through symbolic codes of inclusion and exclusion. Notions of 'civility' depend upon definitions of incivility. All citizens make judgements about who is deserving of exclusion from the public right to speak or indeed who is worth hearing. It has been the strength of cultural studies and post-structuralism that they have been able to highlight the ways in which civil society becomes coded through a multiplicity of often antagonistic discourses (Mouffe 1993). Cultural understandings of citizenship are concerned not only with 'formal' processes, such as who is entitled to vote and the maintenance of an active civil society, but crucially with whose cultural practices are disrespected, marginalized, stereotyped and rendered invisible. As Renato Rosaldo (1999: 260) argues, cultural citizenship is concerned with 'who needs to be visible, to be heard, and to belong'.

What becomes defining here is the demand for cultural respect. Whereas liberalism commonly recognizes that a political community can generate disrespect by forms of practical mistreatment (torture or rape) and by withholding formal rights (such as the right to vote), notions of cultural citizenship point to the importance of the symbolic dimension of community. Cultural citizenship is concerned with 'the degree of self-esteem accorded to ... [the citizen's] manner of self-realization within a society's inherited cultural horizon' (Honneth 1995: 134). These aspects might be linked to whose language is given public acceptance, whose history is taught in schools, which sexual activities are confined in the private and who is permitted to move securely through public space. Cultural citizenship then becomes defined through a site of struggle that is concerned with the marginalization of certain social practices.

Arguably, then, citizenship is both socially and culturally inclusive and exclusive. According to Engin Isin (2002), all historical ages offer a dominant account of the virtues of citizenship that draws discursive distinctions between insiders and outsiders. More often what become celebrated are the glorious self-images of the victorious and the dominant. We might seek to map an alternative history of citizenship to show how dominant groups have defined themselves against others, seeking to 'naturalize' their superiority. To write a history of citizenship from the point of view of alterity is to ask who is currently favoured and protected by its current constructions, and who is excluded. For Isin the twentieth century saw the rise and dominance of the professional classes, who have come to articulate the shape of modern citizenship. Professional groups not only do the work of globalization, whether as lawyers, architects or bankers, but have come to constitute themselves as virtuous citizens. The emergence of 'entrepreneurial professionalization' has normalized the market, individual responsibility, private as opposed to public goods and privatization. The subject is now constituted as an active, choice-driven and risk-reducing individual. Individuals are expected to be entrepreneurial and competitive rather than dependent upon paternal forms of collective welfare. Above all, individuals are expected to 'be flexible' about their working lives, lifestyles, intimate commitments and the cities in which they roam. It is these virtues that are 'threatened' or at least partially disrupted by the presence of the urban poor, refugees, immigrants and beggars. Cultural citizenship then asks us to attend to the ways in which civil society becomes encoded by powerful symbolic codes and discourses.

Chantel Mouffe (2000) has argued that theorists like Habermas who appeal to 'reasonableness' or 'rationality' try to hide the ways in which the 'political' or 'civil society' is constituted through powerful codes and discourses. The idea that participants within dialogue and civic exchange should seek a 'rational consensus' obscures the role played by passion and affect. For Mouffe, a democratic politics depends upon a pluralistic civil society that is constituted through a struggle between adversaries rather than enemies. A polity that sought to homogenize energetic forms of engagement within an overly consensual framework would inevitably promote a largely passive civil society. Democratic civil orders depend upon active forms of identification with civic values, but also with the possibility of passionate encounter. When we encounter others with whom we do not agree the temptation is to portray them as 'irrational'. What is being suggested here is that we might try to understand how different political subjects are positioned within discourses unlike those we currently occupy.

Arguably, these features become even more pressing within the contours of a global society where cultures are no longer anchored to the spot. We should interrogate our own understandings of the 'reasonable' and how they have become constructed, while we seek to encounter views different from our own. For example, Georgina Warnke (1993) argues that what is important is to locate our understanding of the 'good' in terms of diverse interpretations of different traditions. In our dialogue on 'interpretation' and 'meaning' we need not seek consensus. We need to make space for plurality and difference at the beginning and the end of democratic forms of communication. Within this view, we need a more reflexive understanding of the disparate political traditions and perspectives that become activated within a dispute or conversation. Questions of culture and respect remain connected through issues of interpretation. How we seek to understand the 'other' will have a tremendous bearing on our ability to construct democratic conversations. As Alain Touraine (2000) has argued, our passions today need to become less political and more ethical. A post-socialist age is defined less through the need to overthrow a dominant class and more through the creation of public spaces that protect the rights of minorities and establish active forms of communication among those who have become separated. A genuinely cosmopolitan dialogue would need to be underpinned by both the acceptance of universal principles and the recognition of difference. This is the very essence of cultural citizenship. Yet before we can do this we need to understand more fully the role of identity within this process.

Identity, difference and cultural politics

Stuart Hall (1992) has argued that there are two basic ways of speaking about identity. The first is to posit a 'true self' that exists beneath the artificial surfaces of culture, which will emerge once these have been stripped away. Such a view emphasizes identity as a rediscovery, not a cultural production. This strategy produces a view of identity as hard and solid and as either affirmed or denied by society's dominant institutions. The other view of cultural identity is that identities are 'increasingly fragmented and fractured; never singular but multiple across different, often intersecting and antagonistic, discourses, practices and positions' (Hall 1996: 4). Identity within this analysis is never fixed and final, but constructed through the variable resources of language and culture. Such a view of identity dispenses with 'essential' constructions like a single black or working-class culture. The aim is to produce an analysis of the ways in which individuals or groups identify or indeed fail to identify with discursive formations in social contexts that are permeated by power. Here the point is to be able to identify the cultures of power that are able to stereotype or construct subordinate groups as 'other'. A political strategy that aims to resist cultural domination would do so not by seeking to preserve the 'authenticity' of an excluded group, but by seeking to subvert and call into question society's dominant codes. The argument here is that social movements should seek to deconstruct dominant codes and cultures to make them more inclusive of difference.

The discursive strategies of post-colonial and queer theory have criticized the ways in which dominant discourses have helped to construct a number of binary oppositions that reinforce the presumed superiority of 'Western' or 'heterosexual' lifestyles. The aim here is to subvert how ideas of citizenship have sought to mask and normalize cultural difference. Attempts to 'liberate' the 'oppressed group' or subject by appealing to the language of oppressed versus oppressor only succeed in displacing the complexity of contemporary social relations (Giroux 1992). That is, homosexuality, feminism and black politics are not 'minority' issues, but are dependent upon the deconstruction of dominant codes and discourses. The attempt to fix the identities of homosexuals and heterosexuals, men and women, and white and black people is the effect of powerful ideological discourses. Such codes and ideologies seek to impose unitary identities and thereby impose a normalized social order. Here identity is not the product of social construction, but is largely experienced as natural social facts (Seidman 1997). Such a view questions both the simple binaries between self and other and the supposed unity of 'oppressed' groups in order to reveal the ways in which identities are constructed through language and culture.

These considerations mark a shift from identity politics to a politics of difference. Whereas objectivist and interest-based traditions within the social sciences sought to develop a politics based upon unitary identities, these features have been called into question. Identities are increasingly represented as the site of contestation and struggle, and as multiple and fragmented rather than pre-given and natural (Calhoun 1994). Judith Butler (1990) in this context has called for an anti-identity political strategy. By this she means that any attempt to base a politics upon an assumed unitary identity is necessarily exclusionary. This converts the categories of 'woman', 'class', 'race' or even 'earth' into 'permanently moot' points (Butler 1990: 15). Claims to 'identity' are always caught up in the construction of an inside and an outside. It is the cultural production of the abject and the marginal that enforces processes of cultural and symbolic exclusion. For example, the cultural production of dominant versions of heterosexual masculinity seeks to normalize and naturalize cultural difference by appealing to universality and rationality (Bhabha 1995). The implication is that heterosexual men are genderless. However, masculine self-identity emerges through the production of difference, where the fear of the homoerotic and the feminine helps to reproduce a patriarchal masculinity. Masculinity, femininity and homosexuality are seen as the properties of distinct individuals and groups. Women ought not to be masculine, and men are taught to police themselves in order to expel the feminine. Heterosexual masculinity becomes defined through its opposite – that is, its negative relationship with the feminine and homosexuality. These cultural features become 'other' as heterosexual masculinity seeks to produce a view of the self as objective, disinterested and self-controlled.

Yet, as many cultural critics have remarked, homophobia actually implies the existence of the homoerotic (Buchbinder 1998). Homophobia is not just the reaction of 'straight men' to homosexuality, but the possibility that homoeroticism may connect the masculine to homosexuality. The allure of homoeroticism and the regulation and persecution of homosexuality present straight masculinity with potentially troubling forms of affect and identification. Patriarchal discourses seek to protect the category of the masculine through the twin motors of misogyny and homophobia. Whereas heterosexual masculinity will seek to 'naturalize' the connection between men and masculinity, other social movements will aim to introduce the idea that in talking about masculinity we are not necessarily talking about men (Sedgwick 1995). Social movements will attempt to insist that if cultures have no essential origin then they are the product of complex processes of intermixing and hybridity. In response, those seeking to defend the dominant constructions of heterosexual masculinity will seek to present its 'performance' as an effect of biology.

However, as Steven Seidman (1997) has argued, these formulations require a more substantial ethics than is currently available. If the argument is that the rigid performance of sexuality, gender or ethnicity fashions a fear of difference, as well as normative forms of constraint, this entails a form of politics that can deal with these questions. In this context, Butler (1990) offers a cultural politics that seeks to demonstrate that the binaries we commonly draw between men and women, different ethnic groups and straights and gays are ideological and not natural. Here our ethnicity, sexuality and gender are revealed as a performance. We are only able to do this to the extent to which we can reveal that the categories we took to be 'natural' are actually cultural. Gender is not something one is, but something one does. As gender (and indeed sexuality) has no ontological status, Butler is drawn to analyse the ways it has become regulated and normalized within society. Butler's analysis, then, as we saw above, aims to uncouple biology, gender and sexuality by arguing that their supposed stability is an effect of discourse and normative regulation. Here

Butler turns to 'drag' as having powerful political possibilities, in that it reveals the 'performed' nature of sex and gender. If there is no 'original' to copy, reasons Butler, then drag is able to denaturalize the supposed 'naturalness' of heterosexuality by exposing all sexuality as culturally produced. While there has been much discussion on the suitability of a politics of drag, Butler's ethical strategy is deconstructive (Lloyd 1999; Segal 1999). The aim is to unsettle the symbolic norms (and privileges) of heterosexuality, thereby questioning the exclusion of different sexual practices and forms of identification.

The ethical position being advocated here is one that can be traced back to Michel Foucault. For Foucault the development of modernity has been accompanied by the emergence of disciplinary power, which – through the imposition of surveillance techniques – seeks to monitor and normalize the behaviour of individuals. Power in modern society works by targeting the body and by working on the individual personality. In this respect, Foucault (1981) argues that sexuality is not as much repressed as it is examined, monitored and categorized. Power is always linked to knowledge, in that it continually seeks to define the 'normal' by developing specifications of deviant or abnormal behaviour. Both Foucault and Butler emphasize the extent to which sex becomes the product of normative regulation through a multiplicity of discursive practices. However, Butler (1993: 94) seeks to correct Foucault's 'gender neutrality' by focusing upon the imposition of compulsory hetero-sexuality, whose repetition reproduces other desires as 'radically unthinkable'. Further, Butler's ethics of difference seems to flow from Foucault's later work, where he became increasingly interested in the technologies of the self. The concern about his earlier writing had been that Foucault overstated the mono-lithic reach of disciplinary power (McNay 1994). While disciplinary techniques are concerned to produce, discipline and regulate the subject, the question emerges as to how the subject might come to fashion itself. Here Foucault (1997) sought to ask how we might come to 'care for the self' rather than 'know the self'. It had been the desire to 'know the self' in its 'essence' that had prompted the need to seek security in clear rules governing each aspect of everyday life, from deviance to sexuality. To 'care for the self' was to question the need for prescribed moralities that sought to define the self in its 'essence'. The question, argues Foucault, is not 'who am I?', but 'how ought I to live?' In terms of our sexualities, then, the task was not to establish the 'truth' of the self, but to develop our sexuality both pleasurably and responsibly. Instead of finding a true inner self, Foucault urges us to create ourselves as we might works of art. Ethics for Foucault, as well as for Butler, is primarily a form of self-transformation. Normalization is to be resisted by ethical attempts to fashion new patterns and forms of subjectivity (Bernaver and Mahon 1994). Butler and Foucault invite us to make a politics of ourselves.

These reflections open a number of possibilities for questions of cultural citizenship. For example, David Halpern (1995) has argued that a Foucauldian politics offers the possibility of a radical politics that disrupts the normal, legitimate and dominant, thereby radically questioning what is usually accepted as the politics of citizenship. What Halpern has described as a 'queer ethics' is more about the right to be different than anything else. The ability to be able to create new individual and personal possibilities, while becoming free from the normalizing rhetoric of consumer society, social movements or indeed the state, goes beyond attempts to win new legal rights. A Foucauldian politics of the self is concerned with the possibility of lifestyle experimentation and new possibilities for selfhood. The concern here is to promote a politics of the self that does not fall into a prohibition against inventing difference, while seeking to deconstruct the dominant culture.

These questions can also be linked to questions of democratic citizenship. For example, Renato Rosaldo (1994) writes of 'the right to be different' while enjoying full membership of a democratic and participatory community. From this view, the solidified national community sees cultural citizenship as a threat. A cultural citizen is a polyglot who is able to move comfortably within multiple and diverse communities, while resisting the temptation to search for a purer and less complex identity. While questions of 'difference' remain key to cosmo-politan notions of cultural citizenship, they should not be allowed to undermine the necessity of building inclusive and overlapping democratic communities. Here my concern is that a purely Foucauldian ethics remains overly individual-istic (Elliott 2001). To put the point bluntly, Foucault's (and for that matter Butler's) concern with the self and self-transformation neglects to consider our responsibility for others. While I think that we should resist any notion that necessarily argues that there is a zero-sum relationship between care for the self and care for the community, the fear is that Foucault displaces questions of solidarity in favour of the 'modern cult of the self' (Smart 1998: 89). The deconstruction of dominant cultures allows for cosmopolitan cultures of difference, but they run the risk of displacing a politics based upon a concern for the other. The postmodern requirement that we deconstruct many of the hegemonic assumptions of dominant Western cultures needs to be able to distinguish between 'colonizing discourses and convincing ones' (Habermas 2001: 148). We need to be able to separate discourses that foster cosmopolitan solidarity and those that simply homogenize difference. As Nancy Fraser (1995: 71) has argued, critical theory engages with 'both deconstruction *and* reconstruction, destabilisation of meaning *and* projection of utopian hope'. Here we might take human rights as a case in point. The deconstruction of human rights might point to their Western origins, their exclusion of the non-human or the ways they are used to foster Western individualism. However, we would also need to explain why and how human rights have become globally popular. The idea of human rights remains a powerful moral language that enables poor and downtrodden individuals and communities the world over to claim rights that are denied by their locality. Human rights do not necessarily sanction Western cultures or ways of life, but sanction the ability of peoples of different cultures to appeal to a higher law (Ignatief 2001). These questions, which make us look at our responsibilities and obligations as members of a community, have also become the focus of a number of sociological debates in respect of modern individualization.

The challenge of individualization

The growth and development of individualization, which is connected to all six of the transformations I outlined earlier, is one of the most important social and cultural phenomenon of our times. By individualization Beck (1992) means that life is increasingly lived as an individual project. Through the decline of class loyalties and bonds (along with growing income inequalities), individuals are increasingly thrown back on their own biographies, with human relations becoming susceptible to individual choice. For Beck the classic plea of industrial society – 'I am hungry' – becomes replaced with 'I am afraid'. These developments mean that our cultural perceptions become more attuned to what Milan Kundera called the 'lightness of our beings', and ethical questions as to how we should live our lives. What Beck does not mean is that the self is being increasingly determined by market individualism or by social isolation more generally. Individualization means the disembedding of the ways of industrial society and the reinvention of new communal ties and biographies. As more areas of social life become less defined by tradition, the more our biographies require choice and planning. We are living in the age of DIY biographies. Under the conditions of welfare industrialism 'people are invited to constitute themselves as individuals: to plan, understand, design themselves as individuals and, should they fail, to blame themselves' (Beck 1999). Thus, individuals are 'condemned' to become authors of their own lives. The disintegration of the nuclear family and rigid class hierarchies means that we are all released from the structures of industrial society into the uncertainties of a globalized society.

Beck illustrates many of these features by commenting upon some of the profound changes taking place within our personal lives. Industrial society was based upon a strict separation between public and private, with women largely excluded from the public worlds, their identities shaped by a rigid gender system. However, with women entering the workforce after the Second World War we began to witness the breakup of the gender system. This also released men from being the sole supporter of the family and thereby untied the previous connections between work, family and gender. The partial deconstruction of public and private worlds inevitably means that love becomes a more contingent social arrangement. Love, no longer colonized by economic necessity, becomes an empty sign that has to be filled in by the participants within the relationship. In this, argue Beck and Beck-Gernsheim (1995), love has taken the place of religion as the central way in which modern subjects attribute their lives with meaning. Love relationships are the places where we can be ourselves, gain intimate contact with others and find a place where we can belong. However, affective relations, due to the decline of overt class antagonisms, are also the places where individuals are most likely to experience intense conflict. This is largely because more equal relationships imply more freedom for women, but for men imply more competition, more housework, less 'control' and more time with their children.

Arguably, processes of individualization are reshaping all of our lives. As Beck (1997: 99) maintains 'the political constellation of industrial society is becoming *un*political, while what was unpolitical in industrialism is becoming political'. Such a dynamic means that we often look for politics in the wrong place. In this respect, the key antagonism within 'reflexive' modernity lies between a politics that builds upon individualized forms of reflexivity and the reinscription of fundamentalist certitude. Such a politics asks us to think about widespread assumptions in respect of the colonization of economic reason, the decline of values or postmodern forms of fragmentation. That is, modernity has given birth to both 'freedom's children', who have learnt that fun, mobile phones and opposition to mainstream politics can be a force for change, and 'ugly citizens' and moralizers, who seek to reaffirm modernity's perceived loss of security (Beck 1998).

The main political dividing line in the struggles that mark the future will be between those who seek to remake civil society and community out of freedom and those who seek to introduce new forms of discipline and compulsion. Indeed, it is the ethic of individualization when joined with globalization that is most likely to lead politics in a cosmopolitan direction. The decline of national industrialism is increasingly giving rise to a global cosmopolitan ethic, which realizes that the key problems raised by common citizenship can no longer be thought about and experienced in national terms (Beck 1999).

There are, of course, a number of objections to the ways in which Beck has conceived of questions of reflexivity and individualization. The most prominent is the argument that individualization is not about the ethic of self-development, but about selfishness and narcissism. Important here is a communitarian response that modern communities need to be remade through the imposition of shared moral rules. Thinkers such as Etzioni (1997) have argued that the increase in liberty experienced by society since the 1960s has not delivered the good society. A well balanced society requires that we respect the need for both order and autonomy. Hence, he emphasizes that individuals need to be taught a set of shared moral values that clearly distinguish between right and wrong. We need to pull society back from the 'edge of social anarchy' by challenging a social system built upon excessive individualism. Free market economics, sexual liberation, consumer narcissism and the development of mass communications have helped to foster a society of 'me-ism'. This can be seen in rising levels of violence, drug abuse, crime and anti-social behaviour in society more generally. Etzioni argues that his proposals attempt to remake civil society, rather than relying upon economic or state-driven solutions. Society requires not new laws or freedoms, but a consensually shared morality in order to curb excessive social autonomy. We can do this by seeking to recreate moral public cultures through town hall meetings and other networks, all of which should be orientated to rediscovering our collective moral voices. It is, according to Etzioni, time to turn against individualism and rediscover the ethic of community.

In the terms I have outlined thus far such proposals look more like a reaction against reflexivity than an engagement with the new cultural contours of our society. Proposals such as those offered by Etzioni are likely to be socially repressive, and seemingly depend upon 'national' solutions to global problems. They also nostalgically look back to a society that was less contested and uncertain than our own. Arguably, there is considerable moral disagreement about many of the issues that are collectively shaping our futures. Whereas Beck argues that the ethical resources of new individualism *could* lead in more cosmopolitan directions, Etzioni seeks to repress this ethical impulse in favour of consensually managed communities. Yet while my sympathies lie with Beck, I think there might be something to be learned from an engagement with more communitarian patterns of thinking.

If individualization can move in a progressive direction, it also has potentially negative consequences. While such processes open the citizen to new ties and forms of attachment, they also fragment older forms of community. For example, Richard Sennett (1998) has argued that global capital has promoted an uncertain culture based upon short-term contracts, insecurity, risk and superficial communal relations. The self fostered by neo-liberalism is open to the culture of the market, while fostering a pervasive sense of insecurity and a longing for community. If a cultural citizenship based upon cosmopolitan forms of deliberative exchange is to take hold, it must be able to connect with the need for community and belonging. If network capitalism fosters a world of atomized competitive advantage, citizenship needs to be able to offer the prospect of social solidarity with others who are sometimes different from us. Hence, whereas uncertainty and insecurity are good for the market, they are bad for citizenship. The development of a reactivated citizenship and cosmopolitan institutions is not only good for politics, it is essential for deliberative forms of democracy.

Arguably, then, the ideologies of neo-liberalism and endemic instability of the market have played their part in undermining the solidarities of citizenship (Bauman 1999). These questions are poorly addressed by a communitarian politics that seeks to re-emphasize the solidarities of local neighbourhood communities in the ways described by Etzioni. Yet the culture of market individualism, which rewards individual material success and punishes personal failure, undoubtedly requires that we learn to balance a respect of difference with the rediscovery of the art of the common good (Bellah *et al.* 1996). As the market spreads into different areas of social life, citizenship arguably becomes increasingly defined through certain kinds of social conduct. The market views the citizen as having the individualized ability to be able to 'maximise his or her lifestyle through acts of choice' (Rose 2000: 99). The market, under the guise of freedom and autonomy, can act as a mechanism regulating norms and instilling certain forms of behaviour. Citizenship, on the other hand, depends upon the dual capacity to be able to disrupt normative hierarchies while fostering the common ability on the part of institutions and citizens to be reflexive. The question of who our neighbour is in a global society invokes the development of wider patterns of loyalty than those suggested by the nation-state or the particularity of the most fluid lifestyle.

Conclusion

This opening chapter has argued that questions of cultural citizenship need to be understood in the context of social transformation. The development of new conflicts, networks, cultures of risk and reflexivity, globalization and commodification have transformed the operation of citizenship. We have seen how a consideration of cultural citizenship includes rights and obligations, civic spaces of participation, respect, identity and difference and individualization. Cultural citizenship poses the question: how is it possible to maintain solidarity with others while emphasizing the creativity of the self, or indeed to pursue justice while recognizing difference? If cultural citizenship is overwhelmingly concerned with communication and power, how we answer these questions inevitably involves interpretation and conflict. Further, we saw that the development of a critical conception of civil society that is sensitive to difference and the requirements of common dialogue is not easily achievable within modern society. The agendas of moralizers, nation-states and neo-liberal economics are all likely to continue to make such a task a difficult achievement. Yet before we can properly assess the prospects for such a version of citizenship we would need to look more closely at the diverse spaces within which claims to citizenship are likely to emerge.

Notes

1 I return to Williams's idea of culture in common in Chapter 5.
2 Marshall, it should be remembered, also emphasized the importance of maintaining common civilized values, and the link between rights and duties. However, it is hard to resist the idea that for Marshall it is the institutional expression of common rights that is the driving force of citizenship. For a further discussion of this question see Turner (1997) and the excellent paper by Annesley (2002).

Further reading

Butler, J. (1998) Merely cultural, *New Left Review*, 227: 33–44.
Calhoun, C. (1994) Social theory and the politics of identity, in C. Calhoun, *Social Theory and the Politics of Identity*. Oxford: Blackwell.
Hall, S. (1992) Cultural identity and diaspora, in J. Rutherford (ed.) *Identity: Community, Culture, Difference*. London: Lawrence and Wishart.
Honneth, A. (1995) *The Struggle for Recognition: The Moral Grammar of Social Conflicts*. Cambridge: Polity Press.
Isin, E. F. and Wood, P. (1999) *Citizenship and Identity*. London: Sage.
Rosaldo, R. (1999) Cultural citizenship, inequality and multiculturalism, in R. D. Torres, L. F. Mirón and J. X. Inda (eds) *Race, Identity and Citizenship*. Oxford: Blackwell.
Turner, B. S. (1997) Citizenship studies: a general theory, *Citizenship Studies*, 1(1): 5–18.

2 | COSMOPOLITAN AND MULTICULTURAL CITIZENSHIP: WORLD, NATION, CITY AND SELF

This chapter seeks to identify the different levels of 'cultural' citizenship. As we have already seen, the idea of 'cultural' citizenship is dependent upon the emergence of an information or society. The associated processes of the decentring of society, the rise of network capitalism, globalization, risk, reflexivity and consumer culture have all served to reshape and to question the operation of citizenship. This chapter argues that the historical tie between nation, culture and citizenship is becoming increasingly decoupled by these transformations. Cultural citizenship is related to these changes and is more generally the struggle for a communicative society. Arguably, just as questions of citizenship cannot be adequately conceptualized outside a concern for 'culture', the same might be said of spatial dimensions. Increasingly, we will need to be able to differentiate between levels of citizenship that seek to connect the individual to more global levels of identification to be able to understand the practice of citizenship. In this regard, I seek to look at notions of cosmopolitan citizenship across the dimensions of the world–regional level, the nation, the city and the self in order to interrogate these formations.

The nation-state today has to respond to the twin forces of globalism and localism, while the traditional basis for national citizenship is widely reported as being eroded. Yet, as we shall see, it is not that national forms of citizenship are finished but that they are being reconstituted. Our task, then, is to understand what cultural citizenship might mean in these contexts. If the irony of active forms of citizenship is that new rights and demands for democratic forms of participation are being claimed at the very time when global forces makes it difficult to satisfy these demands, then perhaps we need to rethink what citizenship might come to mean in the future. As we shall see, citizenship needs to become as concerned with questions of imagination, identity, recognition and belonging as it has been more traditionally with entitlements and obligations. Through the cultural dimensions of citizenship we need to look beyond the horizons of the nation, outside the concerns of our ethnic group, beyond 'mainstream politics' and increasingly at ourselves. It is in this space that cosmopolitan versions of citizenship are likely to emerge. Yet how we define the 'cosmopolitan' will be a matter of some concern.

Disarmament and European cosmopolitanism

In seeking to understand political cosmopolitanism I want to start before rather than after the end of the Cold War. The current debates often suggest that political cosmopolitanism came to fruition after the collapse of the bloc system. This is not only mistaken, but fails to build upon the cultural production of intellectuals and social movements that sought to dismantle the destructive logics of the two main superpowers. As we shall see, unless we tie contemporary political hopes and expectations to a consideration of past understandings, we will miss an opportunity to learn from previous mistakes and insights. These considerations can also be connected to what I perceive to be the overt philosophical formalism of current political and philosophical versions of cosmopolitanism.[1] That is, while the cosmopolitan ideal remains tied to moral criteria, it also needs to be linked to more ethical and cultural projections.

The fall of the Berlin Wall was the biggest political event of my lifetime. As I was an active member of CND (Campaign for Nuclear Disarmament) since its second coming in the early 1980s, it was the need to dismantle the bloc system that remained at the foreground of my own and others' political imaginations. In particular, an organization linked to CND, called END (European Nuclear Disarmament), was important not only for opposing the destructive logics of the arms race, but for attempting to build an alternative cosmopolitan vision for all European peoples. The key intellectual within this movement was E. P. Thompson, who produced a number of books, pamphlets, magazine and newspaper articles that sought to elucidate a vision of a democratic Europe that was no longer permanently prepared for war.

Thompson (1982, 1985, 1990) argued that both East and West were involved in an ideological mirror stage, where the threat of the 'other' legitimated internal policing and intellectual control. Thompson argued that NATO and the Warsaw Pact mutually reinforced one another. In this way the Cold War was seen as a 'conflictual alliance', because after Europe had been divided following the Second World War there was never any real policy of 'rollback' adopted by the superpowers. Instead, the United States hegemonically sealed its dominance through the Marshall Plan, while the Soviet Union depended more on force than on consent for its authority. Thompson argued that what tended to be sacrificed in the relationship between the two blocs were the interests of third parties. As the superpowers attempted to hold on to their respective spheres of influence, these interests in areas like Eastern Europe tended to be prioritized over demands for democracy. The Cold War promoted an atmosphere of paranoia and hostility, where democracy was the main casualty. In Thompson's assessment it was the imaginary dimension (or the culturally deformed logic) of the Cold War that was pushing Europe dangerously close to nuclear destruction. In arguing that the Cold War had a reciprocal logic there was a need for the peace movement to articulate a 'third space' that could give voice to the common interests of peoples in both East and West. These common interests were for democracy, human rights and ecological survival. The peace movement within Europe was urged to build alliances and promote cultural understanding and intellectual exchange across the blocs. Hence, given that the political elites of both East and West were locked into the ideology of deterrence, the agency for change would need to come from below. Should the bloc system become dismantled, the hope was that this would provide new opportunities for democratic versions of socialism, peaceful relations between nation-states and a reduced threat of nuclear destruction.

The point of revisiting these projections may only be fully appreciated later. For the present, I want to make a couple of related points about Thompson's concerns. The first is that when we are concerned with political questions of agency and strategy, we are inevitably dealing with contingency. That is, the Cold War did not end in the ways that intellectuals like E. P. Thompson and social movements like END imagined. The events of 1989 seem inevitable only with hindsight. Whatever the plausibility of Thompson's reflections at the time, from the vantage point of the present they currently seem no closer to fruition. The vision of a unified peaceful and democratic Europe breathing new life into national democratic forms of socialism was inevitably a 'contingent utopia'. There is a necessary ambivalence within politics, where we have to construct our future plans in the due recognition that they may well be overtaken by historical events, or indeed they may not turn out as we might have hoped or expected. This gives rise to a necessarily postmodern dimension to our thinking. Zygmunt Bauman (1993: 245) further emphasizes this point:

What the post-modern mind is aware of is that there are problems in human and social life with no good solutions, twisted trajectories that cannot be straightened up, ambivalences that are more than linguistic blunders to be corrected, doubts which can not be legislated out of existence, moral agonies which no reason directed recipes can soothe let alone cure. The post-modern mind does not expect any more to find an all-embracing and ultimate formula of life without ambiguity, risk, danger and error, and is deeply suspicious of any voice that promises otherwise.

The breakdown of 'actually existing socialism' has not renewed the prospects for a redistributive politics, but thrown such prospects even further into question. A Europe that is currently marked by the rebirth of nationalism, the impact of network capitalism and most importantly the cultural, economic and political implications of globalization remains distant from Thompson's earlier hopes and projections.

What, then, remains of Thompson's earlier cosmopolitan vision? The most obvious answer would be little in the current context of post Cold War Europe. However, I want to argue that such a suggestion is overly hasty, and neglects to analyse the fact that we may still have something to learn from his projections. First, the reason why Thompson's views struck such a chord with a diversity of peoples across Europe was that they not only articulated a future vision of a less destructive society, but his argument took the cultural and ethical dimensions of politics seriously.[2] Thompson's arguments were tuned to the way the Cold War reinforced both structural and cultural divisions across the continent. His writings consistently opposed the self-destructive logics of what he called 'exterminism' with an alternative symbolic order that prioritized peaceful intellectual dialogue, ecological well-being and cultural exchange. The 'murderous' logic of the bloc system had to be steadily undermined by a multitude of peaceful processes before more sustainable societies could emerge from the ashes. The agency for change in this respect would need to come from beneath the institutional structures of national and international dominance. The possibility of new, less polarized, forms of dialogue actually depended upon the agencies of individuals and social movements. As we shall see, a politics that seeks to reclaim a space for cosmopolitan dialogue requires new forms of civic momentum. In the absence of politically active and motivated citizens, Thompson would have been swift to point out that the prospects for a cosmopolitan world would seem bleak. Yet the paradox of Thompson's views was that he sought to promote transnational cultural dialogues in order to reaffirm specifically national roads to recovery. These, as we shall see, are precisely the political and cultural contours that have come under increasing scrutiny.

The new political cosmopolitans

Since the fall of the Berlin Wall the cosmopolitan view has sought to dispense with specifically national responses. This has largely been due to the argument that processes of globalization have significantly undermined national forms of citizenship. According to Richard Falk (2000a), globalization has minimized political differences within states by converting elections into trivial rituals, while simultaneously weakening the internal bonds of community and consideration. Issues such as growing ecological awareness, the impact of global poverty, feminism and the participation of racial and ethnic minorities cannot readily be integrated into a concern for the declining fortunes of territorial states. Following Held (1995a), Beck (1998) and Linklater (1998), there is the view that without a politically robust cosmopolitan culture, global civil society and cosmopolitan institutions, we will remain a world at the mercy of the interests of nation-states and economic markets.

Citizenship, it follows, has to become a transnational form of governance by breaking with the cultural hegemony of the state. A cosmopolitan political community would be based upon overlapping or multiple citizenships connecting the populace into local, national, regional and global forms of governance. The cosmopolitan polity, guided by the principle of autonomy, would seek to achieve new levels of interconnectedness to correspond with an increasingly global world. These dimensions remain vital, surpassing older divisions in the democratic tradition between direct and representative democracy by seeking to maximize the principle of autonomy across a range of different levels. Within this framework, therefore, the argument for a cosmopolitan democracy is guided by the argument that problems such as HIV, ecological questions and poverty are increasingly globally shared problems.

We are witnessing growing calls for the democratic ideal to detach itself from national boundaries. This is in response to a number of related developments. For David Held (1995b) this is both because specifically national democracies have been undermined by more global flows, and because for local forms of accountability to survive and be revived the democratic ideal must find expression at the transnational level. The task of securing democracy in an increasingly interconnected age must allow for the development of a cosmopolitan democratic law. Held has identified the United Nations as an institution that could play a key role in the transformation of governance from a world system built upon the competing ambitions of nation-states to one with a deeper orientation to cosmopolitan forms of democracy. The UN Charter provides a forum where states are in certain respects equal, offering the beginnings of a break with a world order wherein specifically national interests are paramount. However, as Held is well aware, the United Nations is in need of considerable reform before it is able to generate its own political resources and act as an autonomous decision-making centre.

Similarly, Habermas (1997) and Honneth (1997) locate ideas of cosmopolitan democracy in Kant's (1970) desire to replace the law of nations with a genuinely morally binding international law. Kant believed that the spread of commerce and the principles of republicanism could help to foster cosmopolitan sentiments. As world citizens, individuals would act to cancel the egoistic ambitions of individual states. Kant's vision of a peaceful cosmopolitan order based upon the obligation on states to settle their differences through the court of law has gained a new legitimacy in a post Cold War world. For Habermas (1997), while this vision retains a contemporary purchase, it has to be brought up to date by acknowledgement of a number of social transformations. This includes the globalization of the public sphere and the declining power of states, while also recognizing that it is individuals and citizens and not collectivities who need to become sovereign. Habermas (1997: 127) writes:

> The community of peoples must at least be able to hold its members to legally appropriate behavior through the threat of sanctions. Only then will the unstable system of states asserting their sovereignty through mutual threat be transformed into a federation of whose common interests take over state functions: it will legally regulate its members and monitor their compliance with the rules.

Cosmopolitanism requires the implementation of legal mechanisms that act in the interests of global citizens rather than states. This would build upon the UN Charter model of governance, creating a society of world citizens able to challenge their own governments. Like Held, Habermas sees that the weak link in these arguments is that the UN currently recognizes nation-states as both sovereign and open to challenge. This contradiction is further magnified if we recognize that globalization processes have increased the social and economic divisions across the planet, while also introducing the idea of a global community based upon shared risks.

Similarly, Honneth (1997) argues that the fall of the Berlin Wall, the demise of communism and an increased emphasis upon global interconnection has in the former 'Eastern Europe' led to a rapid increase in the power of civil society. This has simultaneously enhanced the prospects for democratic elections and the rule of law, while also allowing for the explosion of nationalist and ethnic violence. In short, for Held, Honneth and Habermas the prospect of a global cosmopolitan democracy takes on the role of a 'necessary utopia', leading us out of the ambiguities of the present into a new world where international relations become progressively moralized through the rights of individuals rather than states.

The key principle here is that multilevel cosmopolitan governance would offer new opportunities for dialogue across a number of levels. Revitalized local and transnational political structures would seek to provide the institutional basis for conversation that would dissolve older divisions between citizens and aliens. In the absence of an Archimedian standpoint that transcends differences of culture, time and place, such dialogues would provide the basis for a new world society. As Linklater (1998) argues, a cosmopolitan position would need to bring the 'other' into an extended dialogue. A genuinely cosmopolitan dialogue would need to avoid the negative representations of 'alien' cultures, while deconstructing the assumption that 'national' or 'local' conversations have the right to override the interests of 'insiders' over those of 'outsiders'. In these terms, cosmopolitan moral progress can be accounted for when 'they' become 'us'.

Such arguments are not (as many seem to think) dependent upon the replacement of national democracy with a global state. Cosmopolitan democracy requires the creation of institutions (within and between states as well as at the global level) that enable the voice of the individual to be heard irrespective of its local resonance (Archibugi 2000). Further, and somewhat paradoxically, cosmopolitanism is actually dependent upon the social re-empowerment of the national state, while seeking to introduce new voices both internally and externally into the conversation. The downward pressure on public expenditure exerted by financial markets, renewed attempts to include excluded voices within democratic exchange and a widening of our sense of political community all fall within cosmopolitan concerns. What Anthony Giddens (1999) has called the democratization of democracy means the fostering of a strong participatory civic culture, the building of new institutions across a number of levels and the development of more global sympathies and horizons.

However, despite the arguments presented thus far, the project for cosmopolitan governance is not without its own internal sympathetic critics, the most pronounced of which has been the voice of Richard Falk (1995a, b, 2000a, b). Falk has argued that instead of being concerned with institution building as an end in itself, arguments for a cosmopolitan polity need to become focused on the recovery of democratic sensibilities. It is an active citizenry committed to substantive cosmopolitan viewpoints that remains the key agency of change. Cosmopolitanism is therefore actually dependent upon the development of a global civil society that is in itself dependent upon pressure and struggle from below. A democratic identity will have to forge itself in opposition to consumerist inclinations, fundamentalism, neo-liberalism and outright cynicism. The recovery of a substantive ethical agenda in a world driven by consumerism, nationalist sentiment and market calculations is more than a matter of building new institutions. The key to civic momentum in this regard remains the convergence of grassroots activism and the taking of geo-political opportunities by groups that are mostly organized outside the corridors of social and political elites.

Like E. P. Thompson before him, Richard Falk emphasizes the importance of carrying the process of democratization beyond state–society relations to include all areas of power and authority. Such a view breaks with the utopian sentiment that argues that once the world becomes ordered through the formation of democratic law it automatically becomes a more just place. In this, the writings of both Falk and Thompson point to the necessity of connecting the emotional electricity produced by civil society to cosmopolitan horizons and sentiments. To put the point bluntly, a global cosmopolitan civil order is more likely to emerge from the horizons of civil organizations like Amnesty International, Friends of the Earth and Greenpeace than the European Union or the United Nations. While this overstates the case, I think it does point to the necessity of linking the culturally constructed horizons of civil actors to a cosmopolitan politics that is able to link arguments on intimacy and masculinity into international dimensions that serve to criticize the world arms trade and global poverty. Within these arguments, cosmopolitan forms of dialogue would need to be linked to questions of cultural identity as much as institution building. Such a process would require a new kind of 'educative' citizenship that allowed for the negotiation of the self in relation to others, the discovery of cultural plurality and difference, the opening up of more cosmopolitan horizons and our interconnections with nature (Irigaray 2000). For a genuinely cosmopolitan citizenry to emerge they would need the intellectual and emotional capacities to be able to engage in dialogue confidently with others in new public spaces. Unless the 'critical' capacities of ordinary citizens are involved, processes of institution building alone are likely to contribute to technocratic rather than democratic forms of governance.

The cosmopolitan project requires a thicker 'cultural' explanation than has thus far been allowed. This is not the usual call for a turn into more communitarian sensibilities and away from the unencumbered self of liberal thought. As we shall see, there are good reasons for the cosmopolitan project to steer clear of some of the moral prescriptions that have become associated with communitarian patterns of thinking, while recognizing that unless people are able to think and feel like cosmopolitans in the contexts of their everyday lives the project is unlikely to get very far. Cosmopolitanism needs to become part of the soil of culture.

Cosmopolitanism as a cultural ideal needs to be linked into notions of urbanity, the ability to live with difference and a healthy respect for 'otherness'. Cosmopolitanism needs to be discursively and emotionally imagined. How, if you like, do people begin the process of thinking and feeling like cosmopolitans? How might cosmopolitan sensibilities be promoted in communities that are based upon the increased global mobility of some and the more place-specific identities of others (Castells 1996; Bauman 1999)? Perhaps more to the point is to ask how the cosmopolitan project can become orientated around the idea that 'the messiness of the human predicament is here to stay' (Bauman 1993: 245).

Touraine (2000) argues that the modern subject must learn to negotiate successfully between the twin traps evident within global networks of production and the return to community. Market hedonism and the drive towards cultural homogeneity deny the ideals of intercultural communication. Whereas the global market has flooded our lives with standardized goods, our increasingly fragmented world has led to the proliferation of sects that reject universal norms. We are then 'caught between the calculations of the financiers and the fatwas of the ayatollahs' (Touraine 2000: 43). We might take the United States as the model, given that it remains the strongest point of connection for world markets, while also being increasingly fragmented into contested communities of opinion. Similarly to Beck, Touraine argues we are living in the age of the Subject. Rather than submitting to the logics of the market or community, the Subject seeks to defend the self against instrumentalism and communalism. The break-up of national capitalism has led to the weakening of institutions whose aim is to impose collective norms and identities. As our personal lives are less regulated by norms and hierarchies than before, this has led to both increasing social inequalities and enhanced possibilities for freedom and creativity. Within this both Beck and Touraine reject the idea that they are merely describing new forms of individualism available to the middle classes. Instead, the Subject's capacity to be creatively involved in dialogue can only be enhanced by recognition of the threats to 'freedom' posed by communalism and consumerism. The twin dangers of mass culture and cultural nationalism (or indeed communitarianism) are held in check through the rebirth of a cosmopolitan politics through individualization.

A cosmopolitan agenda is emerging out of the cultural contradictions of the present, rather than the need for a 'rational' response to new social conditions. For instance, Beck (2000) argues that from the legal position of non-interference in the 'internal affairs' of states, NATO's response to Kosovo is a clear breach of international law. However, the attempts to stop the genocide expose the tension between human rights and national sovereignty. The second age of modernity is beginning to establish the principle of human rights occasionally taking priority over international law. Whereas in the first stage of modernity human rights were subordinate to the nation-state system, this is no longer always the case. Under cosmopolitan law the bearers of human rights are individuals and not states or nations. According to Beck (2000: 84), this shift posits the possibility of 'a legally binding world society of individuals'. However, Beck takes these questions beyond those identified by Habermas, Held and others by asking: what implications do cosmopolitan institutions and individualization have for questions of cultural identity? That is, whereas the first age of modernity defined identity as given and fixed (usually by national or ethnic groups), in the second age identity becomes 'a creative achievement' (Beck 2000: 92). Stuart Hall (1996: 4) has described cultural identity as 'about questions of using the resources of history, language and culture in the process of becoming rather than being: not "who we are" or "where we come from", so much as what we might become, how we have been represented and how that bears on how we might represent ourselves.'

Questions of difference and diaspora have more recently focused on the settlement drawn by national thinking between location and identity. Rather than rooting identity in place, such questions are rendered 'cultural' rather than 'natural' through the development and recognition of post-national forms of identification. As Pieterse and Parekh (1995: 11) comment, 'at this stage, bicultural and bilingual social forces – typically migrants, diasporas, exiles, returnees – come to the foreground'. Notions of multiple identity question both the assertions of cultural nationalism and the often homogeneous culture of the market place. Yet all political communities must address the patterns of inclusion and exclusion that issues of identity ultimately display. All groupings are concerned with the boundaries of their constitution. As Paul Gilroy (2000) has argued, historically the idea of the nation has sought to resolve these dilemmas by repressing difference and imposing a homogeneous identity. National and ethnic identities in this framework are represented as being 'pure', without the unsettling trace of hybridity.

The question that remains then is how we learn to live together, while accepting, negotiating and constructing our differences. The coming together of globalization and individualization at the same time that nations are losing their defining power makes this a crucial question. This is not an issue that liberalism, with its emphasis on free-choosing individuals, or communitarianism, emphasizing community before individuality, can adequately resolve. Here I want to argue that cosmopolitan concerns have much to gain by being connected to questions of multiculturalism. In making this connection we will need to pluralize and deconstruct discourses of nationhood. Here it is not enough to point to the importance of new levels of governance: we need to connect more fully to questions of identity formation within and between national societies.

National citizenship: liberalism and multiculturalism

Most of the debate around contemporary nationalism makes a clear distinction between ethnic and civic nationalism. Ethnic nationalism holds that citizenship is based upon a common cultural identity. This particular version of nationalism has been associated with the more destructive features of national cultures. It is commonly held that ethnic nationalism's attempt to impose a 'pure' and homogeneous construction on the plurality of the 'people' is connected in late modernity to the cultural barbarism of ethnic cleansing. On the other hand, national cultures and identities are irrevocably Janus-faced, as ideas of nationhood have informed struggles to extend commonly held rights and obligations, and have provided the backdrop for anti-colonial struggles.

This attitude, offering a less pessimistic view of national cultures, brings us to civic nationalism. Here membership and basic citizenship entitlements are tied to a 'legal–political' definition of community. The rights and obligations of the national community are in this respect universal, not culturally specific. For instance, critical-liberals, such as Habermas (1994), have defended a conception of nationalism that he calls 'constitutional patriotism'. Habermas argues that while nationalism and democracy have 'grown up' together, they are analytically separable. Feelings of loyalty and obligation should be constructed around universally agreed procedures rather than specific ethnic groups. Habermas, in this view, comes close to the liberal view that the state or national community should remain agnostic concerning members' particular views of the good life, within, of course, certain boundaries. Similarly, Rawls (1996) argues that political liberalism is the search for a society that can gain the support of an overlapping consensus of principles that are endorsable whatever the individual's respective orientations. Rawls argues that it is basically illiberal to expect a society to be based upon a comprehensive moral or philosophical standpoint. Modern societies are irrevocably pluralist and contain people with different sexualities, religious convictions, class loyalties, ethnicities, political persuasions and so on. For a society to cohere, Rawls argues, it must gain the support of what he calls 'reasonable and rational agents'. Through the use of virtues of tolerance and respect, the aim of political liberalism is the achievement of an overlapping consensus among those who accept the fact of reasonable pluralism. In this sense, the priority of the right over the good ensures that there are collectively held principles of justice that become embedded within the constitution. In questions of dispute, citizens would be obligated to use public forms of reason, seeking to persuade others that their demands or arguments are compatible with the constitution.

While Habermas (1995) has criticized these proposals on a number of grounds, both he and Rawls seek to provide a notion of the good society that is based upon well reasoned universal principles that appropriately involve a diversity of communities within contemporary multicultural society. Both Rawls and Habermas are concerned that the national and international community become structured through shared principles of justice, rather than substantive doctrines. The main point of difference seems to be that whereas

Rawls locates the public sphere within a legal framework provided by the constitution, Habermas is more concerned with the reflexive capacity of civil society. As Benhabib (1996) notes, whereas Rawls's idea of public reason is anchored in the judicial role of the court, Habermas's notion of deliberative democracy concerns the moral grammar of civil discourse. In this it is a diverse, argumentative and contested public sphere rather than the Supreme Court that becomes the embodiment of democratic citizenship. However, within this citizens would be expected to articulate their proposals and policies in a 'discursive language that appeals to commonly shared and accepted public reasons' (Benhabib 1996: 83).

Still, in my view, there remain at least two problems with these formulations. The first is that both Habermas and Rawls are guilty of ignoring the cultural content of national forms of identification. In Michael Billig's (1992) formulation nationalism is a common-sense discourse that makes second nature distinctions between 'us' and 'them'. Nationalism, then, is blind to the ways collective identities are commonly maintained, and presents the division of the world into nation-states as part of the 'natural' environment. Both Rawls and Habermas displace the idea that the meanings of the 'nation' may become a source of contestation (Verdery 1993). This is not a problem that can be resolved by appealing to the fairness or rightness of the constitutional settlement, as it actually requires reconstruction of the ideas, discourses and sentiments that construct our sense of nationhood. A state is not only a political community, but also acts as an imagined community where civic nationalism exists within particular traditions. Inclusive forms of citizenship are as much a matter of symbolism as of formal rights. Following Stuart Hall (1997), this argument asks us to attend to the social codes and conventions that commonly reproduce institutions and identities.

This leads to our second point. Charles Taylor (1992), in an important essay, seeks to link what he calls the 'struggle for recognition' with the politics of multiculturalism. Taylor starts from the view that both personal and collective identities are shaped by the intersubjective processes of recognition and misrecognition. Images of the self are mirrored back by intimate relations and social institutions informing our individual and collective identities. The struggle for recognition is a dialogic process that is negotiated with intimate and distant others. For Taylor, these processes encompass basic human needs that depend upon the recognition of the uniqueness of our identities and notions of equal respect. The problem comes, however, in reconciling the universal demand for equal dignity with respect for differences. The politics of equal respect, which is most often associated with liberalism, requires that we treat others in a difference-neutral way. The difficulty with such a view is that blind universalism is of itself representative of a particular culture, and that if we are not receptive to difference, then this actually suppresses the uniqueness of our identity formations. To return to the culture of liberalism, it has wanted to secure equal respect, while remaining indifferent to the specific identity formations chosen by its citizens. For example, how could difference-blind liberalism help to protect a 'minority' language, or indeed grant the necessary communal resources to a previously silenced and marginalized social group?

Such cultures, it is claimed, in a framework of individual choice, are unlikely to flourish unless they are granted collective or group rights. Brian Barry's (2000) recent claim that 'difference-blind' liberalism is the fairest way of accommodating diversity is no longer acceptable. The view of citizenship that is being advanced here is that it should become as concerned with questions of recognition and difference as it is with the politics of justice and income distribution. Such notions arguably articulate a more cultural version of citizenship. Ethnic and other 'minorities' articulate a double demand for greater equality and social justice as well as recognition and respect of difference and cultural diversity. According to Nancy Fraser (1997), this should lead us to recognize that our integrity as human beings does not flow from our access to material resources, but is dependent upon processes of cultural domination (being interpreted as being inferior), non-recognition (being excluded from the dominant imagery of one's culture) and disrespect (being continually portrayed in a negative or stereotypical way). It is, then, the feelings of having been unjustly treated and disrespected rather than 'interests' that propel attempts to link the ethical self-realization of the community and the individual. The other side of such demands is that cultural identities are recognized in ways that allow 'the goal of undistorted and unrestricted recognition' (Honneth 1995: 171).

Yet we have seen that liberalism's agnosticism on questions of cultural identity both inadequately occupies the ground of national identity and displaces a concern with difference. As we shall see, most versions of multiculturalism are seeking to reformulate specifically national identities while seeking to build more 'inclusive' communities. We might formulate this as the aim to produce a political community without social disrespect. In the following section, I look at three distinctive approaches to multicultural citizenship before emphasizing what I take to be their major weakness towards cosmopolitan concerns.

Multicultural citizenship: Iris Marion Young, Will Kymlicka and Bhikhu Parekh

Here I want to look at three different approaches to group or collective rights, as advanced by Iris Marion Young, Will Kymlicka and Bhikhu Parekh. The argument that mainstream liberalism is inhospitable to 'difference' and fails to address questions of national identity is well made, but does not of itself make the case for the granting of special rights to 'minority' groups. Indeed, while we continue to use terms like 'majority' and 'minority', they are increasingly contested. There has been a move beyond discourses that assume binary oppositions between straight and gay, men and women, and white and black. A politics of difference aims to subvert the potentially normalizing assumptions behind these oppositions. Such a politics attempts to move beyond a sociology of minorities to a study of identity as an ongoing social construction. These theoretical and social tendencies seek to deconstruct what Stuart Hall (1992) has called the 'essential black subject' and Steven Seidman (1997) 'the straight and gay mainstream'. In other words, multiculturalism needs to move beyond simplistic assumptions in respect of the ways that individual and group identity become constructed. Further, we need to consider carefully which kinds of multiculturalism are actually compatible with the view of cosmopolitan politics I defended earlier. Such a concept, we might be reminded, was built upon the recognition of new levels of governance, and the dialogic understanding of questions of cultural identity.

Iris Marion Young (1989, 1990) argues that despite the universal orientations of citizenship, it remains in practice exclusionary. The idea that citizenship is dependent upon a 'general will' necessarily excludes those groups who are not judged as capable of adopting the general point of view, and adherence to 'equal treatment' necessarily privileges certain cultures and lifestyles over others. The dominance of middle-class white males within the public sphere ensures the tone, ethos and substantive content of most political debate. To counteract these tendencies, Young proposes the introduction of a genuinely inclusive public realm that jettisons the practice of citizens dispassionately uncovering a commonly held good society. In this view, the public realm should abandon the search for commonality among different groups, as historically such a practice has masked group and personal difference. The proper recognition that different groups have distinctive cultures, histories and experiences will inevitably shatter homogeneous expressions of similarity. In this the desire for unity that is expressed in common forms of citizenship excludes certain perspectives from the public. Young is particularly keen to include the voices of oppressed groups whose perspectives have been excluded by presumptions of a universal humanity. A genuinely democratic and participatory community should seek to ensure that groups, including working-class people, lesbians, gays and ethnic minorities, have their distinctive voices and perspectives heard. This – given her own account – would be necessarily hard to achieve, given that more powerful social groups tend to behave as though they have a right to speak and others do not.

The proper representation of oppressed and excluded groups would necessarily involve institutional mechanisms that ensured that groups were able to gain a sense of their collective experience, voice numerous policy proposals and have them heard and, finally, be given veto powers regarding the specific policies that affect them. These institutional procedures would, according to Young, ensure that the privileged hear those voices that are usually silenced. Such proposals would constitute the public as a heterogeneous realm, enabling citizens to participate, while having their differences affirmed by society. A genuinely communicative society would not necessarily value the dispassionate and reasoned speech of white liberals and conservatives over others. Instead, a communicative society would seek to institutionalize the voice of the 'other'. Democratic conversation would not as much be orientated around what we have in common, but seek to bring into our common awareness how we differ. It is only when we are able to develop collectively the skills of listening and speaking across difference that we might begin the task of discovering the general interest. It is, then, the 'polite acknowledgement of the Otherness of others' that should guide our engagements, rather than the search for unity (Young 1996: 130).

These views have been widely criticized for inadequately defining what constitutes a group, for essentializing differences and for converting politics into a practice that merely affirms group difference (Phillips 1991; Faulks 2000). While liberalism may be inhospitable to difference, societies still need to be able to articulate principles that give them some semblance of unity. As Alain Touraine (2000) has argued, multiculturalism should not be reduced to an unrestricted pluralism. A genuinely multicultural society needs to be able to establish unity and communication between separated cultural constellations. Without such a principle of unity it is difficult to see why we should be concerned to listen to the voice of the other. Whereas Young seems to assume that certain institutional arrangements can ensure the powerful are 'confronted' with perspectives and opinions that they are hostile towards, nothing could be further from the truth. As Taylor (1992) argues, the provision of minority rights could not guarantee that equal forms of respect are granted towards minority cultures. To be seen does not mean that you are heard.

Missing from Young's reflections are some of the complexities that are involved in the interpretation of the voices and perspectives of others. Her proposal to ensure that oppressed groups gain a footing in a wider conversation could easily have the reverse effect. In a community that lacked universal normative reasons for why the voice of the 'other' should be engaged with, powerful groups are unlikely to be moved to new levels of attentiveness. While 'minority' rights might secure a 'public presence' for previously marginalized groups, they could not ensure that they are respected. Alternatively, guided by some of Young's criticisms of liberalism, I would argue that any community that wishes to call itself 'inclusive' is more likely to achieve this aim if it attends to the voice of the 'other'. It is this, rather than the provision of special rights or the use of public reason, that is likely to foster democratic conversations of a genuinely cosmopolitan nature. The possibilities for an engagement with the 'other' can of course be enhanced by certain procedures, but such an engagement is only likely to be 'effective' if there is a possibility of dialogic forms of encounter.

Will Kymlicka (1995) has also proposed that liberal societies need to become more welcoming than they are currently in respect of group rights. In particular, Kymlicka is concerned about the rights of national minorities, who since the 1970s have sought to have their ethnic particularity accepted by public institutions. These groups are distinctive from the cultural diversity that arises out of individual or familial immigration, where people more typically seek to integrate themselves into the wider society. There are in fact three main ways in which we might think about group-differentiated rights. First, national societies could grant minority communities rights to self-government, which would involve devolved assemblies and parliaments. Second, the recognition of polyethnic rights would involve public recognition and tolerance of the cultural practices of minorities. This could involve the recognition of distinctive patterns of dress or the funding of 'minority' media and cultural festivals. Finally, there are also claims for special forms of representation that could be made, given that the polity tends to be dominated by white, middle-class and able-bodied men. Kymlicka argues that he is mostly supportive of the capacity of 'minority' cultures to make all three of these different claims. A genuinely multicultural community would seek to promote the recognition of national and ethnic difference. Kymlicka, then, connects the term 'culture' to an intergenerational community that shares a distinctive language, connection to a certain homeland and history.

In making these claims, Kymlicka recognizes that many liberals are concerned that the granting of group rights is actually hostile to the recognition of the rights of the individual. In particular, there is considerable fear in liberal circles that group rights could be used by minority communities to police dissent and cultural contestation. However, Kymlicka argues that group rights should be viewed as a form of external protection against majorities, rather than the internal restriction of individual rights. For example, ethnic groups could demand the right to remove children from schools in order to reduce the impact of 'majority' cultures and reinforce 'traditional' cultural practices such as arranged marriages. By way of defence, Kymlicka argues that the struggle for group rights is usually orientated towards the generation of group respect from mainstream society, and that the protection of the rights of individuals would need to be open to the critical scrutiny of the courts. In short, a group-differentiated citizenship is desirable, as a society founded upon the recognition of diversity is more likely to promote the conditions for social unity than a community that seeks to deny or hide group difference.

Jeremy Waldron (1999) argues from a cosmopolitan point of view that Kymlicka's idea of culture is deeply questionable. Kymlicka's notion of culture implies that within modernity we are able to live as if we were the exclusive products of a single national or ethnic community. In other words, Kymlicka is working with a model of culture wherein separate national and ethnic communities impose homogeneous cultures upon their members. According to this model, the integrity of a culture is maintained by its ability to silence external influences and maintain order within its ranks. This, as Waldron notes, leaves very little space for the intermixing of cultures, hybridity and intercultural communication. The cosmopolitan view of culture would emphasize that no community is self-sustaining and that individuals do not live their lives in cultural enclaves. We may indeed want to grant 'special' rights to certain sections of the community, but should we do so we would need to dispense with the idea that cultures act as pre-constituted billiard balls that strike up against each other.

As Homi Bhabha (1992) argues, questions of cultural difference are not the same as those of cultural diversity. Whereas diversity requires a pre-given cultural realm, questions of difference view culture as constituted through struggle and claims to homogeneity and superiority. Questions of cultural difference seek to deconstruct claims to cultural purity and demonstrate that the meanings and symbols of cultural identity require interpretation and enunciation. As Parekh (2000) comments, it is Kymlicka's view of culture that leads him to dismiss the claims to special rights by immigrants. As immigrants have left their 'natural' cultural home, they should have no rights to culture, and are required to integrate into the host culture. Hence, whereas national 'minorities' have specific cultures that require recognition, the culture of immigrants should be denied public expression. Yet in a world of unprecedented cultural mobility in terms of peoples and symbols, it makes little sense to argue that cultures are confined to national and ethnic boundaries. In this respect, Kymlicka's proposals could well lead to a form of cultural apartheid, rather than the intercultural recognition of difference and the necessity of dialogue.

With these considerations in mind, Parekh's (2000) own version of multiculturalism proceeds from the view that unity-creating public spaces are based upon inclusive forms of dialogue. In this we need not make the distinctions between nationals, ethnics and immigrants that Kymlicka finds persuasive. Parekh argues that multicultural societies need to establish a constitutional settlement, implement justice in a way that respects difference and grant group or collective rights. Parekh agrees with Kymlicka that the argument that collective rights can be used to oppress individuals neglects to consider the idea that individual rights can also destroy communities. Collective rights can be granted on a number of grounds, including the respecting of deeply held religious beliefs, to compensate for previous oppression and disrespect, and the maintenance of 'minority' collective identities. However, what makes Parekh's contribution distinctive is his argument that multicultural societies should aim to create a common culture out of difference. Such a culture, he reasons, could grow out of cross-cultural conversations and intercultural dialogue. The key resource to develop such sensibilities among its citizens is the progressive development of a genuinely multicultural education. In terms of European liberal societies, this would involve the enhanced questioning of Eurocentrism and monoculturalism more generally, and the development of an 'educated' curiosity in respect of other cultures. In this, simply to learn about the 'great and glorious' past of a particular ethnic or national society not only breeds racism, but also stultifies the creative imagination. The central aim of a multi-cultural education would be the fostering of sensibilities that were open to the sheer diversity of cultures that make up the general history and experience of a community.

In the promotion of intercultural dialogue, Parekh distances himself from many of the assumptions of mainstream liberalism. Rather than starting from the view that we already know what counts as civilized behaviour, he argues for a transformative dialogue that respects difference. In these dialogues we need to be guided by what Parekh (2000: 267) calls 'operative public values'. While these values are open to question, they are both general and regulative and embodied within the rights and obligations of citizenship, which are in turn shaped by established legal norms and practice. In this, Parekh (2000: 280) argues that 'our decision to allow a cultural practice cannot and should not be based on abstract moral principles or the right to autonomy alone but also on its cultural and historical context'. Such dialogues should have a transformative effect upon both 'minorities' and 'majorities' alike, as they critically interrogate a number of cultural practices.

Parekh best illustrates the possibilities that such dialogues can have through his investigation of the Salman Rushdie dispute. For Parekh, the dispute within Britain was marked by entrenched modes of thinking that failed to make use of the opportunity to gain a more informed understanding of one another. The liberal defenders of *The Satanic Verses* mostly failed to appreciate the sense of harm felt by the Muslim protesters, while they in turn often failed to grasp the significance of ideas about the freedom of speech for liberals. What the dispute actually highlights is the need to formulate new public forums and institutions designed to deal with questions of intercultural conflict and confusion. These dialogues would need to recognize the different cultural associations, fears and cultural projections of both ourselves and others. Parekh argues that such deliberations are not simply the cold exchange of reasons, but would need to be informed by the spirit of compromise, curiosity and mutual respect. Such dialogues are sustained by the idea that all cultures are limited and benefit from dialogue. A multicultural society has the principles of dialogue at its centre, and refuses to privilege a particular cultural perspective (including liberalism). It is the principle of intercultural communication and the recovery of the 'other' that governs a multicultural society, an ethos threatened by claims to cultural homogeneity and ethnic purity. The point here is to foster a society that avoids collapse into either separatism or the tyranny of the majority, while being fully inclusive of the cultural capabilities and capacities of its members.

As we have seen, multicultural societies are likely to benefit from the granting of some group rights and different ways of anchoring intercultural forms of dialogue. While situations inevitably involve the trade-off between universal principles and more contextual forms of understanding, they will inevitably proceed on a case-by-case basis. Such dialogic contexts would also, as many of the critics of multiculturalism have argued, need to address the question of unequal power relations, which lead to some cultures being stereotyped and considered as 'other' (Yuval-Davis 1997). Such forums would need to make sure that 'minorities' within 'minority' communities find a voice and that the diversity of the host cultures is properly represented.

A report called *The Future of Multi-Cultural Britain* (also known as the Parekh report) was published in 2000, the same year as Parekh's *Rethinking Multiculturalism*. Despite being authored by the Runnymede Trust, it takes up many of the themes available within Parekh's more academic work. The report recognizes 'the rights of communities to live according to their own conception of the good life, subject to certain moral constraints' (Runnymede Trust 2000: 37). In this respect, it is critical of mainstream liberalism for promoting monoculturalism in the public and multiculturalism in the private. The report highlights specific ways to enhance intercultural dialogue and the auditing of dominant institutions to ensure their inclusivity. However, as is well known, the publicizing of these proposals in the British press was overshadowed by the report's claim (mentioned only briefly) that Britishness was 'racially coded' (Runnymede Trust 2000: 38). This incident reveals the extreme difficulty of seeking to develop a politics of difference rather than one limited to liberal ideals of tolerance. As Henry Giroux (1994) has argued, multiculturalism inevitably seeks to question the ways in which the national culture privileges certain identities over others. Multiculturalism presents the mutual challenge of seeking to deconstruct the ideas that 'black' and 'white' encode essential identities, and the need to help dominant groups to 'unlearn their own privilege'

(Giroux 1994: 327). Again, multiculturalism points towards the possibility of deconstructing identities of power, primarily by making 'whiteness' visible and by recovering 'other' voices, which are often stereotyped and marginalized. However, these dimensions, as the reaction of the British press demonstrates, will always have to move within less than perfect social and cultural conditions, and these are dangers and difficulties that any version of multiculturalism would inevitably have to face. A dialogic multicultural politics would have to negotiate the dangers of fundamentalist reaction, disengagement by dominant groups and a politics of 'otherness' that sought security in the permanent margin (Gates 1994).

The other criticism that has been brought to bear on Parekh's suggestions is his 'anti-universalism'. Brian Barry (2001: 69) has argued that Parekh's equivocation on these themes fails to recognize the binding force of 'the principle of non-discrimination'. It is this universal liberal principle that should ethically guide a multicultural society, rather than intercultural dialogue. Parekh's (2000) concern with universalism is twofold. First, he argues that Rawlsian liberalism tends to exclude and marginalize practices and perspectives that seem to be 'unreasonable'. That is, liberalism (as we have already seen) is actually inhospitable to cultural diversity, in that it presupposes an individualistic ethos. Second, he argues that universal norms are too abstract to do anything more than offer general norms for guidance. What is actually required is the empowerment of 'weaker' groups in dialogue and the development of multi-vocal conversations. The concern here is that the imposition of abstract norms can be divisive, and indeed may become disputed in practice. While Parekh occasionally bends the stick too far, his proposals are actually a call to develop what Lister (1997) has called a 'differential universalism'. As Parekh (1995) has argued elsewhere, the point where liberalism becomes illiberal is where it finds it difficult to respect those who do not value individualism, secularism, ambition and the pursuit of wealth. The other side of liberalism is that it may come to code those who fail to be 'reasonable' through normalizing discourses. Parekh's concern is less with a minimal universalism than with the cultural insensitivity of liberalism. Yet he is on weaker ground where he fails to recognize that any ongoing conversation or transformative dialogue actually presupposes certain universals, such as equal respect (Benhabib 1999).

Cosmopolitanism and multiculturalism

The construction of common cultures of difference at the national level remains one of the key objectives of multiculturalism. In cultures where citizenship is predominately formulated through national institutions such as the media, education and government, these perspectives remain important. Yet the debate thus far presupposes that multicultural concerns are questions exclusively for national contexts. Such formulations are inadequate, in that modern societies have become marked by multiple and return migrations of people that defy the simple logic evident in talk of refugees and immigration. Further, such questions inevitably highlight the exclusive role of citizenship, given that many nations in the 'First World' are currently tightening their borders against 'outsiders'. As Lister (1997) argues in the European context, the attempt to draw a line between citizens and foreigners creates strong material and symbolic boundaries. The control of borders between different world regions and different nations inevitably impacts upon the dynamics of multicultural societies, given that it raises questions as to who and under what conditions is to be included and excluded (Solomos 2001). For Isin and Wood (1999), such is the centrality of these questions that they prefer the term 'diasporic citizenship' to 'multicultural citizenship'. This acknowledges that the globe is the product of many and varied international migrations.

According to the United Nations, the number of refugees in the world increased from 3 million in 1978 to 18.2 million in 1993. Further, it has been estimated that due to the male nature of warfare, 80 per cent of refugees are women and children (Yuval-Davis 1997). Yet most of the new diversity evident in Western societies is the result of legal immigration rather than the impact of refugees. This has not, however, prevented 'minority' groups becoming the victim of nativist discrimination and violence, which has fuelled the rise of anti-immigrant political parties across Europe. The issue of immigration and refugees is currently one of the main testing grounds for a multicultural society, stressing the ongoing tension between human rights and national forms of citizenship.

The dilemma here has been neatly summed up by Benhabib (1999), in that whereas no liberal democracy can lose its right to determine its own immigration policy, they equally should not close their borders to refugees or asylum seekers. Such considerations take us way beyond the previous arguments in respect of liberalism and multiculturalism, all of which presume the fiction of a closed society. The United Nations 1952 Convention of Refugees proclaimed the right to leave the host nation, without a corresponding right of asylum. Normatively, however, all liberal democratic nations are under an obligation to recognize individually a human right both to enter and to exit nation-states. As Benhabib argues, it makes little sense to claim a right of departure without a corresponding right of entry. While admittance does not give people automatic rights of citizenship, it does presuppose that there are well established procedures to ensure that individuals receive a fair hearing. In other words, multicultural societies are constituted not simply through an ongoing internal democratic and cultural conversation, but also through whom they include and exclude from their borders. These questions inevitably lead back to the concerns of the previous section and point to the enduring link between cosmopolitan and multicultural definitions of citizenship.

Nations are increasingly under pressure in this regard from international agencies that confront states with a number of constraints. Apart from the normative pressure of universal human rights, the state also has to work with different sets of social conditions that are not of its own making (such as the impacts of other states' policies and mediated public opinion), which inevitably move such questions into a cosmopolitan frame of reference (Sassen 1998). Hence, while we might represent multiculturalism as 'the desire to find the cultural and political norms appropriate to more heterogeneous societies across nations', this is likely to be contradictory in practice (Chicago Cultural Studies Group 1994: 114).

Yet if questions of multiculturalism and cosmopolitanism are complicated by introducing the question of the exclusivity of national borders, they are mutually threatened by an identity politics built upon fundamentalism. Indeed, multiculturalism's and cosmopolitanism's opposite is the attempt to build more solid and less fluid identities in the context of rapid social change. Conservative rhetoric in respect of cultural identity is a progressively powerful political force. Defensive reactions to globalization can be seen in a range of fundamentalist and communalist political movements and cultural struggles the world over (Castells 1997). These features provide a powerful challenge to the 'political' forces of multiculturalism and cosmopolitanism. In this way, the 'authenticity' of national and local fundamentalisms is likely to be erected against the intensifying global flows of money, people and identity (Ang 2000). Despite the intensification of the global flows of people and symbols, a number of nationalistic and ethnically based social movements are attempting to reconnect questions of identity and territory. The appeal of 'sameness' continues for many to provide a way of addressing the anxieties of the global age (Gilroy 2000). The trick at the national level remains how to articulate a more fully inclusive society and culture that also recognizes the need to decentre such an identity through the recognition of diaspora and difference. However, there are likely to remain tensions between cosmopolitanism and multiculturalism, given the capacity of 'local' or 'national' forms of citizenship to close their borders against some global flows.

Rejoining cosmopolitanism and multiculturalism, it seems to me, is perfectly possible as long as questions of recognition, respect and cultural identity are taken seriously. Yet we can also point to the continuation of a number of tensions within so-called cosmopolitan perspectives in respect of cultural identity. For example, Turner and Rojek (2001) have recently argued that cosmopolitanism depends upon a cool/thin identity that is able to develop an ironic form of distance from current cultural attachments. Such a view can be contrasted with more 'rooted cosmopolitanisms', which see no necessary contradiction between feelings of loyalty and commitment to particular cultures and an openness towards difference and otherness (Appiah 1998). Such a view would open the possibility of maintaining a commitment to particular national or local identities while seeking to dialogue with others who might have different connections. Here cosmopolitanism and multiculturalism are located less in a 'thin' identity and more in the complex recognition of our loyalties and commitments to dialogue. We should resist the temptation to argue that cosmopolitanism and multiculturalism are best articulated by those who manage to avoid 'thick solidarities' (Turner 2000). It is not too fanciful to claim that a commitment to cosmos is compatible with attachments to both place and dialogue. This will become evident as we consider the city as a key location for cosmopolitan citizenship.

The city as a contested space

As we have seen, to think about the question of citizenship involves different levels of analysis. However, the coordinates of the debate so far imply that cosmopolitan citizenship is required as globalization processes have undermined national forms of citizenship, transferring power upwards into the hands of multinational agencies and out of the hands of national citizens. In this analysis cities become social spaces that are subsumed by the national political arena. However, if we introduce a greater sensitivity to the spaces in which diverse peoples actually live out their relations to larger collectivities, then a more complex picture emerges.

The city is a key location, as it is the place where the maintenance of civility, the acceptance of difference and justice, actually counts (Ignatief 1990). For example, Massey (1997) states that currently half the world's population live in cities, with only three of the globe's largest twenty cities locatable in the 'First World'. The contours of citizenship are progressively shaped by the social and political fabric of the city. As Castells (1996) argues, increasingly the global economy is organized through the command centres of global cities, including Tokyo, Paris, London and New York. These informational cities tend to be the spaces and places of political power, media control and the managerial elite. Global cities are urban spaces where globalization gets done; they are nodes within a network that is globally interconnected, while being simultaneously locally disconnected. These networked global cities tend to be places of innovation and technological sophistication that determine national economic performance, but they are also places where excluded populations gather.

Urban contexts in this view might be said to exhibit a dual cosmopolitanism. First, they are spaces for global cosmopolitan elites to live and consume a diverse array of goods and services that impact upon the city in the creation of arts and entertainment complexes, housing projects, cafes and restaurants in order to attract mobile affluent populations. Second, as Holston and Appadurai (1999) emphasize, global cities have also witnessed sharp increases in socio-economic divisions and have attracted global migrants and immigrants. Especially in the developing world, they are spaces where a poorly housed migrant population exists next door to the mansions of the rich and powerful. These dual cosmoplitanisms built out of wealth and poverty have come to shape globally orientated subjectivities and citizenships.

More generally, although this trend is particularly marked within global cities, the site of the city during the 1970s and 1980s became orientated around a symbolic economy. The city establishes a competitive advantage over other cities through its ability to convert itself into a site of postmodern consumption and spectatorship for the middle and upper classes. These processes have enhanced the social and cultural divisions of the city, with urban spaces aiming to attract a consumption-orientated professional middle class thereby excluding more disadvantaged groups. For Sharon Zukin (1995), the two questions we need to be able to answer in respect of the city are: who constructs the visual images that represent the city, and who determines access to the public spaces of social interaction? In answer to both of these questions, she argues that public spaces are being progressively commodified to meet the needs of capitalism and social elites. While this inevitably means that cities are increasingly becoming contested and polarized spaces, it is arguable that the cultural economy also grants cities new possibilities to respond to industrial decline and reinvent the projected image of the city (Lash and Urry 1994).

This situation invariably offers cultural forms of citizenship opportunities, as well as dangers. It is true that the neo-liberal policies of the 1980s and 1990s sought to develop a lively cosmopolitan life with respect to the cultural industries and other commercial cultural sectors, and more excluded areas suffered as a result. Yet cities are also able to promote intercultural communication and cosmopolitanism as a positive virtue. They can achieve this by establishing venues for cultural exchange, and developing public forums for policy debate and genuinely multicultural arts festivals (Bloomfield and Bianchini 2001).[3]

However, despite these possibilities, the greatest threat to cosmopolitan sensibilities remains the spatial concentration of hierarchy. If there are associated cultures of affluence and poverty then their spatial concentration plays a key part (Byrne 1999). Specifically, this concentration has helped to create fortified urban spaces where private security guards, electronic surveillance and walled communities have carved out enclaves of middle- and upper-class consumption and employment. The closed condominiums are meant to offer islands of calm and security, shutting out the unpredictable urbanity of the city (Davis 1990; Caldeira 1999). These new zones of exclusion within the city are constructed through a fear of the 'other' and can be connected to the systematic privatization of public spaces, which compounds social exclusion. The other side of this process is the construction of urban ghettos, which may become caught in a downward spiral linking disadvantaged populations, an informal drugs economy and the collapse of the labour market and welfare support (Wacquant 1999). While these processes are probably most advanced in North America, they are quickly becoming a global social issue and serve as a warning to alternative social systems. Indeed, the material aspects of exclusion within the city are often compounded by the stigmatization of certain residential areas in the local media. Poor and excluded zones of the city are often relatively powerless to control the ways in which they are represented within mainstream televisual and press accounts. Zones of poverty and exclusion are either absent from media cultures or made present through the reporting of crime or more visual spectacles that usually contain violence (Champagne 1999).

The post-industrial city has promoted a culture of 'hedonism without scruples' among the affluent, and material and cultural impoverishment among the excluded (Webster 1995: 211). Yet the specific effects of social and cultural exclusion vary across a range of different cities and locations. Here two key questions have arisen against the backdrop of entrenched exclusion from citizenship within the city. The first is how we might promote a politics of justice and recognition that does not end as a politics based simply on the assertion of militant particularism (Berman 1997). Second, how can the right to the enjoyment of the city be conferred upon citizens with different identities and subjectivities? In all the talk of exclusion what can sometimes get lost are the undoubted pleasures of the city. The city has traditionally acted as a place where different groups have come to escape the surveillance and order of small communities, to engage in the delight of difference. One of the cultural reasons why cities remain popular is that they provide spaces for citizens to experiment with their identities and participate in a more disorderly existence. The enjoyment of the right to the city is, however, linked to both the 'power to move' conferred upon middle-class populations and the right to feel safe (Wilson 1991; Massey 1997). The dilemma here becomes how to construct a more socially just city without undermining the many features that made it attractive in the first place.

In many respects these issues had already been addressed by Richard

Sennett's (1970) classic little book on the city. In *The Uses of Disorder*, he argued that the desire to bring about the rationally controlled city was an attempt to rationalize and dehumanize the urban landscape. Politically this is often expressed in the search for idealized images of community or an attempt to construct intense feelings of in-group unity. This is actually a way, argues Sennett, of avoiding troubling forms of emotional ambivalence within social relations, and of expelling 'otherness' from our community. As a consequence, the city is becoming not so much a zone for 'multiple contact points', but a space of 'dullness and routine' (Sennett 1970: 135). The desire to live without difference is progressively becoming an everyday feature of urban life, as neighbourhoods became increasingly segregated and as urban planners seek to create conflict-free communities. The attempts to flee difference and ambivalence end in violent strategies seeking either to assimilate or to expel cultural difference. For Sennett, this asphyxiates much about the life of the city that made it exciting in the first place. Similarly, James Donald (1997, 1999) has argued that attempts to plan the city rationally represent the city as a problem to be solved. This is particularly evident in the attempts made within the discourses and practices of urban planners who sought to subject the city to utopian designs. What is required is a different way of imagining urbanity that seeks to foster rather than impose the values of tolerance and difference.

Both Sennett and Donald are pointing to the dangers of enhancing the politics of justice over the recognition of difference. The modernist dream of reordering and imposing the values of justice upon the city ended with the urban planners' imposition of tower blocks in the 1950s and 1960s. The citizenship of the city requires a complex relationship between the politics of justice (which should not become technologically or instrumentally defined) and the politics of difference (which requires that we learn how to negotiate with the other) in shared and often contested spaces. Such a politics would need to negotiate carefully between the fantasy of conflict-free urban space and the evident risks and dangers that are often posed to personhood. An ethical cosmopolitan politics in respect of the city would need to be able to construct dialogue across growing social divisions, while maintaining a shared sense of civility and commitment. Notably, the city is the place where cosmopolitan orientations are most likely to take root.

Cosmopolitan cultures and cosmopolitan selves

There are at least two ways of talking about contemporary cosmopolitan cultures. The first is to suggest that cosmopolitan cultures are the depthless commercial pleasures of the increasingly placeless capitalist elite. In this view, cosmopolitan culture is aligned with a postmodern culture that involves the visual and sensual pleasures of global cities, Hollywood cinema, Madonna CDs and Australian wine. This builds upon a prejudice of certain aspects of Left thinking that presumes that if one moves outside the boundaries of the nation it is to 'wallow in a privileged and irresponsible detachment' (Robbins 1998: 4). Such a notion of cosmopolitanism would tie a fast-moving placeless culture into the rise of a new middle and upper class of cappuccino drinkers. Here cosmopolitanism can be contrasted to the more local and national cultural definitions that are available to poor and working people. Such a view sets up a simple contrast between cosmopolitans and locals. Hence, whereas I have access to the Internet, read European newspapers and listen to world music, the 'less fortunate' members of the city in which I live think that everything English is best, only read local newspapers and listen to lad pop. Cosmopolitanism, on such a view, becomes the everyday currency of global capitalism, whose most obvious effect is the reinforcement of symbolic boundaries between social classes.

However, the second version of cosmopolitanism has a more overtly ethical vision than one motivated by the reproduction of class prejudice. Such a notion of cosmopolitanism would not presume that the globe-trotting journalists are any more cosmopolitan in their orientations than someone who has never left the city of their birth. This is because to conceive of cosmopolitanism ethically detaches it from my ability to access exotic forms of consumption, while connecting it to my ability to live with difference. While cosmopolitanism can indeed be connected to forms of cultural openness, it is more closely connected to what Jonathan Rutherford (2000) has called 'the art of life' than to manic mobility or hedonism.

The version of cosmopolitanism I wish to defend has more to do with ethics and selfhood than explicit concerns with ideology. However, it does retain a sociological point of reference through the many new claims and agendas that are being opened by questions connected to the mobility of cultures, multiculturalism, gender and sexuality (Urry 2000b). Yet there are a number of sceptics in this regard. For example, Friedman (1997) has argued that intellectuals and elites who wish to talk of hybridity and cosmopolitanism are largely writing from the 'particular' viewpoint of 'de-territorialized' identities. The hybridity and cultural sophistication of elite groups is in sharp distinction to the processes of Balkanization and tribalization experienced at the bottom of the system. Friedman makes these points against cultural theorists like Bhabha (1994), whose work seeks to emphasize how all forms of cultural and symbolic production lack the primordial unity or fixity claimed by cultural nationalists. Friedman's view is that this insight is likely to be of little help when faced with nationalist forms of cultural closure and violence. However, Bhabha does point to a connection between questions of identity and ethics missed by Friedman. What Bhabha (1994: 227) describes as the uncovering of the 'contestation and flux' of identity has contributed to the cosmopolitan project. Many post-colonial writers in this respect point to the partial blindness of national habits and traditions, which see only what they want to see. The discursive sin of arguments made in respect of hybridity is to point to the way common identities (not just elite ones) are forged through the unpredictable flows of peoples and symbols. In this respect, Bhabha (1994: 149) argues that pedagogic attempts to inscribe homogeneity exhibit a 'continual displacement of the anxiety of irredeemably plural modern space'.

Such discursive manoeuvres seek to dispel and displace the 'in-between' nature of minority cultures. Bhabha asks that we consider the negotiation of cultural difference, not diversity. Cultural diversity represents cultures as separate islands whose contents are pre-given and frozen in time. The negotiation of cultural difference, on the other hand, requires that we give up notions of cultural purity, and search to uncover the ways in which the meanings and symbols of culture are produced through complex processes of translation, negotiation and enunciation. Again, cosmopolitanism is not well captured by the universal Kantian individual, by certain class or ethnic identities or by becoming a partisan communitarian of a particular community (Waldron 1999).

In terms of a cultural agenda, these questions have been most prominently raised by those writing from a post-colonial viewpoint. Notions of hybridization and mongrelization have been utilized to claim a radical heterogeneity that resists the essentialisms of racialization (Young 1995). Rather than embracing the politics of cultural nationalism or the rhetorics of free-market liberalism, notions of diaspora have sought to break the simplistic links between place and culture. Processes of transcultural dialogue, difference and displacement emphasize how we are all 'out of place'. Whereas supremacist thinking seeks to fortify boundaries of racial particularity, this is challenged by popular forces that seek to articulate more ambivalent, less settled identities (Gilroy 2000).

Such projections then break with the idea of the self as embedded within any one community or as being atomized and individualistic. Cosmopolitan politics requires a dialogic view of the self. As the social world loses its capacity, once and for all, to fix moral hierarchies through tradition, this opens the cosmos to the difference of others. For Habermas (1979), the fully developed ego should in principle be capable of questioning the authority of previously held identities and communally transmitted norms and values. As Habermas recognizes, such a notion of selfhood has been most fully outlined by Mead. The self in this account emerges through a three-way conversation between the I, Me and generalized other. Mead (1934) argues that human selfhood develops out of our capacity to be able to view ourselves from the generalized attitude of other people. Once we learn to take 'the attitude of the other' we are able to view ourselves from the position of the community. This is not a description of moral conformity, but the recognition that the dialogic self can only handle community disapproval by setting up moral standards that 'outvote' currently held social norms. Hence, in cosmopolitan terms an individual or social movement might be required to come into conflict with the immediate community in the defence of a universalistic morality. Mead, in such a view, consistently represents individualism as the flip side of universalism.

However, while central to the cosmopolitan project, such a view of the self can only take us so far. The dialogic model of the self is unable to account for the creative productions of the unconscious. According to Elliott (1992), self-hood is not only shaped by the to and fro of conversation between the self and community, but is also dependent upon the pre-linguistic configurations of the psyche. Arguably, then, psychoanalysis has a great deal to contribute to a cosmopolitan understanding of the self, given that it has been able to identify much that is creative and destructive about human beings. The dialogic view of the self cannot explain a fear of difference and otherness that may come to obstruct ongoing cosmopolitan conversations.

Psychoanalysis introduces a cosmopolitanism of the self, given its rejection of the idea of a unitary or homogeneous psyche. The conflictual alliances of the id, ego and superego introduce a level of complexity into the under-standing of the self missing from many sociological and psychological accounts. Indeed, as many have begun to consider, psychoanalytic under-standings of the self bring questions of feeling, phantasy and subjectivity into citizenship (Elliott 2001; Frosch 2001). 'Cultural' citizenship becomes an investigation into irrational and psychic investments and not just the more formal sphere of rights. For example, Jessica Benjamin (1998) has argued that a purely cognitive view of the self cannot explain omnipotence. By omnipotence, we mean a mental state where a person is unable to accept that the other does not want the same. In psychoanalytic terms such a view is connected with violence, as the other becomes assimilated within the wishes of the self. This is a denial of recognition and respect. These features are related to the political question of whether a community can accept the 'other' without expecting them to conform. Benjamin seeks to explain this disposition through the capacity of the mind to split objects into good/bad, excluded/included. If the other is either idealized (as the good object) or repudiated (as the bad object), these features cancel the intersubjective tension required by mutual recognition.

Michael Rustin (1991) has demonstrated how fear and anxiety often invoke the paranoid splitting of objects into loved and hated. Building upon the work of the psychotherapist Melanie Klein, he describes how these features are commonly evident in the first two years of life. Much of Klein's work focuses upon how paranoid mechanisms are evoked through intimate contact with the primary carer (usually the mother). These primitive phantasies involve getting rid of unwanted feelings into others (projective identification) and the taking of the attributes of others into the self (introjective identification). Rustin suggests, not unreasonably, that these mechanisms can be linked to racism, where uncomfortable feelings are projected into others, and where different ethnic groups are idealized and denigrated.

The fear of ambivalence evident within attempts to promote purity or the 'objective attitude' could be due to a fear of the feelings that are involved in recognizing the complexities of our personal investments within politics and society (Samuels 1993). The argument here is that whether these are feelings of anger, contradiction, disappointment or estrangement, they may well be experienced as threatening by the political subject, who prefers to take shelter in either the politics of purity or objectivity. The desire to rid the self of ambiguous feelings is indicative of fundamentalist as opposed to cosmo-politan politics. As Christopher Bollas (1992) argues, in order to combat fundamentalist politics we need to combat the fascist within each of us. This view offers a different set of political and personal considerations from arguments where authoritarian tendencies are seen as connected to some groups rather than others. The fascist personality will seek to expel doubts and counter-views from the self and replace them with more coherent ideologies. The fascistic mind values the clarity that is to be found in both purifying and purging the self. These violent forms of purification are prefigured within everyday encounters between the self and others, as well as within the self. Each time we denigrate or caricature another we are participating in a form of emotional violence. By this Bollas is looking at the ways certain political viewpoints are prefigured in the self, not arguing that this is what brings oppressive ideologies into political space. To refer back to the connection between racism and the psyche, the argument is not that the self is inherently racist, but that conditions of insecurity and upheaval may strengthen the appeal of racist views. Indeed, as Rustin (1991) suggests, to call these feelings paranoid is to suggest why racism is often difficult to counter with rational arguments. Similarly, Bollas is arguing that the capacity of the self to be destructive is linked to the need felt by the self to project difficult feelings into others.

While Habermas and Mead seek to construct an intersubjective view of the self, they do so without paying sufficient attention to the subject's capacity to be destructive. To open up the relationship between the self and other is to ask whether we can avoid assimilating the other to the self. Can we recognise the other's alterity without normalizing difference? Similarly, Kristeva (1992) has argued that the projection of rage and hatred on to strangers within the community involves the removal of feelings that cannot be held internally. That we are, to borrow her phrase, 'strangers to ourselves' may mean we become caught up in similarly destructive psychic processes. As Jung (1946: 8) famously put it, 'anything that disappears from your psychological inventory is apt to turn up in the guise of a hostile neighbour'. Other than the recovery of responsibility, psychoanalytic writers often point to the need to recognize our own internal mystery in this respect. Stephen Frosch (2000) argues that the ability to resist cultural fixity, while being alive to your own strangeness, is a deeply moral project. It is a common human experience to have feelings of despair and panic when we are unsure of what we feel and hunger for coherent identity. The ability to be able to recognize what we do not know about ourselves may prevent us from attempting defensively to construct a coherent in-group identity. The other side of not being able to tolerate 'not knowing' and of misnaming the self's and the 'other's' internal state means breaking with the practice of being able to predict the experiences of others and ourselves. To be open to difference entails that we are able to retain an openness to the often unpredictable human natures of ourselves and others (Ogden 1991; Bollas 1999).

These considerations point to the fact that the cosmopolitan project is as defined by an ethical agenda as it is by a certain level of emotional complexity. Such considerations arguably point to the links between post-colonialism and psychoanalysis. As Said (1999: 295) has commented:

> I occasionally experience myself as a cluster of flowing currents. I prefer this to the idea of a solid self, the identity to which so many attach so much significance. These currents, like the themes of one's own life, flow along during the waking hours, and at their best, they require no reconciling, no harmonising. They are 'off' and maybe out of place, but at least they are always in motion, in time, in place, in the form of all kinds of strange combinations moving about, not necessarily forward, sometimes against each other, contrapuntally yet without one central theme.

Psychoanalytic perspectives on the self point to the ways in which inner and outer reality are connected to one another. This brings to the fore the idea that aggression, hate and envy are as much part of the self as the more positive virtues often associated with citizenship. Yet we are not the passive victims of unconscious processes but creative agents in the construction of personal meaning and identity. A cosmopolitan view of the self and citizenship necessarily shares the view that we need to conceive mutually of society and each other beyond the ambitions of the nation and the ego. Both are radically

decentred through the operation of flows and processes that they can never fully control.

Conclusion

This chapter has argued that a cultural cosmopolitan citizenship needs to recognize four different levels of analysis. The dimensions of the global, national, city and self all display questions that are potentially cosmopolitan. We have seen that issues of justice and difference constantly move across these levels. The multiplication of citizenships beyond exclusively national concerns has revived a number of different positions that connect the personal to the global. It was noted that the struggle for a communications-based society or cultural citizenship is dependent upon the emergence of republican institutions and the emotional and cognitive capacity to engage within intercultural conversation. It may also require the introduction of new group rights in order to protect minorities from the effects of dominant cultures. However, there are many dangers in this respect, and here I have argued for the setting up of new democratic forums to empower the voices of the marginalized. These might include public forums and staged television debates that empower the voices of refugees, marginalized religious groups and poor ethnic communities. Cosmopolitanism is best served by seeking to bring the 'other' into the debate. I have also argued that cosmopolitan citizenship depends upon certain models of culture and identity that emphasize hybridity and difference. We also saw how models of cosmopolitan and multicultural citizenship face challenges in the guise of fundamentalism and the presumption that such ideals are the property of certain sections of the community. In the next chapter, I aim to explore how similar levels of analysis are transforming the relationships between nature, culture and society. Just as cosmopolitan citizenship needs to break with the boundaries of the nation-state to introduce more complex social relations, the same might be said of ecological citizenship.

Notes

1 The argument that many Kantian-inspired attempts to reformulate democracy in cosmopolitan terms are overly disconnected from diverse political contexts revisits some of the criticisms made by the early Frankfurt School.
2 On Thompson's ethical and political positions see the excellent paper by Michael Kenny (2000).
3 This question is explored in more depth in Chapter 5.

Further reading

Appiah, K. A.(1998) Cosmopolitan patriots, in P. Cheah and R. Robins, (eds) *Cosmopolitics: Thinking and Feeling Beyond the Nation*. Minneapolis: University of Minnesota Press.

Beck, U. (1999) *World Risk Society*. Cambridge: Polity Press.

Donald, J. (1999) *Imaging the Modern City*. London: Athlone Press.

Giddens, A. (1999) *Runaway World: How Globalisation is Reshaping Our Lives*. London: Profile Books.

Held, D. (1995) *Democracy and the Global Order: From the Modern State to Cosmopolitan Governance*. Cambridge: Polity Press.

Parekh, B. (2000) *Rethinking Multiculturalism: Cultural Diversity and Political Theory*. London: Macmillan.

ECOLOGICAL AND CULTURAL CITIZENSHIP: ACROSS THE NATURE/CULTURE DIVIDE

3

Those trees, those useless trees produce the air that I'm breathing.

(Pulp, The Trees 2001)

Images and icons of our blue planet can be seen on office walls, posters within schools and logos to sell goods. These pictures originally taken by the Apollo space mission in the late 1960s directly led to the discovery of the biosphere – the ten miles or so of water, soil and air that wraps the globe and without which life for humanity and other species would not be possible. The biosphere, which is currently threatened by a hole in the ozone, acid rain and global warming, has paradoxically been made visible by some of the same technological inventions that are threatening its existence. This ambivalence can also be seen in representations of the globe. Images of the blue planet promote ideas of global interdependence, where we are all interlinked by planetary webs of life. Such images can remind us of the fact that processes of globalization and technological development are indeed crucial in helping us to understand and imagine our shared hopes and vulnerabilities. Yet we might equally argue that the ability to look upon the globe from on high promotes an omnipotent fantasy in which the earth can become the subject of our will and technological mastery. Such projections encourage the view that we might come to fix technologically the problems of our shared planet given our ability to master nature.

These two cultural projections on to the same image can be related to two different views of globalization. The first is a moral–ethical view of the limits of the Earth's resources and the need to find a way to live sustainably with the rest of humanity and other species. The other is a neo-liberal project that seeks to impose the operation of free markets, thereby removing the geographical and cultural boundaries to competitive accumulation. Both ecological considerations and the market are currently urging us to think globally (Sachs 1999).

Yet despite the dominance of global capitalism we are currently living in an age where definitions of personal and collective 'success' are being radically rethought. Modernist ideas of more, bigger and better are increasingly coming under personal and collective scrutiny. Complaints of stress, overwork, illness and insecurity are becoming common among society's economic winners. The contrast between the desire to accumulate wealth and engage in overt patterns of conspicuous consumption, and the ethics of self-fulfilment and personal responsibility, has become the everyday fare of television chat shows and the newspapers' lifestyle sections. The ability to be able to make our own accommodation with still dominant views of personal and collective success is increasingly important. Elsewhere, the growing realization that ever higher levels of economic growth have presided over the poisoning of our oceans, the depletion of different animal and plant species, the global widening of income distribution and the undermining of indigenous societies has made us question previously accepted forms of societal development. Add to this the widely reported (although still contested) consequences of global warming and climate change, and it is clear to see why human societies are becoming sceptical of models of growth that have become associated with ideas of progress connected with modernity. Hence, the question of what it means to be a 'successful' society or person is currently a matter of global debate and concern.

There are many responses that are possible to these and other related questions. Some argue that we need to renew our faith in the abilities of experts and liberal democracy more generally. The 'free market' and the official representatives of government bureaucracies need to be trusted to guide humanity through its darkest days (Fukuyama 1989). This is particularly evident as we enter a new century hoping to avoid the barbarism evident within national and state socialism. The triumph of liberal democracy over competing social systems is not a matter we should treat lightly. We might choose to view some of the gloomier predictions made by modern society's detractors as lacking the necessary faith in our technological ability to overcome common problems. We can develop greener solutions to our shared problems, while still enjoying the prosperity of network capitalism. In stark contrast, others suggest that we should return to 'nature' by seeking to recover humanity's balance with the ecosystem.

Such perspectives seek to renegotiate the relationship between diverse human cultures and nature, thereby recognizing that our attempts to dominate and control our shared environments have had a destructive effect upon our relationship with ourselves, other species and the Earth (Merchant 1992). Green or environmental movements have been at the leading edge of those developing a more ethical relationship with nature, criticizing dominantly held views of progress and success. Such an approach would argue that the environmental crisis requires a complete break with the social and political ideologies that have governed the modern period. While the diverse networks of the ecological movement cannot be reduced to a single philosophy, they have undoubtedly helped to open up a number of repressed ethical questions in terms of our relation to our own bodies, the food we eat, the kinds of transport we use, our relationship with other animals and our understanding of risk more generally.

Yet whichever path we decide upon, it is hard to maintain that either 'business as usual' or the 'recovery of nature' is an adequate response to eco-logical questions. The idea that we need to learn how better to manage or live in nature reproduces a binary split between nature and culture. If we view 'nature' as an external set of material relations that requires more efficient management or planning, it breaks the circuit through which we would recognize ourselves as part of the planet. Such a view would seek to displace the problem of sustain-able development and species diversity on to the more efficient running of the state or market. Indeed, much green thinking is governed by a suspicion of technical fixes and the attempt to rethink humanity's relation to the web of life (Trainer 1991). Alternatively, the attempt to stage a 'return' to nature inadequately appreciates the fact that strict distinctions between the cultural and the natural are increasingly difficult to make in modern society. As Anthony Giddens (1994) has pointed out, the natural and social worlds have become so entangled that all attempts to remoralize our relationship with nature must start from this position. If we are thinking of questions of climate change, the impact of new technologies or questions of sustainable development, we are intimately concerned with the links between 'nature' and 'culture'. Bill McKibben (1990: 54) writes: 'we have changed the atmosphere, and thus we are changing the weather. By changing the weather, we have made every spot on earth man-made and artificial.' Talk of the 'natural' and the 'fabricated' is pressed to breaking point. This would mean abandoning talk of a 'return to nature', and raising critical questions as to what would constitute appropriate forms of human responsibility in respect of nature.

Hence, an ecologically informed citizenship depends not as much upon 'nature' as upon the links between 'nature' and 'culture'. We need to come to terms with the limits of our bodies, our 'use' of 'nature' and our relations with the other life forms with which we share the planet; this requires a new cultural language within which we might reinterpret ourselves. If we are to resensitize ourselves to biological rhythms, the capacities of other species and the life cycles of which we remain a part, this necessarily involves the development of new narratives and discourses through which we experience our 'naturalness'. The paradox is that the recovery of 'naturalness' depends upon the orientations of 'culture' (Melucci 1996a, b).

Culture and nature

The question as to whether it any longer makes sense to distinguish between culture and nature is central. Are we involved in an investigation that looks at ways in which 'culture' and 'nature' overlap with one another, or are they still separable phenomena? This ambivalence can be seen within the writing of Raymond Williams (1989b), who more than most sought to problematize questions of 'culture' and 'nature'. Notions of 'culture' and 'nature' have been historically projected on to our ideas and images of the country and the city. The 'country' is held to signify the 'natural' and unchanging features of our shared biological condition, whereas the 'city' is usually linked with progress, modernization and development. Part of Williams's project was to point to the ways these binary divisions reflected a division of labour that reinforced the dominance of the city over the country, and to search for ways of pointing towards their reconciliation (Williams 1985). Ultimately, Williams did this by locating the 'natural' within the 'cultural' while also arguing that there are 'natural' limits to the constructions of 'culture'. This points towards an argumentative strategy where the 'cultural' and the 'natural' are implicated within each other, but are ultimately separable. This ambivalence is evident within his discussion of the origins of the term 'culture' in meanings such as 'cultivation' and 'husbandry'. Hence, we can think of gardening as partly natural and partly cultural. In redesigning our backyard, Williams would argue we are likely to employ variable aesthetic and instrumental criteria in a process of creative transformation. Planting a seed is no more 'natural' than writing a poem, as both involve material and semiotic relations.

Further, Williams argues that by recognizing our shared biological natures we might better appreciate our ecological vulnerability and interconnection with nature. We are caught up with the natural world, while having distinctively human features, capacities and characteristics. From this recognition, Williams (1980) sought to develop a materialist ethics, which held that much of our experience might appropriately be termed 'passive', given the agency that can be granted to a common biological inheritance. In this way, we might seek to problematize the suffering that can be associated with old age, hunger, lack of shelter, disease and infant mortality. This would build a politics on the interconnections between 'culture' and 'nature'. By this Williams does not argue that recognition of our shared 'naturalness' would automatically deliver certain political positions rather than others. Elsewhere, Williams argues for a model of democratic community built upon difference and dialogue, allowing for a range of voices to be heard (Stevenson 2002), so that a shared community could be based not upon a homogeneous culture but on one of dialogue and complexity. Yet what was important was to recognize that 'nature' operates as what Terry Eagleton (2000) has described as 'a kind of inert weight' within culture. Again, this means that while 'nature' is undoubtedly culturally constructed, it continues to signify 'those material structures and processes that are independent of human activity' (Soper 1995: 32). For Williams, then, we make the webs and significations of 'culture' out of a common vulnerability that is delivered by a shared nature. In Williams's many novels and critical works he seeks to reveal the ways in which the dominant culture seeks to obscure these features, which – if more consciously and dialogically recognized – could lead to a renewal of human sociability and community.

There continues to be much that is germane in this way of thinking. To talk of 'culture' and 'nature' as becoming indistinguishable is surely to bend the argumentative stick too far. It is still possible, I think, to discuss the material–semiotic processes of 'nature' that work independently of human design and intention. To suggest otherwise flies in the face of an Earth and a cosmos that predate our arrival and that will probably outlast our extinction as a species. It is also to suggest that the human condition continues to be determined through the cycles of death and birth that invariably structure our experience. The idea that we might somehow escape these processes is evidence of a failure to appreciate the ways in which human beings are integrated into a number of 'natural' cycles. Yet such an approach does not really address the social and cultural transformations that have intensified the interconnections between 'culture' and 'nature'. As many recent commentators have pointed out, nature is currently being redefined in terms of doing rather than being. Here Sarah Franklin (2000) argues that genetics, for example, has converted biology into a form of reprogrammable information. The cloning of Dolly the sheep in 1997 points to a relationship between 'culture' and 'nature' that is poorly described by metaphors like passivity. Instead, we might talk of the ways in which human interventions into genetic codes are being used to redefine what we take to be 'natural'. These processes offer a way of thinking about the interconnections between culture and nature that are continually being historically and politically redefined. While 'nature' in certain respects remains the 'other' of culture, we can also talk of the naturalization of culture and the cultural fabrication of nature as important contemporary processes.[1]

Cosmopolitan and ecological citizenship

Presentation of the environment as a globally shared responsibility points to a diversity of ways in which 'nature' is becoming politicized. According to Howard Newby (1995), environmentalism in Britain has historically developed through a number of distinct phases. From the mid-1880s to the turn of the twentieth century, the dominant aim was to preserve nature as a form of national heritage against the threat of industrialism. During the inter-war years there was an increasing focus upon the state to regulate, plan and control the environment. Among the suburban middle class there developed pressure groups who sought to develop national parks and expand green belts. The 1960s saw the rise of radical environmentalism. This brought in a post-materialist emphasis upon less consumer-friendly lifestyles and the need to break with an unquestioning belief in science and technology, coupled with a loss of confidence in 'progress'. While these currents can still be discerned today, the 1990s saw the emergence of ecological questions within a global context. Talk of a global environmental commons points to the complex and interconnected chains of causation that connect human activity, different world regions and the fortunes of nature. This evokes a community of fate that escapes the sovereignty of nation-states. No state has the capacity alone to control the quality of its atmosphere, prevent global warming and reverse the poisoning of its seas and air (Held *et al.* 1999). In recognition of this fact, the period since the 1960s has witnessed the rise of international environmental regulation, with major conventions and treaties being signed to reverse the impact of the global industrial system. This has been done in the recognition that no humans or animals can be said to be exempt from questions related to environmental degradation. For example, CFCs sprayed in Manchester can impact upon the loss of ozone at either of the two poles. These questions have led many to argue that environmental destruction requires a cosmopolitan form of politics that involves binding national agreements in the interests of humanity as a whole.

However, the fact remains that while the responsibility to protect the environment is a global responsibility, it is not the case that those most responsible for environmental harm and those most at risk from the destruction of nature are the same. It is well known that the United States is the world's greatest contributor to global warming and pollution, yet it is likely that the least wealthy and powerful societies are those who are most likely to suffer the effects of these practices. There is also evidence to suggest that as Northern countries became more aware of the environmental threats and hazards of waste, they export toxic substances to countries in need of revenue. Universal values and global responsibilities can help to mask inequalities in respect of the impact of environmental degradation (Yearley 2000). Further, the failure to ratify the

1997 Kyoto convention on the reduction of greenhouse gases has led many to question the commitment of the world's governments to addressing such processes (Gray 2000). That ecological questions take us beyond the nation-state does not mean that the impacts are necessarily universally the same, or that existing forms of governance have adequately responded to these issues. While there is a common need to take responsibility for the global commons, such a view is necessarily informed by the different contexts and locations referred to in the slogan 'act locally, think globally'.

The duty to care for the environment also by-passes the nation, in that it suggests individual obligations and responsibilities. This duty has consequences for the ways in which we choose to live our lives both individually and collectively (Steward 1991; van Steenbergen 1994). Such an outlook seeks to persuade us to rethink the ways in which we view human relationships with nature. In particular, the ecological case, as many have remarked, opens a challenging vision for sociologists, who have tended to see humans as separate from nature and embedded within a social as opposed to a natural world (McNaughton and Urry 1995). Ecological thinking asks us to examine how different societies have constructed the relationship between country and city, society and nature, and humans and animals (Williams 1985; Soper 1995).

Arguably, it is only when we learn to tell a different story about ourselves that we become open to rejoining our identities, as consumers and citizens, in such a way that places our relationship to 'nature' at the 'centre' rather than at the periphery of our thinking. The resensitization of our relationship with nature, rather than quasi-religious deference or instrumental reason, remains key in this regard. We are much more likely to become attuned to our obligations in respect of more sustainable development if we are able to reconfigure imaginatively our place within the 'natural' world. For example, McKie (1999) suggests that reductions in biodiversity (mainly through pollution and intensive farming) undermine the capacity of different animal and plant species to aid each other biologically. In other words, biodiversity promotes sustainability, whereas a reduction in planetary complexity has a negative knock-on effect. Alternatively, we might consider the recent case of the reduction in the number of species of wild flowers evident in the British countryside (McCarthy 2000). At first sight this might appear to be an issue only for the flower lovers among us. Yet we may view this differently if we consider that the depletion of wild flowers can be tied into the use of chemical fertilizers and pollution from car exhausts, and may have consequences for other species and human well-being.

The framing of human relationships with nature in terms of responsibility and obligation questions representations and practices that would ask us either to conquer or to submit to nature. Of course, such claims do not automatically tell us what our obligations should be towards the environment, or how we might best care for the planet in globalized settings. Such questions cannot be decided by searching for technical solutions or by converting 'nature' into an object of worship. Our desire to preserve 'nature' against the effects of industrialism can be evoked on a number of different grounds in ways that might suggest different practices of care and obligation (Dobson 1998). Castells (1997: 127) reads these developments positively, in that green culture 'is the only global identity put forward on behalf of all human beings, regardless of their specific social, historical, or gender attachments, or of their religious faith'. Castells's argument is that 'green culture' offers the possibility of a new kind of politics that creates a new identity based upon our species membership, and that is locally based and resistant to the cynicism, spin doctoring and ideas of strategic advantage that are promoted by more mainstream political and social concerns. Green websites run by a computer literate elite play a role similar to that of artisan printers at the beginning of the labour movement. Green citizenship aims to widen the circle of responsibilities commonly assumed by human beings to include global communities, animals and other 'natural' life forms, all of which may be distant within time and space. Within this, ecological citizenship is necessarily more concerned with obligations than with rights. It is our care of 'nature' rather than the 'rights' that we can claim against nature that is the subject of ethical concern. Yet, as I have indicated, there are many processes and forces that are currently preventing ecological issues becoming converted into questions of cosmopolitan concern. These can be connected to existing inequalities and, most crucially, some of the more substantial features of Western modernity.

Modernity, progress and consumption

The idea of 'progress' is both normative and tied up with the economic, political and cultural development of modernity. In terms of Western societies, it can be linked to our ability to develop technologies to control an 'outer' nature, and the beliefs that 'experts' will necessarily solve our problems and that cultural differences will fade away once people discover the benefits of Western science/culture (Norgaard 1994). Such views are now widely discredited and perceived to be ethnocentric. Western ideas of progress have seemingly legitimated the destruction of the environment, but also privilege the production of Western forms of control and production of knowledge. The power relations signified by notions of 'progress' and 'development' may silence different approaches to culture and the economy that do not seek to legitimize current patterns of economic growth and relations of expertise (Tucker 1999). The systematic exclusion and 'othering' of different perspectives on questions of progress and development have until now sought to run the world in the interests of the powerful. Yet there is no easy escape from Western modernity. The recovery of questions of 'difference' and 'otherness', which has been so important in contemporary social theory, does not present us with readily defined paths to follow. While we may wish to break with the binary logic that categorizes the world into developed/underdeveloped, traditional/modern and backward/advanced, no alternative model seems to be readily available. Traditionally ideas of progress and development offer the notion of human progress through economic growth and cultural homogeneity. If we are to decouple the idea that success equals money plus power, we will need to develop a substantial ethical vision that recognizes the continued resonance of this equation. This ethical vision, however, should not attempt to identify new universal rules of progress regulating our social lives under a revised set of hierarchies and controls. Such a project is likely to be perceived (mostly correctly) as authoritarian and would fail to build upon the many positive gains that are evident within cosmopolitan individualism. In terms of ecological arguments, the key issue, in my view, is whether global tragedy can be averted without authoritarian forms of state control. The question an ecological citizenship must be able to answer is how might we live sustainably without a parallel increase in the control and surveillance of citizens. As Touraine (2000: 147) argues:

> Our late modernity is primarily worried about its survival and the risks it is running. It aspires to being neither a society of order nor a society of progress, but a communications-based society, and it is therefore more afraid of intolerance than of poverty or illegality.

It is only running with the increasing capacity of individuals and institutions to become reflexive about the links between nature and society that opens the way to more sustainable futures. There are good reasons to think about the ethical limits of more traditional forms of development and to seek to develop a global society along sustainable lines. Yet there are evident dangers if such discussions are allowed to breed moralist enclaves and authoritarian reactions. A cosmopolitan approach seeks to develop a society based upon collective and self limitation, where the values of citizenship and democracy are regenerated, while opening up a dialogue across different civilizations and cultures. Ecological thought would need to break with the idea that the 'West' is necessarily the 'best', while seeking to place ethical considerations more centrally. In competition with ideas of success, we need to cultivate notions of human frailty and interdependence, responsibility and a respect for difference and 'otherness'.

However, the problem is that these ethical concerns often sound like demands for collective austerity. Whereas the market offers fun, pleasure and choice, ecological viewpoints suggest restraint, punishment for our previous excesses and insecurity. Considered globally, according to Sachs (1999), 'the best one can say is that development has created a global middle class with cars, bank accounts and career aspirations'. If we were to enter a more sustainable century then the lifestyles of the majority of citizens in the North, along with the elites of the South, would need to be transformed. The overall size of this group is currently estimated to be 20 per cent of the global population (Sachs 2002). Yet such pronouncements are usually built upon the idea that processes of everyday consumption involve the satisfaction of false or at least manipulated needs. Dobson (1994) reasons that the green argument is built upon the idea that we are ethically stunted by the growth economy's refusal to acknowledge the loss in the quality of life for our own and future generations. The ecological case is not helped by labelling the evident pleasures of fashion, music, cinema and the rest as the 'specious satisfactions of consumption' (Dobson 1994: 90). For example, Friends of the Earth argue that reductions of at least 80 per cent are required in the consumption of key resources and polluting goods within modern industrial societies. The radical nature of this demand becomes apparent if we consider that governments of Left and Right regard high levels of consumer expenditure as a key policy objective.

The ecological argument here is the need for 'downshifting', which involves the emergence of new lifestyle patterns emphasizing second hand goods, cycling and not driving, recycling waste and the buying of durable goods. As Michael Jacobs (1997) has argued, such measures often presume a neo-liberal assumption that the consumer acts as an atomized individual. Individualization processes open up questions of responsibility necessary for ecological reflection, while simultaneously contributing to environmental dangers, given that the meanings involved in consumption are important sources of modern identity (Ropke 1999). Similarly, Rosalind Williams (1982) has argued that the positive collective morale needed to counter the narcissism and pleasant illusions of consumption should be found in the re-energization of collective bonds. The reforging of community would require a 'shared austerity' that seeks to distinguish different levels of destruction that can be connected to the various practices of consumption. The problem is that such measures would be difficult to enforce within an increasingly individualized and global society. What would start as an attempt by the community to pull together is likely to end in the demonization of some groups rather than others (usually the least powerful), and in the imposition of technocratic or statist rather than civil solutions. The attempt to separate 'real' from 'false' needs, as previous generations of social theorists have discovered, is extremely complex even given democratic procedures.

This is not to underestimate the extent to which global capitalism is currently seeking to present itself as the saviour of the environment. 'Nature' has become part of an accumulation strategy on the part of corporate interests. Industrial capitalism has progressively 'sentimentalized' nature as something to be consumed during vacations or at the end of the working day (Pred 1998). Corporations take on the guise of ecological concern, while acting to privatize public environments. For example, the development of 'world wildlife zones' by cordoning off a preservation area can promote the idea of nature as a luxury consumer products while distracting attention from the environmental degradation outside special sites (Katz 1998).

Arguably, then, a cosmopolitan approach to questions of ecological sensitivity and consumption might be better served by conceding that we need to balance the evident pleasures (and indeed dangers) of mass consumption against judgements and assessments that can be related to the survival of the planet and the various life forms that inhabit it. This would, as I have already indicated, be more attainable through the constitution of a substantial ethical domain than through an attempt to demonize everyday consumption or retreat into an authoritarian politics. As Raymond Williams (1989: 220) has argued, new forms of resource allocation 'can only be very carefully negotiated'. It is the political attempt to reconnect nature and culture that is at stake in these debates. However, while resisting the urge to demonize consumption, we should not underestimate the ability of the market to impose the normative imperative to consume. Consumerism, observes Baudrillard (1998), works through the liberation of needs, enjoyment and freedom. The expansion of credit and the decline of puritan attitudes to work and saving have fostered a society based upon the principle of enjoyment now and payment later. The paradox of this new society is that this has become a new cultural imperative. It is our duty to consume. To follow Foucault, new forms of environmental ethics would need to suggest that subjects maintain a capacity to be able to transgress the forms of subjectivity offered by consumerism (Darier 1999). This would suggest a new green politics of the self that refused moralism and the idea that there was any final liberation from consumer society. In terms of the environment, 'the target nowadays is not to discover who we are but to refuse who we are' (Foucault 1982: 216).

A reflexive ecological citizenship would need to be aware that all our actions are likely to have unintended ecological consequences, however well intentioned. Here there is an ongoing need to refuse fundamentalism (in whatever guise) while holding on to the capacity to reinvent ourselves. How we might begin this process is highlighted by a reconsideration of the relations between the politics of risk, science and democracy.

Risk, science and democracy

Living in the contemporary world means learning to live with the possibility of large-scale hazards that throw into question attempts at bureaucratic normalization, the imperatives of the economic system and the assurances of scientific experts. Not only are we learning to live in a post-traditional society, we are constantly haunted by the possibility of large-scale hazards like Chernobyl. Despite the end of the Cold War we are currently living within the shadow of our own annihilation. No one really knows what the long-term consequences of ecological destruction will be or the level of risk that is environmentally sustainable. Politics and economics in such a society can no longer be conceptualized as a struggle over resources, and environmental degradation is not easily dismissed as a partial side-effect. The international production of harmful substances, the pollution of the seas and the dangers of nuclear power all call into question the mechanisms of national governance, and our relations of trust with society's central institutions. Ulrich Beck writes on the escalating risks of the modern era:

> The more pollutants are put in circulation, the more acceptable levels related to individual substances are set, the more liberally this occurs, the more insane the entire hocus-pocus becomes, because the overall toxic threat to the population grows – presuming the simple equation that the total volume of various toxic substances means a higher degree of overall toxicity.
>
> (Beck 1992: 66)

The risk society is predicated on the ambivalence that science has both produced and legitimized these risks, while being the primary force, other than popular protest, through which these dimensions can be made visible. In this respect, the ecological movement cannot afford to be anti-scientific, but has to turn science back on itself. Scientific rationality and judgement need to be open to the community as a whole, as modernity is revealed to be a more uncertain and fragile construction than was previously assumed to be the case.

The pervasive power of technical reason has given birth to a new form of politics that Beck (1996) calls 'sub-politics'. The humanity-wide project of saving the environment has actually been brought about through the destruction of nature, as well as the accompanying culture of risk and uncertainty that has become wrapped around human conceptions of well-being. The politicization of science and technology is rapidly introducing a reflexive culture in which politics and morality are gaining the upper hand over scientific experts. Thus a shared environment of global risk enables the formation of an ecological politics that seeks to recover democratic exchange. Whereas struggles for citizenship have historically been organized in material settings like the workplace, sub-politics is much more likely to be symbolically shaped through the domains of consumption, television media and the repoliticization of science. In this new political arena it is cultural symbols that determine who are the winners and losers in the world of risk politics. Beck argues that disputes over risk involve consumers in a form of direct political participation. As the public attend to daily reports about the risks and dangers of eating beef, using mobile phones or living near electric pylons, products are boycotted and positions quickly adopted and discarded in what Beck (1999: 46) calls 'the world fairground of symbolic politics'. In this, the ecological movement has sought to develop a 'cultural Red Cross consciousness' (Beck 1999: 44). Organizations like Greenpeace and Friends of the Earth have fostered a sense of public trust in their own declarations, taking a moral stance that is seemingly above the daily scraps of political parties. In this world of 'judo politics' yesterday's winners soon become tomorrow's losers as unpredictable spirals of information are circulated on a 24-hour basis. The speed at which different viewpoints and perspectives are literally turned over means that the cultural definition of risk plays a central part within these disputes.

If the ecological movement asks us to attend to the obligations we have to the Earth, it also raises the question of the regeneration of public spaces and democratic dialogue. This is particularly pressing given some of Beck's remarks regarding the fast moving world of media definitions of risk. Beck (1995) exhibits an awareness of these dimensions through a discussion of the possible emergence of an 'authoritarian technocracy'. Here he argues that industrial society (as we have seen) responded to the problem of ecological risk through the formal development of certain laws, and belief in 'cleaner' technology and more informed experts. The deep uncertainty that is fostered by media spirals of information could mean that states seek to close down areas of debate and discussion, and give their citizens false feelings of certitude. That is, states may decide to protect the public from contestation and debate. For Beck what is required is a repoliticization of these domains. Citizenship – we should remember – is cancelled if politics is subservient to the market, becomes defined by the state or presents the world as a confrontation between fixed interests. In this view, citizenship becomes possible through the development of republican institutions and civic forms of engagement. Beck's case is that democratic dialogue needs to introduce into its repertoire the principles of doubt and uncertainty. As Adam and van Loon (2000: 2) comment, 'risk is not that it is happening, but that it *might be* happening'. Risks are constructed and contested and move public debate beyond certitude. Only by considering worst case scenarios and the idea that technical rationality is dangerous can we begin to have a proper discussion. As Beck (1995: 179) argues, 'caution would be the mother in the kitchen of toxins'.

Yet both Bauman (1993) and Smart (1998) have argued that the 'revival of reason' offered by reflexive modernization will do little to offer a future more riven by doubt and ethical complexity. As Beck defines it in his early work, the recovery of reason is just as likely to foster as undermine what Bauman (1993: 204) calls 'the suicidal tendency of technological rule'. Beck's analysis remains dependent upon the continued domination of scientific reason, rather than engaging in a more ethical politics. Bauman expands this point by arguing that the most likely response to public expressions of risk is the systematic privatization of risk, not the remoralization of public space. For Bauman, Beck seems to presume that more, not less, modernity would necessarily undermine attempts by 'private' consumers to avoid public risks. Bauman points out that privatized risk-fighting, from attempts to lose weight to taking vitamin tablets, is big business. In a consumer society there is a strong temptation to buy oneself out of the debate privately, rather than publicly engaging in the construction of shared moral and ethical norms. There is no direct connection between the public acceptance of risk and the political action necessary to deal with these questions. In their different ways both Bauman and Smart point to the need for a wider ethical recovery, which is not addressed but undermined by the new individualism and scientific reason.

These are substantial criticisms that are both right and wrong. As we shall see, the privatization of risk within contemporary culture remains a real possibility. Yet the argument that a remoralized culture is dependent upon the jettisoning of science and scientific forms of evidence is surely false. As Donna Haraway (1997) argues, the implosion of science, technology and nature, especially within the post-war period, has fundamentally altered the make-up of contemporary society. The webs of knowledge and power connected to the development of technoscience have reshaped the boundaries between humans and non-humans. For example, the development of genetic engineering since the early 1970s has redefined the boundaries between culture and nature. The development of transgenetic organisms within life forms from tomatoes to fish provides a 'cross-cultural polyphony' that violates notions of natural integrity. The transferring of genes between different species disrupts notions and categories of species differentiation supposedly authorized by nature. This deconstructs ideas of genetic and species purity that can be found within racist discourses. To object to the 'unnaturalness' of these processes is politically problematic, and fails to recognize the ways in which human–non-human relations have already been transformed. Yet the power to define what counts as technical or political is a key consideration. The point is not to rid ourselves of science, but to seek to politicize the ways in which biotechnology is increasingly commodified and globally dominated by commercial interests.

For example, the funding of science and research within the United States (the main global player) has significantly shifted in the direction of large corporations. This is not necessarily a conspiracy, but nevertheless it severely limits the public discussion and understandings of the ways in which science is reshaping our shared world. Such processes determine the current construction of science by the agendas of money and power, and disallow the public emergence of different areas of priority from less powerful sectors of the population. Rather than allowing science to be determined by the state, capital and the military, a voice needs to be found for the public. For Haraway this could be achieved by establishing citizens' juries that would seek to debate the ethics of animal research, genetically modified food or pollution, allowing a public space for different and diverse knowledges. Rather than assuming that science is the master discourse, the aim would be to include the ways in which science is contested and determined, and is currently reshaping our common world in open forms of discussion. Invariably, this would include a diversity of knowledges, thereby helping to democratize the practice of science. As Haraway (1997: 114) puts it, 'technoscience is civics'.

However, as Adam (1998) has pointed out, a major problem for democracy is not just the legitimation of a diversity of ecologically sensitive knowledges, but also that discussions of risk tend to be concerned with past problems. What is needed is the introduction of a respect for the diverse temporal dimensions that inform our understandings of these questions. In rejecting the idea of the Earth as a man-made machine for which we can easily find replacement parts, we need to be aware that ecologically the past is a poor guide to the future. We need to become publicly aware of the time lags that are evident in our dealings with 'nature'. The timespan of democracy is at odds with the temporal dimensions of nature. Elected governments usually have a four- or five-year period of responsibility, whereas environmental degradation may not become a problem for over a hundred years. The public legitimation of a diversity of knowledges about the relationship between science and technology would need to be both ecologically and temporally sensitive. We would need metaphors other than clock time in order to make sense of and gain a new respect for past and future that is not strictly calculable. In this, the recovery of a sense of responsibility for future generations, spatially distant others and other species should guide our actions.

How, asks Adam, should we proceed under circumstances where we cannot know the long-term effects of our actions? For example, while principles like the 'polluter pays' can be useful in certain instances, they are not helpful when dealing with an indeterminate number of causes and time lags. Indeed, as Beck

(1995) argues, sometimes principles like the 'polluter pays' or 'individual culpability' actually allow pollution levels to rise. This is because it is often difficult to attribute pollution to any one source, as such a causal relation may evade scientific demonstration and there is often a struggle over who is actually to blame. Key to reclaiming responsibility is not only to consider our actions within temporal and spatial coordinates, but also to develop a different relationship with and sensitivity towards the fragility of our shared natures. Arguably, this fragility comes to the fore when we consider our capacity to impact on and intervene within the environments and beings of others. Democratic talk on the environment needs to move beyond talk of the need to protect nature or save the world. Such paternalistic rhetoric not only represents the environment as 'other' to ourselves, but blinds us to the ways in which we are nearly always uncertain about the long-term consequences of our actions.

Cinematic representations of risk: *Safe*

A number of other critics of the risk society thesis have sought to investigate ways in which 'risk' is translated into more popular forms of understanding. The concern is that Beck's theories remain connected to an instrumental and technocratic agenda that seeks to 'manage' an environmental crisis. Beck describes the risk society as a social crisis, demonstrating little concern with the way in which different populations, cultures and political movements might reinterpret and interrupt dominant conceptions of the natural. According to Lash (1994) and Wynne (1996), Beck's analysis stays on the side of the technocratic professionals (including politicians, scientists and government bureaucrats) by failing to connect with the different frames and projections that are currently available to more grass-roots organizations. As Mary Douglas (1992: 48) has argued, 'there is no intrinsic reason why the analysis of risk perception should not engage in comparisons of culture'. By failing to make this move, Beck is accused of unintentionally reinforcing the divide between experts and lay opinion. Beck ends up producing a view of the subject that is not far from a calculative-rationalist approach, in that he fails to problematize the complexity and cultural variability of different risk cultures within and between diverse social groups and societies. Rather than developing notions of reflexivity through an explicitly aesthetic set of concerns like Lash, or seeking to attend to many of the reservations and resistances that 'ordinary people' might have to the agendas and cultures of scientists, he is arguably more concerned to introduce the principle of responsibility into elite discussions.

Within these coordinates I want to focus briefly on the 1995 film *Safe*, directed by Todd Haynes. This is because it seeks to address many of the complex issues related to science, risk and responsibility that I sought to open up in the previous section. In my discussion of the film I am seeking to demonstrate not only that we are indeed living in a world of hazard and risk, but also that there are many different personal and collective narratives available to us as consumers and citizens in making sense of this world. This is to argue not that the film simply reflects a more popular domain, but that it provides a critical response to many of the questions of individualization and risk that the analysis has traded upon thus far. Here I aim to investigate some of the ways in which 'risk' becomes signified, represented and made meaningful in our culture (Hall 1997). This is important, as dominant discourses aim to 'rule in' and 'rule out' ways of perceiving risk. The film is centrally concerned with the ways in which we construct our identity through narratives of well-being and health. Haynes, as an openly political and gay film maker, seeks to open questions about the way that certain recovery and treatment therapies in relation to AIDS have become individualized. Yet the film also seeks to target a specifically 'left-wing' culture that argues that ideas of 'truth' can be read off from social positions within society. This view holds that the more marginalized a viewpoint, the more 'truthful' it becomes.

The film itself is focused on Carol White, who lives in the San Fernando Valley in California with her husband Greg and adopted son. In the early part of the film we see Carol going to the gym, talking to her domestic help, arranging the delivery of a new sofa and discussing the possibility of a new fruit diet with a female friend. Carol's world seems extremely 'safe', given that she does not work and lives in a wealthy and exclusive part of the city. Yet the film's genre is probably closest to that of a horror film, in that there is a powerful sense of impending doom, which is mainly signified by the musical score and the way the film is shot. There are very few close-ups in the film, which creates a sense of distance and coldness that is reflected in Carol's personal relations. In the first scene we see Carol having sex with her husband in a way that draws attention to her emotional detachment. The cinematic effect is to individuate Carol and emphasize her vulnerability.

As the film progresses Carol becomes ill. The first sign that there may be anything wrong is when Carol has a coughing fit after driving behind a truck on the freeway; this is quickly followed by a nose bleed caused by a hair perm and her collapse after walking in on a dry cleaners while it is being sprayed. Despite Carol's frequent trips to see her doctor, they cannot find anything medically wrong with her. Eventually Carol comes across a leaflet on 'environmental illness' while she is visiting the gym. After a series of meetings, she progressively learns to give her illness a name, in that it is her everyday tolerance of chemical substances that is breaking down owing to a general rise in the level of toxicity. The social movement that Carol joins is populated by a number of people who are suffering from similar illnesses that have defied explanation by the medical profession. The social movement is seemingly made up of marginalized groups, including women and people of different sexualities and ethnicities, within American society.

The rest of the film is concerned with the ways in which Carol becomes socialized into a New Age group that lives in a remote place called Wrenwood. This alternative community asks that its residents dress moderately, refrain from sexual activity and concentrate upon 'personal growth'. However, the sect that Carol joins offers a form of safety through fundamentalist certitude. The community ultimately rejects the complexities and ambiguities of the modern world and instead seeks to socialize its inhabitants into blaming themselves for their illnesses and ridding themselves of all negative thoughts. For example, the guru of the retreat, Peter, stands up in front of the other members to proclaim that 'I've stopped reading the papers. I've stopped watching the news on TV.' Through group therapy sessions and personal reflection the members of Wrenwood are asked to rid themselves of any potentially negative stimuli that might come to damage their immune system and hence impair their ability to fight disease. That the community rests upon a form of communalism is cleverly demonstrated: when Carol is asked by Peter to share with the group, she uncertainly replies that she is 'still learning the words'. To this Peter replies, 'The words are just a way of helping you get to what is true.' That Carol eventually 'learns the words' is made clear when on her birthday she gives a faltering speech that begins to mirror Peter's sentiments. However, despite Carol's progressive socialization into this alternative community, she ends up as lonely and isolated as she was at the film's beginning. Carol retains a constant concern with her own health, in that her cabin is downwind of a highway, and she eventually moves into a purpose-built toxically cleansed white igloo. The final scene of the film shows Carol standing alone in front of a mirror in the igloo repeatedly telling herself, 'I love you.'

One of the many interesting features of the film is that it does not descend into a cynical commentary upon the New Age. While it takes a questioning stance towards certain features and aspects of New Age therapies, they are not completely disregarded. As director Todd Haynes says in an interview with Larry Gross, 'I felt the least interesting thing you can do with New Age stuff is totally accept it or totally dismiss it. So I really tried to look at it' (Gross 1995). Haynes goes on to say that Carol, in this respect, came to 'represent the most vulnerable part of identity, the most uncertain and fragile part of myself'. In this, the film asks questions about what safety and risk mean in the context of modern society. It deliberately avoids taking a moralistic stance that simply argues that Carol is deluding herself, but does suggest that 'individualistic' or 'communalist' responses to risk can bring a closing down of critique and what

As Haraway (1991: 154) puts it, 'a cyborg world is about lived social and bodily realities in which people are not afraid of their joint kinship with animals and machines, not afraid of permanently partial identities and contradictory standpoints'. The myth of the cyborg is created out of the fictions, imaginations and discursive realities that have helped to construct a world of domination and transgression where science is simultaneously reaffirming relations of oppression and calling into question binaries between culture and nature. The cyborg as a matter of science fiction and lived experience takes 'pleasure in the confusion of boundaries and responsibility in their construction' (Haraway 1991: 150). The story of modernity that promised increasing domination and control over nature has been breached by the mixing of humans and non-humans. In this, the boundaries between humans, animals and technology have become increasingly blurred and discredited. We are no longer certain as to what counts as a machine, human or animal. This means that our identities are currently constructed out of a number of differences that defy essentialist attempts to reconstruct boundaries that have begun to implode. The idea of the cyborg is intended to engage in a form of politics that is more appropriate to an information society, while providing a critical analysis of webs of power that simultaneously delights in the ironies and complexities of transgression. In this respect, our politics needs to form a complex understanding of a range of interrelated organisms that are biologically, technologically and culturally constituted.

For Haraway, the cosmopolitan imagination would seek an ethical response to the ways in which technoscience operates in terms of global forms of power and the emergence of ambivalent zones between culture and nature. This involves not an uncritical celebration of all things cyber or an ideological rejection of the operation of science, but the critical exploration of ambivalent possibilities and transformations (Haraway 2000). The research stimulated by Haraway's projections seeks to uncover how science, nature and culture have become progressively intermeshed in a way that destabilizes a number of previously assumed dichotomies. For example, Bryld and Lykke (2000) look at how the dolphin has become an ambivalent icon of our age. In this analysis they trace how the dolphin is embedded in the structures and cultures of capitalism, while also offering the possibility of transgression. For example, in the context of the Cold War, the dolphin was used in research by the military, who apparently believed that if they could establish conversations with dolphins they might also understand aliens from other planets. Yet Bryld and Lykke note that in New Age culture the dolphin is often used to signify pre-technological feminine values, while it is also used as a symbol of Internet communication. If the dolphin is viewed as a cyborg then it signifies the ruptures between culture and nature that Haraway views as being central to the contemporary world.

Science has had a dual role, seeking to reaffirm human distinctiveness and separation from nature, while simultaneously calling into question these very distinctions. For example, Haraway (1997) gives the example of OncoMouse as unsettling simple oppositions. Haraway describes OncoMouse as a bio-engineered being that is the result of a transplanted human tumour-producing gene. In this, OncoMouse is an invented animal, but also one that has been patented. As Haraway points out, the ethical dimensions of OncoMouse are complex and difficult to decide. On one level OncoMouse is a real being that suffers, yet the mouse has been specifically developed to fight breast cancer in women. Transgenetic animals, which are increasingly being made to order for those involved in scientific research, can be seen as both part of a profit-making industry and a sustained attempt to defeat cancer. Is OncoMouse an attempt to relieve human suffering or a high-tech way of causing even further suffering? Such questions, Haraway cautions, cannot be decided within a political matrix that makes simple divisions between issues of resistance and complicity. Instead, these issues open out questions of responsibility: we need to ask who is suffering and to what ends. In accepting our responsibility for OncoMouse, we would need to decide whose suffering should 'count' in a way that dispenses with simplistic distinctions between humans, animals and technology. Such questions, Haraway asserts, are necessarily open-ended, and cannot be easily decided upon.

Against Haraway's cosmopolitan focus, others have suggested that the argument about our relationship with animals needs to be viewed through a more concertedly linguistic or material dimension. In this regard we might see the concerns of Tester (1991) and Benton (1993) as viewing the so-called animal question through a lens that is either overtly cultural or materialist in approach. Tester and Benton disagree as to what might count as the sociological basis for a consideration of animal rights in modern society. For Tester (1991), all human societies seek to establish human uniqueness as distinct from the 'otherness' of nature. In this we view the world not naturally, but through cultural classifications and social definitions. Animals are 'blank pieces of paper' upon which humans have historically projected a range of distinctions (Tester 1991: 42). By giving animals rights we are actually naming the ways in which animals are different from ourselves, in that they cannot claim the entitlements of citizenship for themselves. In this, animal rights are not as much about animals as about the desire of human societies to 'improve'. This means that animals remain permanently subject to the wishes, fantasies and cultural projections of human society. Similarly, Salecl (1998) argues that animals and humans differ because of language. For example, a human may be said to differ from a dog because humans are constituted through a symbolic order in ways that could not be said to be true of dogs. In this respect, our love of animals is actually about our perceived loss of freedom and animality, or it is due to the fact that a pet can take on the role of the ideal other. Again, we are able to project our desires upon animals, but in this there is no return for us to a 'natural' state. In short, both Tester and Salecl argue that our ethical concern for animals is nothing more than an overriding concern with ourselves. As the 'other' in respect of animals cannot talk back in a language that we would understand, the values we 'choose' to give animals can only be those that we project on to them.

Alternatively, Benton (1993) argues that rather than animals being viewed as the 'other' of society, they can be said to share both differences and similarities with human beings. In this, Benton (1993: 24) offers 'a view of humans as both sharing a common nature and conditions of life with other species, and as joined with them in bonds of ecological independence'. We might view each species that currently exists upon the planet as having both its own distinctive pattern of need and forms of life that meet those needs better than others. This is not to deny that there is a range of activities – including composing symphonies and building nuclear weapons – that we might argue are distinctively human. Yet we can also point to certain continuities between animals and human beings, in that they share a limited lifespan, develop emotional bonds with others, reproduce sexually and are dependent upon others during the early part of their lifespan, among other features. Benton hopes to introduce into the conversation a range of understandings about what could conceivably pass as 'living well' across a range of species.

However, neither the culturalist nor the materialist response gives us an adequate way of thinking about our obligations and feelings towards animals. The culturalist response seems to be based on the denial of the ways in which the fate of humans and animals might be mixed in together, and of 'animals' being a legitimate subject of ethical concern. While the ability to use language is indeed an important distinction between humans and most animals, this is not a reason to exempt them from concern. In this respect, culturalist arguments can be defined as exhibiting a form of speciesism. As Mary Midgley (1983: 101) suggests, speciesism is not the claim that there are distinctive boundaries, but 'the supposition that species boundary not only makes a difference, but makes a gigantic difference of setting limits to morality, of deciding whether a given creature can matter to us at all'. However, the 'ontological naturalism' of Benton inadequately appreciates the cultural problems evident in the search to determine the needs of other species. As I argued earlier, such attempts usually depend upon distinctions between 'real' and 'false' needs, which are difficult enough with fellow humans, but carry an added difficulty with animals, given their exclusion from language. Benton seemingly underestimates how the ways in which 'we' might decide upon the needs of, say, cats as opposed to lions will inevitably be contestable and culturally variable.

In this respect, the strength of Haraway's perspective is that it seeks to position both humans and animals within a shifting set of material and discursive relations that recognizes that we view nature itself as a material semiotic actor. Her analysis steers clear of the moral certainty of Benton and punctures the 'indifference' of Tester and Stercl. However, the weakest point of Haraway's argument, in my view, is her lack of focus on the ethical dimension. The argument that technoscience has socially transformed the relationship between culture and nature is a compelling one, but such is her desire to point to the complexity of these new relations that she understates the point that more cosmopolitan forms of understanding are indeed dependent upon the responsibility and ethical agency of humans. Animals are a 'problem' for us in a way that cannot be said for them. Haraway is, however, right to point out that our ethical concerns will be shaped by our affinities with other living creatures. In this I would agree with Soper (2000) and Hayward (1994) that only humans can have values, but this does not mean that 'other' species and natures should not become the object of our concern. Despite the emergence of cyborg relations and identities, environmental concerns remain distinctively human concerns. While the development of technoscience, hazards and risks may have posed questions about the maintenance of clear distinctions between culture and nature (acid rain affects both humans and non-humans), these remain issues that are genuinely 'our' responsibility.

Further, as Midgley (1996) points out, despite the implosion of technology, animals and humans, we continue to display greatest concern for those animals that are emotionally closest to us. That we are generally more concerned about the well-being of cats than earthworms or robots is owing to their enhanced capacity to suffer. While humans are likely to continue to exhibit a loyalty in respect of our own species, it is the capacity of 'animals' to sustain complex emotional bonds with one another that converts them into objects of concern. The question that continues to guide our moral and ethical concerns depends upon the degree of suffering experienced by other animals, rather than, say, their ability to use language. In short, in answer to the question of why we are concerned for other species, we continue to be more motivated by their capacity to exhibit a shared vulnerability or experience hardship than anything else.

In this respect, cultural citizenship would need to emphasize these features, while being attuned to the way distinctions between different forms of life are currently being transgressed. To view other species and nature through the nexus of obligation and care means that we are dealing with a form of 'otherness' that is like, as well as unlike, ourselves. This means that we should be sceptical of some of the claims made by deep ecologists, which suggest that humanity is just another part of nature. For example, Roszak (1992) proposes that it is central to the environmental ethic to discover ways in which nature works within the self. Yet the idea that we simply need to discover our continuity with 'nature' obscures the 'otherness' of nature. As Plumwood (1993) reminds us, we can do this by either incorporating 'nature' by obscuring the differences between 'nature' and ourselves, or excluding the notion that our planet may indeed have 'natural' limits and that animals can suffer in ways similar to ourselves. Both of these strategies lead to the erasure of the 'other' and the blunting of very real and problematic questions that our relationship with our own and other natures inevitably brings.

Vulnerability, voice and community

The new forms of cosmopolitan thinking and feeling in respect of the environment that are being addressed here rely upon an ethical agenda that could emerge between the individualist escape attempts offered by the market and the communal assurances of identity politics. An ecologically informed citizenship is dependent upon a dual strategy, where obligations are given priority over rights, and new zones of citizen involvement based on dialogic exchange are created. The politics of the environment is also a politics of communication and public space. Further, it is a politics that would depend upon a very different view of the human subject from that currently envisaged by mainstream politics and sociology. By this, I mean that a greater awareness of our interconnection with nature, other species and different cultures from the ones we currently inhabit points us towards a deeper concern with questions of human and species frailty. Ecological thinking is interesting in this context, given its attempts to preserve different forms of life that are threatened by industrialization. It has been my argument that ecological thinking is better secured through civic initiatives and an exploration of different narratives and discourses that aim to politicize nature. It is the recovery of an ethical agenda in respect of nature that this chapter has sought to emphasize. Questions of citizenship are not well served by a renewed faith in the market, science or technology. A resensitized relationship with questions of risk, culture and nature depends upon deeper forms of democratic engagement, and a more explicit concern to uncover the different cultural narratives of environmental concern and connection. This is what I have called cultural citizenship.

These features are likely to open up difficult feelings and questions for which there are no easy solutions. As we have seen, the troubling picture of environmental degradation is likely to be resisted by both political and consumerist escape attempts. The ability of citizens to look the other way in respect of these questions is not to be underestimated. As psychoanalytic accounts have sought to stress, processes of individual and collective denial are far from straightforward. Stanley Cohen (2001) has argued that denial may be active (repudiation) or passive (turning the other way). More often, when it comes to the environment we are not dealing with simple fraud. Instead, we are vaguely aware of the changing climate and associated risks, but without fully acknowledging what we are trying to avoid. We turn a blind eye to what we feel we cannot change. Such an attitude stops short of outright innocence (although some may try), but retreats from a recognition of the risks involved in the maintenance of contemporary lifestyles. The effort of citizenship (similar to that of the therapist) would need to seek to uncover what mobilized this denial in the first place (Bollas 1992). My hunch, as I have indicated throughout, is that this might be located in the mutual fear of increased forms of state control and the desire to protect the pleasures of consumption. Further, it is only when we break with the illusions of development, growth and an unquestioning attitude towards experts that it becomes possible to address pressing ecological dimensions.

Yet the question remains: how might human vulnerability become reimagined in a context that has politically sought to deconstruct the oppositions of nature and culture? Michael Young and Lesley Cullen (1996) have suggested that to break with the individualization of death would be to find a new role for the community and ritual within these processes. In an ecological age this would link the individual to both the community and the cycles of life and death that relate to the blue planet. The moment of death and the associated processes of mourning and loss would need to find a means for both communal and planetary identifications. In this respect, it is an awareness of our own common vulnerability that often enables humans to attend to the sufferings of others. The ecological case takes these questions further and asks us to reimagine ourselves in terms of complex natural processes without which we would come to our end. 'Nature' is not the backdrop to our actions or to be only located within ourselves, but is produced, sustained and destroyed in our common world. Similarly, psychotherapy teaches us of the possibility of finding strength within weakness. The 'good enough' therapeutic relationship allows the patient/client to become aware of their limits. In an age of rationalized health care it is worth reminding ourselves that the 'health' of the person undergoing treatment often depends upon a healing relation, rather than any technique. It is dialogue that creates the possibility of self-criticism and thereby the recognition of our own limits (Gadamer 1996). The 'change' brought about by therapy and other healing relationships enables the patient to be able to recognize their own vulnerability and generative capacities along with connected others (Melucci 1996a, b). The consideration of the vulnerability of the body points to the fact that environmental concerns are connected to our relationships with the community and us. We need to be able to address questions of ritual and practice that 'engage' lived experience, not merely operating at the level of ideas (Szerszynski 1997). The argument here is not that new communal rituals and practices will solve the environmental crisis, but that the recovery of ethical relations may develop new civic relationships. These rituals would need to convert 'nature' into culturally recognizable processes. As I have indicated, these might include new ways of handling life and death, but could also include special environmental days and ways of marking seasonal change. Citizens' initiatives therefore depend not only upon the formal opportunities to participate, but also upon intersubjectively maintained cultures that seek to reconnect culture and nature.

Conclusion

This chapter has argued that the deconstruction of 'culture' and 'nature' is necessary to refocus ecological questions in terms of citizenship. Culturally rediscovering ourselves as both part of and responsible for 'nature' depends upon changes within mainstream thinking. Ecological citizenship places its faith in the recovery of public space and human responsibility in order to attend to the environmental crisis. Neither the market nor state institutions are likely to offer adequate responses to these issues without an enhanced role for the citizen. The keys to a more ecologically sensitive society are new forms of public space and ritual that allow new narratives and perspectives to be shared by concerned citizens. The challenging of experts, the recovery of the 'other' and an expanding circle of concern are all important in this regard. However, the environmental movement needs to be careful not to lapse into a form of moralism in pressing its case. Much of the anti-consumerism rhetoric, while well intentioned, seeks (as socialism before it) to replace the market with the state. Much of the resistance to ecological ideas within civil society can be located within a fear of state control and regulation, and the need not to know. Alternatively, ecological citizenship would be better served by linking personal and international responsibility in a way that emphasizes the capacity of citizens to 'learn' from diversely constructed experiences. This will involve the dual practice of recovering a relationship with 'nature' and more fully appreciating what we are seeking to deny.

Note

1 On the vitality and agency of nature see some of the excellent work by Nigel Clark (1997, 1998). Unlike many current theorists, he manages to respect the mutual global agencies of biology and culture.

Further reading

Adam, B. (1998) *Timescapes of Modernity: The Environment and Invisible Hazards.* London: Routledge.

Beck, U. (1992) *Risk Society: Towards a New Modernity.* London: Sage.

Clark, N. (1998) Nanoplanet: molecular engineering in the time of ecological crisis, *Time and Society,* 7(2): 353–68.

Dobson, A. (1994) *Green Political Thought.* London: Routledge.

Sachs, W. (1999) *Planet Dialectics: Explorations in Environment and Development.* London: Zed Books.

4 MEDIA, CULTURAL CITIZENSHIP AND THE PUBLIC SPHERE

The development of the media of mass communication over the course of the nineteenth and twentieth centuries ensured the construction of one-way forms of communication within national public spheres. The arrival of the press, radio and television developed a specifically national basis, as elites utilized various media to promote a sense of loyalty and obligation towards individual states. Notably, these developments became the source of a popular cultural citizenship, which involved certain rights of communication, participation within the cultural life of the nation and a sense of community with others. Media had a democratizing effect upon public life, as they allowed more inclusive definitions of the public. Whether one is listening to a sports event, the voices of political leaders or the daily weather report, the nation is symbolically constructed as 'home'. The media communicate collective identities as ongoing events. Historically, the core message of national broadcasting has been the dominant tone, language and style of everyday life (Schlesinger 1991). Media across the globe have been responsible for giving people a taste for the meanings, gestures and tone of nationality (Martin-Barbero 1993). Hence, a diversity of media becomes a key focus for claims to citizenship and for developing a sense of solidarity among strangers.

However, there is a growing concern that through a number of key trans-formations these identifications are being restructured by economic, tech-nological and cultural developments. The arrival of new forms of electronic communication has partially deconstructed the assumed links between media, culture and citizenship. Here two developments are central. The first has been the emergence of transnational media organizations whose power and reach are more significant than those of any single nation-state. The new media order is characterized by conglomerates like Time Warner and News International, which have become international players across a range of different media (including books, television, films and other media), and whose webs of power stretch across different parts of the world. Second, the intensification of globalization processes means that the world is now a more interconnected place. The global trade in information and entertainment, the capacity of technology to compress time and space, and the enhanced traffic of people and symbols have all sought to develop a different communications environment, beyond that of the nation.

Yet what is not currently clear is what kind of mediated public sphere is emerging. Some have argued that a global public would need to be constructed at the planetary level in an attempt to mirror the development of a global political economy (Garnham 1992). Others have suggested that a global public sphere will be necessarily elitist, given that only a tiny minority among the world's population have access to the different levels of cosmopolitan information necessary to make sense of a global polity (Sparks 1998). Various commentators continue to resist the idea that a public sphere could ever exist beyond the nation, given its continuing power to shape citizens' loyalties and identities (Smith 1995). My argument is that we should challenge these constructions, and try to understand more carefully some of the evident ambivalences, complexities and indeed possibilities of the current situation. Here I briefly trace some of the arguments in respect of citizenship that have emerged at the level of the nation-state. This includes a consideration of the idea of a national public sphere and the fears that it is currently threatened by more global flows and governances. From there I propose a different understanding of global and cultural citizenship in respect of the media from the one that has emerged at the national level.

It is because many commentators have sought to replicate a national media politics at the global level that the idea of a global public sphere has been prematurely rejected. In this respect, I build upon some of Geoff Mulgan's (1997) ideas about *connexity*, which focus on the capacity of media technologies within a global world to enhance a cosmopolitan mentality. My analysis seeks to tie the possible emergence of a global public sphere into the ordinary ability of citizens to be able to forge ethical links, solidarities and connections with others who are distant in time and space. The development of communication that is not dependent upon face-to-face interactions on the surface seems to allow for the possibility of cooperative forms of human conduct that transgress national boundaries. However, my analysis, unlike that of Mulgan's, is alive to some of the less utopian and generative political consequences of these transformations. Further, such reflections are not intended to substitute for the need to develop a substantial public sphere at the level of the nation. The public sphere, as we shall see, is increasingly differentiated both spatially (local, national and global) and technologically.

The emergence of a cosmopolitan/global public sphere is dependent upon an active civil society that has been able to deconstruct oppositions between the local, national and the international. In such a view, civil society not only comprises the realm of voluntary organizations, legal rights and elections, but also encompasses the realm of symbolic communication. The media of mass communication in modern societies are important resources in the development of diverse civil societies that construct public narratives, symbols and identities, providing the ground for a number of imagined communities (Alexander and Jacobs 1998). Hence, the construction of cosmopolitan civil societies depends upon an intersubjective framework of human rights, political activism and common symbols and markers, which might be stretched to include common rituals and media events that help to raise questions of solidarity and identity across a number of divides (Sreberny 1998). Notably, such a view of civil society would take us beyond the usual distinctions between information and entertainment, and quality and commercial broadcasting, to encompass the normative and cultural horizons of everyday life. Within such contexts, an inclusive cultural citizenship or public sphere not only depends upon our shared attempts to critique official politics rationally, but also involves symbolic attempts to construct boundaries between 'insiders' and 'outsiders' through a variety of mediated cultural forms (Stevenson 1999). If the construction of a cosmopolitan civil society is not exclusively focused upon oppositions between civil life and pleasure, or upon the local as opposed to the international, how might we understand the current contours of our communicative universe? Further, the study of the media of mass communication should aim to deconstruct ideas of the public and the private. Feminist accounts have argued that we need to revise notions of the 'public' that neglect to analyse the ways its construction connects with the 'private' (Walby 1997). The feminist idea that the personal is political should lead us to question ideas of the public that exhibit an exclusive concern with the working of money and state power, neglecting more intimate dimensions. Public space has in more recent times been transformed through the emergence of stories and narratives that are concerned with intimate questions. Gay and lesbian communities and the women's movement(s) have in this respect fostered a new kind of intimate citizenship (Plummer 1995). Here, I seek to analyse media power, taking account of interconnections between the public, private and popular media culture.

Media, citizenship and cultural power

The idea of a genuinely public as opposed to a private or commercial system of communication usually makes reference to Jürgen Habermas's (1989) seminal study of the public sphere. Here Habermas famously traces the historical emergence of a critical domain that upheld the principle of open public discussion on matters of universal concern. Across seventeenth- and eighteenth-century Europe there emerged coffee houses and salons where male members of the bourgeoisie met to discuss works of literature. Despite the exclusive character of these debates, Habermas argues that they continue to have a normative relevance. We can judge contemporary media by the extent to which they facilitate free and open debate. The tragedy of the bourgeois public sphere, however, was that the very social forces that brought it into being would eventually lead to its decline and destruction. The instituted dialogue of the salons and coffee houses would give way as communication became increasingly organized through large commercial concerns. The progressive institutional elimination of private communicative individuals coming into conversation emphasized an increasing separation between public and private life.

From this point on commercial culture was consumed in the private, requiring no further debate or discussion. Unlike the print culture of the discursive bourgeois salons, much of the new media that emerged in the twentieth century (television, film and radio) disallows the possibility of talking back and taking part. Just as modern mass culture is received in atomized contexts, so the technical development of new cultural forms promoted privatism. Along with the 'privatization' of culture, Habermas adds, there has also been a corresponding trivialization of cultural products in order to gain a large share of the market. For Habermas, the operation of the market is best seen as a dual and contradictory process that has both emancipatory and dominatory effects and implications. For example, the video market provides a small strata of viewers with access to high-quality films. However, the lowering of entrance requirements has meant that film has had to be accommodated to a mass leisure culture that encourages passive relaxation and ease of reception. Modern cultural forms integrate subjects into a depoliticized culture, which by-passes the public sphere, where claims related to rightness could be discussed. This has led to what Habermas has called the refeudalization of the public sphere. Most of the visual (and print) culture consumed by the citizens of Western societies is increasingly dependent upon manufactured drama, media spectacle and the voyeuristic consumption of images. Habermas's concern is that such a culture both reaffirms the private sphere as the principle site of political engagement and by-passes a moral engagement with the voice of the other. The more sensational the output of television news, the more the public sphere withers on the vine.

Habermas's model has attracted a good deal of critical dialogue.[1] Yet, despite the numerous criticisms, many media scholars have sought to develop Habermas's model of the public sphere as a means of defending public service models of communication (Stevenson 2002). The idea of the public sphere has proved to be important, as it offers a model of democratic communication. This model, however, has taken on a different set of meanings depending upon the spatial context to which it is applied. For example, some commentators have argued that Western Europe has a tradition of public service broadcasting that needs to be defended against market penetration (Weymouth and Lamizet 1997). Within Britain, the tradition of public service broadcasting has aimed to provide licence fee payers with access to quality information, universal reception and a diversity of entertainment. From the 1960s and beyond, cultural critics like Raymond Williams (1962) and Richard Hoggart (1995) have sought to defend and revise this model. This has been primarily through calls to make public service broadcasting representative of the wider society, and to enhance its autonomy from the state. In the United States, Daniel Hallin (1994) has argued that while there is no tradition of the public sphere to point back towards, Habermas's views continue to display a critical purchase. Whereas the press has always been defined by commercial interests (linking partisan political views to elites from their inception in the eighteenth century), the media have become progressively depoliticized. News media journalists in this respect have come to view themselves as professionals who search for objective facts. The consequence of this is that most news media tend to value objectivity over discussion. Whereas the early newspapers had a built-in expectation that the audience would respond, contemporary news media assume the passivity of the audience. Hence, the problem with US news media is not the quality of the product, but that it is offered as a form of privatized consumption that disallows the participation of the public.

In this respect, intellectuals like Douglas Kellner (1995) have turned to the Internet and new communications media to provide new possibilities for critical citizens who are largely excluded from dominant media institutions. New computer technology is less hierarchical and more dialogic than traditional media. By this, Kellner means that whereas the technological form of television imposes passivity on the audience, the net allows users to construct their own web pages, send messages, download interesting material and visit the websites of their choice. Building on Habermas's theory of the public sphere, the problem with commercially orientated and centrally organized media is that they disallow the possibility of dialogue. Yet, and despite the impact of the Internet, most of the media we consume disallow the possibility of directly participating within their construction. It is a fundamental feature of most forms of mediated communication that they are essentially one-way communication. My argument is that this need not be a problem. I think we should accept in a global culture that dialogue is neither necessarily just nor practical.

John Durham Peters (1999) has argued that the search for the kinds of reciprocity implicit in the public sphere model need not necessarily be democratic. The need to be reciprocal within a mediated culture should not be allowed to overshadow other principles, such as responsibility, imagination and the capacity to voice our solidarity with others. Rather than searching for consensus, as is implicit in the Habermasian model, it is perhaps better to imagine communication 'as a dance in which we sometimes touch' (Peters 1999: 268). Further, as J. B. Thompson (1995) has argued, it is no longer clear what practical relevance discourse ethics has for global media cultures. Discourse ethics applies to those who share a common social location and who are able to engage in dialogue directly with one another. But under global conditions where the media are able to recontextualize imagery into local contexts, what would an all-inclusive conversation look like? How could the millions of spatially diverse people whose lives are affected by issues from poverty to pollution and from AIDS to the proliferation of nuclear weapons make their voices heard? The media of mass communication has fostered a non-localized and non-dialogic form of publicness operating across national contexts. Taking the points about the one-way nature of most mediated flows, and the lack of practicality evident within the model of the public sphere, a more sustainable model of communications would institute a framework that sought to mediate a diversity of views and in which the powerful could be challenged.

In these terms, Graham Murdock (1992, 1994, 1999) has argued that publicly owned and operated communication needs to be both conserved and extended in order to defend a common idea of citizenship. For Murdock, public service broadcasting is part of an ambivalent heritage that has provided a publicly funded forum where viewers, listeners and contributors are addressed as though they are citizens in a national community. Hence, whereas public systems have a responsibility to the public as broadcasters, commercial media institutions are primarily concerned with the selling of either air time to advertisers or subscriptions to fee payers. Public broadcasting, then, is a relatively decommodified realm that needs to be defended against the market. Murdock maintains this position despite his recognition that public broadcasters like the BBC have often displayed elitist dispositions towards certain forms of popular culture, and a hegemonic version of Englishness that excluded many on the grounds of class, ethnicity, age and gender. Public systems of broadcasting need to be extended to become less exclusive, while protecting people's rights to participate within a shared cultural space. Here Murdock identifies four basic cultural rights that should be commonly shared within a national community. These are rights to information, knowledge, experience and participation – all of which require public protection from commercial interests. That these rights require explicit protection is largely because of the enhanced role of the market within communications.

Pierre Bourdieu (1996a) has argued that where public broadcasters aimed to civilize the general public in the 1950s, by the 1990s the aim was to gain the largest possible audience. For Bourdieu it is market competition (rather than questions of ownership and control) that ensures the dominance of tried and tested formulae and the communication of banality. The media – like education, health, welfare and other social goods – require common forms of protection from a neo-liberal agenda.

In the US context there have been calls to develop a system of publicly funded communication systems as a means of strengthening civil society (Giroux 1999). The dominance of commercial organizations over the communicative structures of society serves to promote excessive consumerism and undermine the possibility of public forms of reflection. Here the struggle for public dialogue becomes the struggle against commercially run media.

The primary effect of the new media age in this reading has been the deregulation and privatization of public media. The commodification of public space has led to increasing numbers of channels and communications services, and has also pushed 'public' media into commercial ventures of their own (Herman and McChesney 1997). The development of digital broadcasting will improve picture quality, lower production costs and increase the available number of channels. The neo-liberal agenda has directly determined the communications agenda in the interests of global corporations like Time Warner, Disney and News International, all of which are likely to profit from an increasingly commercial culture based upon cross-selling, cross-promotion and conglomerate merger. In this analysis, globalization and trade liberalization are rendered equivalent, as commercial competition progressively seeks to undermine the operation of public media. Such is the connection between the freedom to communicate and the free market that the operating logic of the market and communications policy becomes 'Let people watch what they want' (Mattelart 2001).

Further, if national public broadcasting is being eroded from above by globalization processes, it is being eroded from below by subnational developments. Morley (2000) reports that whereas in 1995 only 4 per cent of the French population subscribed to satellite television, 21 per cent of Arabic-speaking households had access to these new channels. In other words, new channels of communication are popular not only because they talk in the popular language of consumption, but because they allow minorities to escape from the perceived restrictions of national media systems. Diasporic communities are able to maintain a sense of ongoing connection to an absent homeland through the transportability of videos, films and television programmes (Gillespie 2000; Sreberny 2000). Arguably, these features question the ability of 'national' public systems fully to 'represent' overlapping communities within an increasingly post-national age.

Cultural citizenship in a global mediated culture

So far, I have argued that public systems of broadcasting need to be repositioned in terms of both global and subnational developments. Yet we also need to be aware that many cultural theorists have pointed to the media's ability to enhance international dialogue, empower minorities and potentially construct solidarity at a distance. The globalization of the mass media is inherently ambivalent. While it has increased the power of media conglomerates, it has also tilted questions of citizenship away from exclusively national concerns. Global forms of mediation – as should now be clear – are poorly appreciated by a tradition of public service broadcasting that seeks to preserve 'authentic' forms of communication against the corruption of the popular and the market. That is, we need to be attentive to the media's capacity to shift information through time and space, which opens the possibility of what J. B. Thompson (1995) has described as 'intimacy at a distance'. The audience's relations with celebrities, media events and politicians are different from those with persons who are co-present. A non-reciprocal relationship of intimacy depends upon the scrutiny of the celebrity or news event by the audience, and not the other way round. For many, the media's capacity to enhance *connexity* holds out the possibility of enhancing surface forms of cosmopolitanism. It is the capacity of media cultures to move perspectives and images through time and space that contributes to the making of 'fuzzy' cultures (Hannerz 1992). The globalization of the media might mean that we are likely to become more tolerant of the 'other', or that our capacity for reflexivity will become enhanced, and that such developments will help to foster a society of 'clever' people who are no longer bound by parochial geographies (Giddens 1994; Mulgan 1997; Urry 2000a).

These projections hold out the possibility of a form of citizenship that is no longer contained by the nation-state. The main problem with the way in which citizenship has been constructed by the public service tradition is that it is inattentive to the ways in which social movements, events, lifestyles, consumer products, human rights abuses, religious ideas, risks, hazards and ethical beliefs all struggle for visibility within a global media culture. Here we might follow John Urry (2000b) by making a distinction between a citizenship of stasis and a citizenship of flows. The desire to defend and deepen the culture of public service broadcasting can be linked to a membership of certain nation-states (not all nations/states have such traditions). Alternatively, a citizenship of flows is more concerned with the capacity of mediated material to cross borders. The movement of refugees, viruses, images and symbolic material involves questions of rights and responsibilities that take us beyond specific national societies. Yet while we cannot escape our symbolic inclusion in a media culture that multiplies the possible worlds of our experience, there remains a diversity of personal and collective reactions to these new contexts. In other words, if media cultures are diversifying our possible worlds of experience, we will need to be attentive to the complex ways in which these are interpreted. If in the twentieth century the cultural bonds of the nation were maintained by communication technology, we can no longer assume this to be the case. The cultural connexity of technological society is constructed through networks that are discontinuous (Lash 2001). This holds out the prospect, as we shall see, of a complex dialectic of identification and disidentification. Hence, returning to Mulgan's (1997) idea of connexity, we need to study the complex circuits of information that the new media order makes commonly available. This will mean abandoning any simple idea (evident in Mulgan's original formulation) that new forms of technology necessarily enhance cosmopolitan mentalities. We cannot simply assume that because we are living in a global age people will become less local in the construction of their horizons. There is indeed evidence that the paradox of globalization is that the flow of culture has been met by the stasis of perspective. Instead, along with others, I prefer the metaphor of the network, where circuits of information simultaneously promote connection and disconnection (Castells 1997; van Dijk 1999). For example, the new media order has rapidly expanded the amount of information made commonly available, while enhancing the capacity of citizens to choose their own level of interaction. Yet we can equally argue that the commercialization of the media has exaggerated the divisions between a global information rich and a global information poor (Schiller 1996). As we shall see, what remains crucial in respect of these dimensions is not the global construction of public systems of broadcasting or the need to return to more dialogic forms of communication. A more globally orientated cultural citizenship should be more concerned to explore the ambivalent connections, disconnections, miscommunications and possibilities global systems make commonly available.

In the remainder of this chapter I investigate these questions. I briefly examine the ways in which the global flows of the media of mass communication can be connected to questions of cultural citizenship in respect of: (a) the global struggle for human rights; (b) the impact of new media; (c) the enhanced speed of modern communications; (d) the fostering of indifference and cosmopolitan connection; and (e) the impact of popular commercial media.

Human rights, social movements and global media

One of the most significant moral and political achievements of humanity remains the 1948 Universal Declaration of Human Rights. The principles laid down in this document recognize that everyone, irrespective of national boundaries, is entitled to the rights and freedoms held out in the Charter. The Charter has provided the basis for international law, setting out common standards that might reasonably be expected by all peoples (Falk 1995a, b). Article 19, for example, contains a defence of the freedom of information and rights of expression, including the right to impart and receive information irrespective of frontiers. These universal rights to communication have provided the inspiration behind attempts by Third World nations in the 1970s to challenge western media dominance. This led to a series of commissions and reports that issued declarations on the rights of peoples and the responsibilities of the global media.

More recently, Cees Hamelink (1994, 1995) has argued that the globalization of mass communication has led to the disempowering of ordinary people when it comes to exerting power and control over their communicative environments. Globalization processes have increased the power of large-scale media conglomerates and flooded the world with cheap, standardized media products. These processes can only be reversed through a human rights initiative that enables participation within cultural and political life, by providing people with access to information so that they might make autonomous decisions. Whereas global media empires are disempowering, in that they infringe upon local cultural space and privatize access to information, human rights approaches treat knowledge as a collectively owned common good to be shared, debated and contributed to by equal citizens. The reduction in cultural space enables the West to control the flow of information and disempower 'other' peoples from developing their own sense of identity.

Starting from local networks, the world's peoples are encouraged to search for alternative sources of information exchange that emerge underneath the disciplinary power of the state and the commercial imperatives that govern global media empires. The development of a genuine people's media through community radio and newspapers and the burgeoning of a people's community network over the Internet could form the beginning of local and global sources of information that provide alternative sources of communication. Politically, we can afford to be optimistic about such movements, due to the 'revolt of civil society'. By this, Hamelink means that alternative networks of communication will arise alongside social movements like ecology and feminism. The emergence of a 'double citizenship', or what Albrow (1996) has termed 'performative citizenship', means that such movements point to a new form of politics that seeks to link national internal struggles to more global levels of interconnection. As a first step in building upon these civic initiatives, Hamelink proposes the worldwide adoption of what he calls a 'People's Communication Charter'. The main aim of the charter is to raise the awareness of individuals and social movements with regard to the shared importance of securing both human and cultural rights. The charter then builds upon Article 19 of the 1948 declaration by granting people rights freely to form an opinion, gain information, enter into public discussion, distribute knowledge, protect their cultural identity and participate in a shared public culture, among others. The aim is both to make this a movement of non-governmental forces (groups such as Amnesty, CND, Greenpeace) and to have the charter adopted by the United Nations.

The most obvious and immediate objection to such arguments is that the Declaration of Human Rights is not legally enforceable, and without the reform of the United Nations itself such charters have historically had little impact. The 'People's Communication Charter', from this cynical viewpoint, ends up adding to the meaningless pieces of paper that are produced by the United Nations bureaucracy. These proposals could be further criticized for being unlikely to have any lasting impact on the dominant rationale and structures of the global media. Yet such arguments are as insightful as they are mistaken about the politics of human rights and their connection to questions of democracy, citizenship and the media of mass communication.

The first point to make is that the widespread acceptance of a 'People's Communication Charter' is not solely dependent upon its ability to produce legal effects. Like other human rights that are widely accepted among non-governmental organizations, its 'cultural' existence gives groups something to appeal to and build a social struggle around. It is undeniable that in terms of its perceived moral legitimacy such a process would be greatly enhanced if the charter were accepted by the United Nations. This would give social movements a platform on which to perform immanent critique, whereby signatories could be embarrassed by their refusal to uphold the principles they had formally agreed. Human rights documents in this respect are important, in that they help to create a set of general political and cultural expectations that – when violated – potentially attract the attention of the media and political movements alike.

There are of course no guarantees in this respect, but if movements for social change are able to point to international treaties or other collectively agreed documents it will aid them in making interventions in the global televisual arena. Their claims will be given an added normative weight if they are able to claim that a state's actions are breaking international agreements. The argument being proposed here is that the economic (wealth and resources), political (influence over public policy) and cultural (modelling stocks of discourses and concepts) power of the new media order is such that an international recognition of people's rights in respect of information exchange could indeed have an empowering effect upon the interrelation between local, national and more global public spheres.

Yet it is likely that Hamelink presses the case of the colonizing effect of media conglomerates too far. As J. B. Thompson (1994: 94) notes, currently global media cultures subject the world's nation-states to a form of *global scrutiny*. By this he means that the exercise of political power increasingly takes place upon a visible world stage. The medium of mass communication makes the actions of despotic states visible to the globe's citizens. This process can also be coupled to the global remooring of images and perspectives that give individuals some idea of forms of life different from their own. This surface knowledge of other cultures, Thompson (1995) argues, gives individuals a social resource, enabling them to distance themselves from more official state-driven viewpoints. To claim that the globalization of the media places restrictions on the activities of nation-states is undoubtedly correct, but this remains dependent on social context, as states still have considerable powers to isolate themselves from the internal impacts of global criticism, no matter how self-defeating this might prove over the longer term. More globally orientated forms of mediated citizenship need to challenge agendas that seek to move against the formation of international law, ensure the development of peaceful dialogue free of damaging stereotypes and seek to affirm other principles, such as self-determination and a commitment to human rights more generally.

Further, and perhaps more crucially, there is considerable evidence that post-colonial media cultures continue to promote ideologies of superiority and dominance (Bhabha 1992). This is not, of course, to adopt a mode of theorizing that points towards a progressive Americanization of world media cultures. Post-colonial thinkers have questioned such images in the name of hybridity, multiple identity and diaspora. Popular culture considered along these lines cannot be contained within the frameworks of Americanization or nationalism. With these features in mind, Pieterse and Parekh (1995) have called for the 'decolonization of the Western imagination'. While such a perspective dispenses with one-dimensional views (like those advanced by Hamelink) that media cultures promote Westernization, this does not mean that they are free from ideologies of dominance. Much media culture, as my own research on the televisation of the Rwandan genocide revealed, makes binary distinctions between the civilized West and the barbarism of the 'other' (Stevenson 1999). My research uncovered that in reporting Rwanda, news discourses coded the Rwandans as essentially either 'violent' or 'innocent', failing to take account of the historical and social context. The television media failed to uncover the national and international context relevant to state-driven murder. While 'official' media cultures continue to trade in these terms, they serve to mask more complex sets of narratives of exile, travel and intercultural dialogue. In mediated terms, then, cosmopolitan media are those that have deconstructed a host of stereotypes that remain the common fare of journalism.

Finally, the faith that we might have in the 'People's Communication Charter' is undermined not as much by the trust it places in institutions as by people's initiatives generally. Civil society is currently made up of organizations that aim to reinstate patriarchy, ethnic nationalisms, religious fundamentalisms and all kinds of other causes that Hamelink would find himself out of sympathy with. This begs the question as to whether a charter that emphasizes the 'right' to be heard can really solve the communicative crisis within civil society today. However, the politics of mediated human rights remains a key area for contestation and debate within a global arena where citizens are able to appeal for help, publicize suffering and make terrorist and state-driven acts of violence visible, thereby seeking to attract the attention of a 'global community'. While a globally mediated human rights culture can enhance post-national forms of interconnection, we should be aware that such agendas continue to be subject to the power of transnational media empires and the nation-state.

Technocultures, media and community

Current debates in respect of the development of new media technologies have a strong overlap with the nature of connexity. The media of mass communication are rapidly diversifying just at the point when old communal relations are increasingly open to question. Are new media technologies responsible for undermining a sense of community by robbing people of participatory public spaces, or are they the sites where more diversified relations of solidarity can be made? Crudely, we can divide arguments over the effects and transformations brought about by new media into opposing optimistic and pessimistic schools of thought. The pessimists propose that the development of new media technologies can be coupled with the continuation of modernity, the destruction of communal forms of identification and the progressive privatization and commodification of public life. On the other hand, more postmodern frames see the emergence of the net, video, mobile phones and portable stereos as opening out new possibilities for voices that have been traditionally excluded from public cultures. New, more affective attachments can be formed through underground networks, fan magazines, MUD (multi-user domain) sites and phone chat lines. Unlike traditional communities, in which individuals are born into co-present local relations, so called postmodern communities are more likely to be the result of 'individual' choice and the product of mediation. Whereas one set of critics views the global triumph of capital as destroying the communal identifications that allow people to resist capitalism, the other views community as a more fluid site and a potential place of radical politics. To overstate the point, where one set of critics is mournful at the passing of old ties, the other is celebratory in the hope that new ones might be made. The debate concerns the ways in which people are connected and disconnected from a spatially complex media culture. I will now unpack these viewpoints.

The pessimists' camp houses a wide spectrum of political viewpoints, from old-style radicals to cultural conservatives. For instance, Julian Stallabras (1996) argues that the information superhighway and cyberspace will offer not a utopian domain of free communication, but the perfect market place, which can operate through space and time at the flick of a switch. Those who are currently excited about the future possibilities of the net are failing to ask who will control the information, work out to whom it is going to be made available and in whose interests it is likely to be run. The answers to these questions are all traceable back to the needs of global capital. For instance, so called virtual communities are places built upon irony and play, unlike real communities, which are places of obligation and responsibility. If within cyberspace we are able to disguise our identities, this effectively denies the possibility of a genuinely democratic communicative exchange, where the particularity of the 'other' has to be engaged with. Instead it creates a 'kingdom of information, whose palatial halls we may wander without fear, free from chaos, dirt and obscurity' (Stallabras 1996: 67). Cyberspace becomes a zone of irresponsible consumption, where the poor will never appear as subjects in their own right and only very occasionally as 'objects' for discussion. Indeed, the desire to create 'virtual' communities over the web points both to the disappearance of 'real' communal relations, which are trampled under the atomizing effect of commodity capital, and to the fact that humans desperately need a sense of belonging and will create it with whatever tools they currently have to hand.

Further, according to Robins (1997), new media technologies are invested with omnipotent fantasies and feelings. Cyborg relations promise to melt the distinctions between humans and technology while offering the 'thrill of escape'. In the new media universe we are invited to choose disguises and assume new identities, thereby distancing ourselves from 'real' human relations. The capacity of technology to solve human predicaments magically offers us an 'instant' solution to the problems of self and community. The net can both promote the warm feelings of community while we are being atomized and deliver us the fantasy of self-creation free of actual social encounters. In cyberspace we become blind to questions of difference, as we only encounter the privileged, retreat from the brutal realities of late capitalism and escape from the burden of geography. On the net there are few real surprises and little that is unfamiliar. Rather than dealing with the otherness of the 'other', cyberspace is based on the governance of corporate capitalism (Robins and Webster 1999).

Significantly, the development of new communications technologies has been read differently by writers who occupy less traditional frames of reference. Maffesoli (1996) questions the pessimistic projections of those who are concerned with the fragmentation and privatization of the modern subject. He does this by articulating a notion of the subject that is continually searching for emotional connection with intersubjectively related others. Maffesoli rejects the idea of the isolated individual split away from others through the operation of mass culture, and points to what he calls the 'tribalization' of the social. By this he means that through the creation of football teams, self-help groups, friendship networks, Internet sites and religious associations individuals are increasingly likely to belong to a number of diverse and contradictory communities. What we are currently witnessing, therefore, is the deindividualization of modernity and the growth of more affective communities based less on utilitarian notions of self-interest than on sociality. The new tribes are based upon shared sentiments, whether they are regular visitors to an Internet site, members of international human rights forums or even occasional viewers of a soap opera. These new emotional communities are constructed more upon fleeting identification and periodic warmth than upon the stability of traditional ties. Hence, the argument here is not as much to bemoan the ways in which capitalism has destroyed traditional forms of association as to investigate the creative ways in which social solidarity might be reimagined in the late modern age.

Yet, as these remarks suggest, we need to be able to view new media beyond the binaries of utopian possibility and sociological nightmare. Global cultural citizenships are likely to be formed through the power of technology to connect and disconnect the globe's citizens in a multitude of ways (Featherstone 1999; Stevenson 1999). These questions will undoubtedly be driven by questions of symbolic power, representation and disconnection. However, within this we should be careful not to assume that access to technology automatically makes for cosmopolitan horizons or that a 'rootedness' to locality invariably spells parochialism. Alternatively, we should also be careful not to assume unproblematically that the Internet can be read exclusively through the prism of connection or disconnection. Instead, the Internet is likely to play an important part in the construction of social movements. The progressive shift away from a print culture within modernity can be linked to the pluralization of voices and the popularization of a wide range of perspectives. The Internet has already played an important role in a range of globally orientated civil actions, including the international ban on landmines. Here non-governmental organizations (NGOs) targeted the globe's media with emotive images of children in wheelchairs and truckloads of crutches, while also setting up influential websites (Warkentin and Mingst 2000). The Internet was part of a media strategy designed to establish a global network between NGOs and sympathetic states, helping to promote a momentum for social change. However, we could equally point to the very real problems of Internet and technological access that will inevitably be encountered within a global context. It was estimated in 1999 that 80 per cent of Internet users were from North America and Europe. Again, it is the Internet's ability to foster complex circuits of engagement and silence, and interaction and exclusion, that holds the key to understanding its considerable power.

Speed and communication

The temporal dimensions of media cultures have strong connections to processes of globalization. For instance, in the mid-eighteenth century it used to take letters approximately 40 days to cross from Europe to the United States. Today, through the intervention of telephones, the world wide web and live broadcasts, we have entered the age of instantaneous and immediate communication. The experience of what Giddens (1990) has called 'time–space' compression has meant that the increasingly 'event'-driven nature of media reporting has become exaggerated, in correspondence with its global spread. Newspaper stories, television news items and radio programmes are no longer determined by their proximity to the location of their production. The linear and sequential nature of time that, according to Benedict Anderson (1983), allowed the nation to imagine itself collectively progressing through history is being displaced by a global time of instantaneous transmission. The idea of historical progress through time by a hermetically sealed nation-state has been undermined by simultaneous global happenings and the blurring of strict boundaries between past, present and future. This new structure of feeling is propelled by a media culture of nostalgic revivals and pastiche, where firmly distinct historical periods and sensations are difficult to maintain in an increasingly mongrel world. The displacement of the linear and sequential temporal frames associated with modernity by the speeded up, disorganized dimensions of postmodernity has important consequences for the way we understand global media cultures. This can lead to a situation where the rational forms of reflection necessary for participatory citizenship are undermined by the formation of immediate opinions, collective forms of forgetting and a wider culture of uncertainty.

Paul Virilio (1997, 2000a, b, c) has argued over a number of publications that the impact of new technologies of communication on the human senses is mostly negative. The 'real time' of modern media communications has fundamentally altered and distorted the subject's conception of reality. What Virilio (2000a: 57) calls the 'industrialization of vision' has not as much added new realities as displaced our sensitivity towards different temporalities within modernity. The real-time of television has come to dominate our shared definitions of reality. The showing of events 'as they happen' has meant that a society of images and spectacles has come to replace public forms of dialogue. Within this, the linear time patterns of modernity have become displaced by the hegemony of instantaneous communication. The speed of modern communications in this regard has a number of consequences.

First, speed destroys thought and the possibility of democratic deliberation. Ideas concerning the possibility of using technology to enhance democracy are mistaken, in that what is more likely is a culture of conditioning, where communications are used to control the responses of the public (Virilio 2000b: 109). Second, the global spread of information and computer technology introduces the possibility of the 'terminal citizen'. With the destruction of temporal relationships between near and far, human beings become more concerned with the reality of the screen than the actual physical proximity of their more immediate personal and communal relationships. Society then becomes divided between two distinct temporalities, which Virilio (1997: 71) describes as the absolute and the relative. The radical divide is between those who live in real-time, whose economic, political and cultural activities are driven by speed, and those who become ever more destitute while living in 'real' spaces. For the 'terminal citizen' virtual reality, event-driven media and the frantic mobility of information have come not to supplement 'reality' but to replace it. Third, the paradox of the information society is that it leads to an increase in virtual mobility and physical inertia. The 'terminal citizen' does not have actually to move about, as technology is increasingly modelled to fit the contours of the human body. The new interactive space that is facilitated by the Internet, television and virtual reality means that the home becomes a cockpit that receives the world without the occupant having to move. We are, then, not as much in the age of mobility as in the age of paralysis. This induces the subject into a 'vegetative state', or culturally induced coma, where the search is not for the possibility of public action, but for the 'intensiveness of sensations' (Virilio 2000a: 69).

Fourth, the speeding up of 'reality' in real-time has an individualizing effect, whereby information becomes increasingly focused in on the self. This process, coupled with the replacement of reality, means that we actually pay less and less attention to our ecological landscapes, which support all life forms.

The collapse of space turns us inwards, away from the world and into the increasingly simulated world of new technology, fun and cyber fantasies. The televisualization of reality delivers not a cosmopolis but an omniopolis, which enhances the possibility of a global accident that could destroy large sections of humanity. As we become distanced from our own naturalness and vulnerability, the perceived possibility of global catastrophes through economic collapse, nuclear war or the spread of viruses comes ever closer. Technological imperialism pushes us closer to disaster, while robbing our common human senses of the ecological sensitivity necessary to resist such changes.

Finally, the global spread of 'real-time' technologies increases the possibility of a new phase of totalitarianism by putting us under constant forms of surveillance. Live cams set up on the Internet from people's kitchens and bedrooms are not about information or entertainment, but about the exposure and invasion of the individual. The monitoring of human activity now takes place on a global basis and makes us constantly visible, imposing upon us a 'technological vigil' (Virilio 2000b: 62). The spread of new technologies of surveillance, from mobile phones (which abolish the distinction between public and private for employees) to the orbital surveillance of enemy territories, subjects us all to global forms of control. Control, as demonstrated by the war in Kosovo, is now not as much a function of state sovereignty as the capacity to determine who occupies air and space. This enhances the possibility of global powers (like the United States) launching an information war through the presence of satellites (monitoring population movements) and live broadcasts that spread disinformation. This control is also linked to the ability to pollute information exchange through disinformation. By disinformation, Virilio (2000c) does not mean the control of information through shortage and distortion. In the Kosovo war disinformation was more the product of over-information: the constant 24-hour supply of television news does not as much divide opinion as confuse it with contradictory data. For Virilio, technological advance is the opposite of democracy.

Rather than answering all of Virilio's charges on the information age, I want to concentrate on how he links technology, speed and cultural impoverishment. Technology, as Virilio points out, is intimately concerned with speed and efficiency. The quickening of the time allowed for opinion formation can often lead to the production of superficial perspectives in place of those that should have taken a deeper and more substantial view. We might then be in a position to receive more information more quickly than ever before, but be denied the interpretative opportunities to make the world more meaningful. For example, the increased speeding up of events interferes with our capacity to feel empathy and disappointment. The media are always moving on, restlessly searching for fresh news and different viewpoints. This makes the achievement of responsible and meaningful forms of reflection increasingly difficult in the modern age.

Yet it is a mistake to proceed as if the media only colonize society's shared capacity to construct meaningful relations with others. For instance, the culture of immediacy and speed can also feed the idea that we, the nation or international alliance, in a time of crisis, ought to do something. This can be invaluable if, say, we are considering offering immediate humanitarian aid to the victims of a disaster. But it can also have other, perhaps more negative, consequences, given that speed can be used to displace the necessary labour of democratic discussion. The rapidity at which these decisions are made might mean that a wide-ranging public discussion has not yet taken place and that not enough 'quality' information has been made available to make a judgement. Here I am struck by a basic ambivalence between the need to receive information quickly and the consequences this might have for human reasoning. The wider point is that the temporal bias introduced by media cultures disrupts our capacity for critical reflection, as well as providing a necessary service to and influence on contemporary political culture. The issue here is to hold an intellectual concern regarding the lack of slowness in our culture against an appreciation of the political necessity of speeding up information exchange.

Second, I think that the daily overturning of opinion in the modern era has led to a tendency for collective memories to be shortened. This can also have unpredictable effects and consequences. In political terms, it might result in similar mistakes being made and an increasing inability to make sense of larger historical patterns and trends. This might lead to a 'forgetting' of the historical struggles that have granted us certain citizenship entitlements, producing a culture of complacency and neglect. It can also give the impression, as we become caught up in the immediacy of the present, that events that happened only a number of years ago are temporally distant. Yet, again, I think it important to stress the ambiguous nature of such processes. The unintended consequence here might be an opening of human horizons free from the dead weight of the past that can offer new hope and energy to emancipatory groups of various kinds.

This paradox can be illustrated by looking at ecological movements. As Barbara Adam (1995) has expertly argued, ecological concerns have focused collective attention on time lags and latency periods between cause and effect. By this Adam means that modernity has increasingly made us aware of the risks that our present actions are shoring up, if not for ourselves then for future generations. This again points us towards a different conception of temporal dimensions from the one that existed with sequential and linear causality. However, the main problem for the green movement is that they have to get people to think over a longer period of time than is evident in a world fostered by speed capitalism and mass communication. The need to consider the material conditions of future generations, however, rests uneasily with the current desire to satisfy the immediate and the short term. In this respect at least, Virilio is right to point our attention to the connection between ecological issues and time. Yet his analysis is surely too sweeping in the suggestion that speed is obliterating our appreciation of different temporal frames.

Sachs (1999) has argued that the time frames of industrial modernity clash with those that govern the Earth. Industrialism is based upon acceleration, whereby technological innovations are fostered to increase the yields of animals, nature and humans. The paradox is that while modernity has introduced so-called time-saving devices, people are increasingly expressing a concern that they lack time. In this, Sachs comes close to Virilio in identifying inhuman time as the time of industrial development and progress, whereas sustainability requires the nurture of different time frames, with a renewed emphasis placed upon slowness. Yet to complicate the situation further, in ways that are absent from Virilio and Sachs, the concerns of the ecological movement have undoubtedly been shaped by new levels of global interconnection that the media regularly make available. The compression of space and time, it seems, has both revealed global interconnections that were previously obscured and opened out a concern for wider collective futures. In short, the global media make planetary identification possible.

Finally, the changing temporal dimensions of our culture has helped to foster a shared sense of the future that is deeply uncertain. The breakdown of narratives of progress and security that can be connected with linear time frames has produced anxiety about the future. Baudrillard (1994) has argued that fear in the face of the future can be discovered in the arguments that abounded about the 'end of history' as the twentieth century drew to a close. This can be detected in what he calls an 'event strike', where the aura of historical events has declined through the repetition and simulation of the twentieth century in the media. By this Baudrillard means that the history of our time is currently being rerun through a culture of ecological recycling, nostalgia for the French revolution (evident in the 200 years celebration) and the rebirth of liberalism after the fall of the Berlin Wall. The desire to impose an 'end to history' and the current cultural rerunning of the twentieth century exhibits a generalized global fear about what the future might hold. However, while I think that Baudrillard's reflections are interesting, they displace what I take to be the key issue.

The break with linear time evident in the globalization of the media and related processes reveals a sense of the future that is likely to be chaotic, disorganized and increasingly unpredictable. The event-driven nature of the global media helps to foster an impression of a violent conflictual world that is running out of control. This sense could perhaps be linked to fundamentalist desires to reorder the world, a greater moral concern with the sufferings of others, passive forms of voyeurism or even increasing indifference. Obviously, then, the handling of these different responses to globalized uncertainty will depend upon a variety of social and psychic responses of which the media make up only a small part. The mistake that Virilio makes in this regard is that in his polemical assault on a culture increasingly determined by technology, he makes little space for different cultural and social mediations.

Moral indifference and cosmopolitanism

We have already seen that the connexity of the media can have ambiguous effects in respect of the links between media and politics. A different way of exploring these questions is to ask what effects the televisualization of suffering has upon our shared moral landscape. We might argue that practices of time–space compression make it increasingly difficult to ignore the plight of the 'other'. The daily screening of images of suffering on our television sets means that it has become increasingly difficult to shrug off our responsibilities towards others in a shared world (Adam 1996). Through televised appeals on behalf of people we will never meet we become aware that a donation 'right now' could have an immediate impact upon the well-being of distanciated others across the planet's surface. Television and new media technologies arguably make cosmopolitan compassion and moral solidarity more possible. This is especially the case when such concerns become connected to the emergence of a cosmopolitan civil society that includes the global spread of human rights, charitable agencies like Oxfam and the globalization of communication networks.

However, there are a growing number of more sceptical voices in this respect. Keith Tester (1995: 475) argues that television cannot actually create moral solidarity, but it can provide a cultural resource for those who have a predisposition towards 'moral leaps of the imagination'. The images and perspectives of the media do not have any automatic moral consequences. The representation of murder, war and suffering on television has no necessary connection to the development of cosmopolitan solidarity. In this respect, Zygmunt Bauman (1993) offers the notion of *telecity* to explain some of these aspects. Telecity, Bauman argues, is where objects and subjects appear only as forms of pleasure and amusement. The television screen may allow us to go travelling without leaving home – but its integration into privatized leisure patterns means that our experience of the alterity of the 'other' becomes blunted. The space opened up by telecity is one based upon individual pleasure – one that allows the subject to wander through a variety of media texts without any strings attached.

Tester (1995) continues that a world awash with images helps to foster a blasé attitude among the audience, where they repeatedly fail to be shocked by the pictures of horror and distress that are the daily diet of the television news. Television images are too fast and fleeting to leave any lasting moral trace of their presence. The box presents the moral issues and problems of living in an interconnected world as crumbs that can be easily swept off the collective table. The television screen in this regard can be seen as a 'door' that we stand behind, rather than a 'bridge' directly connecting the viewer to the sufferings of others. In this the screen is not really a 'window on the world', but can literally be seen as a barrier between the viewer and those whose lives are represented. If the media are a door rather than a bridge, we can keep it shut in order to maintain our social and moral distance from the sufferings of others (Tester 1999). In this scenario, the act of giving is largely a means of maintaining rather than closing social distance. Tester (2001), along with Devereux (1996), argues that global news, telethons and documentaries are more often concerned with the cleansing of suffering and the sanitization of the 'other'. In Lars von Trier's film *The Idiots* this is demonstrated through ordinary middle-class people constructing barriers of 'niceness' and 'politeness' to avoid being too close to what they perceive to be people with mental health problems. Money or polite behaviour in this respect is a way of keeping the 'other' at a comfortable distance.

Mestrovic (1997) has taken these views further by arguing that we are currently living in a post-emotional society. This is a society of synthetic feeling where we have all become progressively indifferent to the suffering of others. How else, charges Mestrovic, are we to understand the West's indifference to the practice of genocide in Rwanda and Bosnia? Civilization in the Western world has come to mean the ability to exhibit refined manners alongside a cool indifference to televised murder. The post-emotional society values 'being nice' over the collective ability to be able to act on our emotions and to intervene to help others. The capacity to be able to feel deep emotions in an age that end-lessly simulates sentiment through news bulletins, talk shows and soap operas is being progressively undermined. The display of feeling is short-lived, useless, aesthetic and luxurious, and rarely becomes connected to a sense of justice and a genuine concern for humanity. Our emotions are becoming progressively regulated by pre-packaged sentiment and the crocodile tears of journalists reporting from war zones. Post-emotionalism disallows the possibility of emotions becoming chaotic; instead, they are increasingly subject to 'politically correct' forms of regulation. This cleaned up universe leaves little room for the strong passions and commitments necessary to intervene in humanitarian disasters.

While the language used by Tester and Mestrovic is deliberately designed to shock, such perceptions have an important case to press. If, as I argued earlier, a global civil society depends upon the activation of a cosmopolitan connexity, then the issues raised here have a clear importance. If we take the mediated charity event 'Red Nose Day', which appears on British screens biannually, it may illuminate our understanding. Red Nose Day seeks to coordinate different fund-raising activities during the day, with the emphasis being placed upon showing concern for others while having fun. In the evening these activities are supplemented by a five- to six-hour television programme that runs continuously through the night. The programme is presented by well known celebrities (giving their time for free) who present 'serious footage' from people 'in need', which is supplemented by guest appearances, comedy sketches and interviews from participants involved in charitable activities. On one level, Red Nose Day is a mediated example of cosmopolitan solidarity enjoyed by 'freedom's children' (Beck 2000). Indeed, when I asked my students to view the event as part of a media course, their reactions were mainly positive. In 2000, Red Nose Day dedicated a third of its resources to helping the genocide victims of Rwanda. Many of my students reported how the clips of film (interspersed by celebrity appearances) from Rwanda had made them aware of the sufferings of others. The plight of the people from Rwanda was confirmed by comedian Lenny Henry, who kept reminding the audience that 'we are all brothers'. Undoubtedly, then, the information and knowledge provided by Red Nose Day tap into a latent cosmopolitan sensibility. Yet the students also reported other feelings further away from the surface. There were concerns that the shocking images could be used to guilt trip the audience, and further that such help as 'the needy' received might be short term. There was a concern about the moral distance between the givers and receivers of the money that is donated.

What was not commented upon was the lack of depth, voice and complexity available within many of the images. To treat a person or a community justly we would need to take seriously their commitments, concerns and ethical complexity. More global forms of cultural citizenship that failed to do this could not expect to sustain relations of solidarity. Typically, the plight of the Rwandans was represented as that of a homogeneous people united by suffering. Within the images and representations that Red Nose Day made available, 'the victims' were given little opportunity to speak for themselves or be connected to a recognizable political or social context. Further, many of the students (and myself) found it difficult to distinguish the reports from Rwanda and other stories of suffering from different African locations also presented on Red Nose Day. While such criticism would need to take into account the limitations inherent within the genre of the telethon, many of the facets of Red Nose Day seem consistent with the observations made by Tester and Mestrovic. Such events could be characterized as 'carnivals of charity' in which giving takes place outside of lasting relations of solidarity (Bauman 1998).

While these perspectives pose difficult questions for a mediated global citizenship, they are in need of further discussion. Modern society is not as afraid of strong feeling as it is of moralism. A global citizenship in an information society would do well to steer clear of moral certitude, which is less concerned with dialogue and difference than it is with its own claims to rightness. Indeed, in Mestrovic's view, emotions that do not directly lead to immediate forms of action are labelled as useless. Such a view takes as its touchstone an idealized masculine subject who has banished uncertainty and is able to act confidently in the world. The values of introspection, ambivalence and doubt are quickly dismissed as a form of cruelty that is indifferent to the sufferings of others. However, read differently, the assembled views of Tester, Bauman and Mestrovic open up different questions that speak of the inequalities and injustices of globalization. Morley (2000) has argued in this respect that whereas privileged consumers can progressively delink themselves from a national territory, the same cannot be said of the planet's poor. It is the ability of the planet's relatively privileged to withdraw into the pleasures and comforts of their own living rooms, away from their obligations towards those that are suffering, that troubles Tester, Bauman and Mestrovic.

Despite the media's capacity to bring in the 'other', this is blunted by the effects of commodification, the nature of television and wider social divisions. Here we need to understand the role of television as a specifically domestic medium. Roger Silverstone (1994) has argued that television (like other media) operates within a boundary between the domestic and the public, private and collective, and intimate and more distant social relations. In many respects, television has grown up as part of a post-war, privatized, suburban culture. Television (like other mediums such as radio) functions within a social and political context that seeks to domesticate the 'other', where conflicts are avoided, homogeneity is embraced and ideological contestation is shut out. Here, the 'other' is unable to shock, as it becomes assimilated into the predictable domestic routines that constitute modern living. Similar objections have also been made in connection with the spread of so-called 'compassion fatigue', where the world's privileged, despite being awash with images of poverty and deprivation, are accused of retreating behind the walls of closed communities and the pleasures of consumer culture. In this scenario the winners of global capitalism are becoming increasingly indifferent to the plight of both local and global losers.

However, I think that these arguments, while asking important moral questions, are also in danger of being overstated. Images of suffering still have the capacity to move some of the people some of the time into political concern, expressions of sympathy and care. As Stanley Cohen (2001) has argued, it is not information overload or a pervasive culture of indifference that affects relatively privileged populations, as much as demand overload. If we take the estimates that 46 per cent of the world do not have access to clean water, that 8.5 million African children by 2010 are likely to be orphaned due to AIDS and the current total of 16 million refugees, the question is often where to start. Such statistics do not induce indifference as much as the impossibility of knowing how to act. For instance, Tester's example of television culture's ability to foster a blasé attitude is misleading. Like most people, I find that I respond to some appeals for help but not to others. That people do not respond to every appeal for help does not necessarily mean that the public is indifferent.

Further, the sheer fact of actual moral distance is often difficult to close. This raises the question of how 'strangers' are represented in media cultures more generally. The problem with simply assuming that the globe's affluent have turned their back on the poor is that there is a deal of evidence that contemporary journalist cultures have on the whole contributed towards amplifying this sense of 'distance'. The global flow of images that have helped to deconstruct simple divisions between the 'First' and 'Third World' has not necessarily brought an end to ethnocentrism (Julien and Mercer 1996; Stevenson 1999). The argument here is that a sense of social distance or compassion remains at least partially determined by our access to knowledge, images and information about others. Within this context, a journalistic culture that regularly promotes stereotypes about the world's poor, replays similar images of hopelessness over and again and substitutes the voice of sensation and shock for more complex and informal perspectives is unlikely to foster a culture of sympathy across different cultures.

Finally, we might also point to the political rise of what Ulrich Beck (2000) has called responsible globalization. Such a view does not just tie the relation between media cultures and globalization into the inevitability of exclusion, but seeks to focus upon political and cultural responses to such processes. Beck argues that the politicization of global networks seeks to open a new transnational civil society built upon consumer boycotts, cross-cultural communication and organizations like Amnesty International, Greenpeace and others that work within a post-national world. A global citizenship on this understanding is one that is full of paradoxes and ambivalences. Contrary to the impression created by some of the perspectives reviewed above, it is a world that constantly reveals the closeness of seemingly separated worlds. The circulation of information, viruses, hazards and culture more generally actually reveals the impossibility of retreating behind so-called safe zones. The world is governed more through interrelation than it is through separation.

This heralds the real possibility of compassion becoming global, where the citizen is no longer trapped in the framework of the nation-state. In this respect, we might think of recent campaigns on the Internet and in the high streets against global brands such as Gap and Nike, which seek to convert shopping into what Beck describes as a form of direct democracy (Beck 2000: 70). It is through the deepening and widening of democracy and citizenship to other areas, such as science, the economy and shopping, that the leading edge of cosmopolitan society might be developed. Yet, as Beck freely admits, it is not as though the world has resolved the problem of how social justice becomes possible in the global age; the point is that we are gradually waking up to the question. Perhaps we need to be able to hold a line between recognizing some of the very real exclusions enhanced and reinforced by media technologies, and recognizing some of the new possibilities and dangers that are opened by time–space distanciation. While the television screen itself cannot force us to act politically, there are political movements within civil society that are beginning to ask these questions.

A better metaphor than either blankness or engagement is suggested by Jose Saramago's novel *Blindness*. The novel tells the story of humanity's panic when it learns that 'blindness' is contagious. Blindness is an ordinary human ailment that is passed on much like the common cold. As the story unfolds, the state attempts to limit the spread of the disease by placing the blind in guarded prisons where the afflicted battle against one another for survival. The novel suggests that we are all blind people (whether sighted or not) who have the capacity to 'see' the sufferings of 'others' if we attend to the voice of the other. That is, Saramago poses that the 'visibility' of suffering has a deep connection with the moral and ethical capacities and engagements of modernity's citizens. The ambivalence within this account suggests that a global civil society remains both less and more possible than considerations that exclusively point to global connections or disconnections routinely think. Our capacity to be able to 'experience' the pain and grief of another will ultimately depend upon the ethical resources of the self and the community.

Media, popular culture and the deconstruction of public and private

The global traffic in images of deprivation and suffering takes the analysis of a global public sphere beyond the opposition between entertainment and knowledge. While there are evident dangers that the imperatives of the market will come to replace the diverse sensibilities of civil society, we need to be alive to the ways in which complex frameworks of knowledge and power become displaced once we reduce our analysis of media systems to a direct conflict between public and commercial systems. We need to move beyond the supposed divide between the civic virtues of public broadcasting and the 'innocent' entertainment of the market. How media cultures help to foster different identities, which representations are invited and excluded and whose pleasures become validated are easily displaced within this logic (Giroux 1997).

Commercial organizations seek to hide behind a rhetoric of providing mere entertainment, and public systems shelter behind a discourse of quality. This does not mean, of course, that certain kinds of civic communication are not better catered for if they are protected against the market and the state. The freedom of communication within civil society requires a constitutional defence that safeguards minimum standards in respect of ownership, funding and freedom from political interference (Keane 1991). A vibrant media culture is not best served by a communications universe that has become overly controlled by powerful communications conglomerates that place profit before civil exchange (Giroux 1999). Yet we need to tread carefully here, as many critics have tended to neglect the ways in which popular media (fiction and factual) produce a wide variety of subject positions beyond that of the privatized consumer. This again points to the limitations of those forms of analysis that perceive only the colonizing effects of popular media cultures, without appreciating the complexity of the sheer diversity of positions that more popular formats potentially introduce (Dahlgren 1998).

Joke Hermes (1997, 1998) has argued that the media have transformed citizenship by constructing us as members of overlapping communities (not necessarily national in focus) that have opened new forms of subjectivity and identity through the domain of popular culture. A defence of public communication systems by commentators on the left and right has often been accompanied by a sharp disdain for popular culture. In this argument, robust systems of public communication are required as a defence against the encroachment of a feminine 'other'. The attempt to defend commercial systems against the logics of emotionalism, irrationality and passivity becomes the defence of a beleaguered masculine identity. The binary that constructs media cultures through access to substantive information versus the banalities of consumer culture operates through specifically gendered forms of thinking. A renewed definition of 'cultural' citizenship would need to be open to the different fantasies, hopes and utopias that are more often the traces of popular culture. Such a view would move our ideas about the construction of public knowledges beyond oppositions between reason and affect, quality and trash, hard news and popular entertainment. This crucial move deconstructs the gendered oppositions that would neglect to analyse the role of popular dramas, soap operas and talk shows in the construction of the 'public'.

A non-gendered conception of citizenship would need to investigate the ways in which popular forms of media entertainment help to construct the variable horizons of everyday life. John Fiske (1989) has gone furthest in this respect, arguing that the art of everyday life is commonly involved in the 'transformation' of mediated products. All popular media are sites of struggle, where meanings are never controlled by the producers, but are actively and pleasurably produced by the consumers themselves. In a reprinted interview, Fiske describes his own theoretical output as being concerned to articulate 'a socialist theory of pleasure' (Fiske 1989). These irreverent forms of *jouissance* that erupt from below are opposed to the disciplinary techniques utilized by the power bloc. Here there is a double pleasure involved in the audience's reading of popular texts. The first is the enjoyment involved in the symbolic production of meanings that oppose those of the power bloc, and the second concerns the actual activity of being productive. In this scenario, the market, unlike the declining high culture of the powerful, brings certain cultural products within the critical horizons of the people. A progressive strategy should steer clear of 'preachiness' (Fiske 1989: 178) and advocate pleasurable texts that refuse the temptation of imposing certain socially correct meanings.

Yet while Fiske has usefully concentrated upon the ways in which mediated forms are used to interrupt dominant norms, he has been widely criticized for romanticizing popular resistance (Stevenson 2002). If we redraw our boundaries as to what gets to count as public discourse and knowledge to include more popular forms, this inevitably has an unsettling effect on distinctions between public and private. The global spread of daytime talk shows is probably the best example of this process, given that they regularly seek to bring issues of 'private' identity, like parenting, the experience of unemployment, bad neighbours, friendship, sexuality and illness (among other topics), into the public realm. Lunt and Livingstone (1994) argue that talk shows are a valuable contribution to public life, in that they are a less overtly authoritarian form of television, and open up spaces for the voices of ordinary people. While there are many different formats for the talk show, they at least introduce the possibility of raising a range of questions ignored by more 'officially sanctioned' forms of communication, and of interrupting the discourses of experts.

However, Shattuc (1996) argues that the critical potential of 'talk shows' in the American context is currently in decline. Talk shows since the 1960s have been key in allowing working-class, black, bisexual, lesbian and gay people a form of public visibility that shattered the image of happy smiling nuclear families presented by much popular entertainment. Yet the political possibilities opened by these popular forms significantly narrowed in the 1990s through the arrival of shows like *Ricki Lake*. This has meant that the talk show format has become more overtly constructed by agencies, with different shows trading in participants, overly simplified categories of good behaviour versus bad, a faster paced style and a mode of address that asks the studio and home audiences not to take the discussion too seriously. Talk shows, in effect, can offer the illusion

of participation, while offering those at home the *possibility* of less judgemental narratives to navigate their personal experiences (Dahlgren 1998;
Morley 2000). The mode of talk television exhibits potentially democratic and
cosmopolitan tendencies as it deconstructs oppositions between the serious
and the popular and public and private, without ever finally escaping from a
wider sets of concerns that impact upon programme makers as they struggle for
audiences in a global television market.

The cultural coding of magazine cultures, celebrity, popular television and
other forms of 'entertainment' should be viewed, in my opinion, as a form
of popular cultural citizenship. These dimensions often exhibit pleasures and
ideological complexities that translate political concerns into a commercial
culture. My own (along with others') study of men's lifestyle magazines sought
to demonstrate how material cultures position masculinity in terms of a
number of different and contradictory locations. It is the magazine's capacity
to be able to accommodate both more 'open' and reflexive aspects of modernity
and the certitude of traditional features that explains their appeal (Jackson
et al. 2001). This enables male consumers to 'open up and close down, to
move into and withdraw from the flow of messages' (Melucci 1996a: 51). The
magazines represent the commodification of contemporary gender anxieties.
These popular texts are sources of cultural power in respect of the speed
at which network capitalism simulates new markets and helps to inform the
changing definitions of contemporary masculinity. The magazines are neither
harmless forms of entertainment nor the location of new forms of resistance.
Instead, we need to maintain a 'political' reading of the magazines that opens
up questions of gender, sexuality and commodified desire within contemporary
society. Instead of popular media being read through the lens of 'dumbing
down', a more sophisticated understanding of the gendered nature of media
products is available if we seek to understand the ways in which they commonly
seek to construct and disrupt gendered assumptions and practices.

Conclusion

The media of mass communication commonly exhibit a form of cultural power
that symbolically constructs popular horizons and investments. We have seen
how the contemporary public sphere simultaneously works at the local,
national and global levels all at once. Here we need to be careful not to assume
that media cultures can be exclusively captured by commodification and
privatization or popular forms of resistance. Questions of cultural citizenship
connect intimate social relations to human rights disputes, which are commonly
mediated through a cultural realm. Today there is no knowledge of citizenship

that has not passed at some point through the media. In this respect, cultural citizenship is centrally concerned with media institutions, cultural texts and the perceptions and practices of audiences. Our capacity to be able to form an understanding of ourselves and others in our shared world is increasingly shaped by the ambivalent technological presence of the media.

Note

1 For a more extensive discussion of Habermas's writing on the public sphere see Stevenson (1995, 1999, 2002).

Further reading

Murdock, G. (1999) Rights and representations: public discourse and cultural citizenship, in J. Gripsrud (ed.) *Television and Common Knowledge*. London: Routledge.

Stevenson, N. (1999) *The Transformation of the Media: Globalisation, Morality and Ethics*. Harlow: Longman.

Stevenson, N. (2002) *Understanding Media Cultures: Social Theory and Mass Communication*, 2nd edn. London: Sage.

Tester, K. (2001) *Compassion, Morality and the Media*. Buckingham: Open University Press.

Thompson, J. B. (1995) *The Media and Modernity: A Social Theory of the Media*. Cambridge: Polity Press.

5 | CONSUMERISM, CULTURAL POLICY AND CITIZENSHIP

The global development and spread of commodity capitalism has provoked a number of different responses from those concerned with questions of citizenship. As we shall see, many commentators have argued that the culture of the market has come to erode the practice of citizenship. The seductions of pleasurable commodities are arguably displacing the more educated and serious forms of deliberation that are required within mature liberal democracies. Others have argued that processes of commodification are more complex and contradictory than this model would allow, with the diverse practices of consumption opening the possibility of combining questions of pleasure and politics. Today, in the early twenty-first century, there is little agreement on whether commercial cultures are destroying the practices of political engagement or changing the focus of citizenship by opening up new questions. In cultural policy, the question becomes: given the increasing dominance of the market within the determination of the cultural field, what role should the state and other institutions play in the governing of culture? Whose 'culture' is deserving of protection and funding? In a world where we can no longer look to tradition to settle these questions, they are increasingly pressing. Issues of cultural citizenship are raised in terms of the role played by consumer societies in the development of certain 'political' questions, and in helping to determine the policies that are necessary to regulate contemporary cultures. What remains crucial to our discussion of citizenship is the relation between common rights and responsibilities, and questions of difference. How might we begin to reconcile questions of justice and difference in terms of our increasingly commodified and globalized culture? How do we make sure that questions of justice (when applied to culture) do not merely protect the tastes and preferences of dominant groups? Alternatively, how might we politicize the pleasures of consumer culture without becoming either moralistic or indifferent about the effects of the global market? Finally, how might we best protect the spirit of aesthetic innovation from the pressures of the market? These questions and others are explored in the contexts of consumerism and cultural policy.

Consumer culture and the death of citizenship

As I have indicated, in this section I aim to explore the relationship between consumerism and citizenship. In doing so, I want to build upon and establish a more complex relationship between these terms than currently appears to be available. We need to avoid polarizing the debate between two of the perspectives prevalent within the literature.

The first perspective is that consumerism merely undermines the practice of citizenship. Such arguments posit that the declining fortunes of Western democracies are tied to a culture of 'contentment' among the middle-class population, or that a substantial aesthetic and political culture is currently swamped by synthetic commercialism. The argument here is that practices of democratic engagement have been replaced by visits to shopping malls, channel hopping and the culture of cool interactivity to be found on the web. As we shall see, such views have a persuasive logic, but remain blind to the ways in which the practice of citizenship may have changed within contemporary societies.

The second perspective is that consumerism provides a new basis for the practice of citizenship that is largely unappreciated by mainstream political parties and more traditional frames of analysis. Those holding this view would argue that the popularity of consumerism among 'ordinary people' speaks of a popular democratic revolution waiting to happen. Again, such a view opens interesting dimensions into the debate, while being insufficiently appreciative of the ways in which consumer societies undermine the quest for justice. My argument is that we need not make a choice between either perspective.

The American social critic Daniel Bell (1976) has identified some of the historical and cultural transformations and contradictions that led to the emergence of a consumer society. The most evident contradiction within capitalism today is the division of the economic structure (based upon efficiency and functional rationality) and the cultural sphere (orientated around the aesthetic point of view and the pursuit of diverse lifestyles). Bell argues that capitalism was built upon a culture of self-discipline and hard work; this was opposed by modernist avant-garde movements that propagated a desire for new and anti-bourgeois sentiments more generally. The culture of modernism was guided by the principles of lifestyle experimentation and innovation, which sought to critique the restrictive nature of the common culture of capitalism. For Bell, there are clear links between the more expressive culture originally propagated by artistic movements and what he calls the 'consumptive ethic'.

Today the culture of the modernist avant-garde, on this reading, constitutes, rather than opposes, bourgeois culture. The war between the culture of self-expression and the conservative disciplines of hard work is over. The ideals of the Protestant ethic (saving, industriousness and thrift) have been displaced through the operation of the free market and the celebration of new consumer freedoms. The rise of consumer culture has built on the displacement of the forms of self-control exhibited by smaller, less commercially defined communities. The new capitalism, developed out of mass marketing, rising standards of living and the expansion of debt and credit, destroys the ability to defer gratification and replaces it with hedonism.

Similarly, following a different historical lineage, Colin Campbell (1987) has argued that we need to explain how the ethos of luxury and hedonism came to displace the puritan virtues of hard work and deferred gratification. The ordered and disciplined life of the Puritans that Weber (1932) had identified as being so crucial for the early stages of capitalism was gradually displaced by more aesthetic sensibilities. This key cultural transformation was brought about through artistic and religious movements that sought to legitimize beauty, imagination, spirituality and aesthetic pleasures more generally. In particular, the Romantic movement's emphasis upon emotionality and the craving for new sensations sought to place the imagination more centrally within the context of everyday life. What is provocative about Bell's and Campbell's emphasis upon the cultural roots of consumer society is that it offers a more complex model than those accounts that simply mention the power of marketing, advertising and a capitalist visual culture. Despite their differences, for Bell and Campbell the willingness to consume has more complex aesthetic and cultural roots than many seem to appreciate (Agnew 1994). These dimensions are critical of any account of consumerism that reduces the desire to consume to the 'effects' of capitalism. More productively, Bell and Campbell seek to develop a complex historical narrative that points towards the aestheticization of everyday life.

For instance, Featherstone (1991) argues that the postmodern blurring of barriers between art and everyday life has created a culture that is continually searching for new tastes and sensations. Like Bell and Campbell, Featherstone suggests that the project of turning life into a work of art is no longer a purely bohemian project, but connects with the dominant ethos of consumer society. Fashioned by artistic movements like the Romantics, Dada and Surrealism, the carriers of the new culture of consumption are to be found in the new middle classes. The 'new cultural intermediaries' (following Bourdieu 1984) that propagate a culture of lifestyle and appearance are most likely to be found within a range of occupations, including media, design, the new cultural industries and education. Notions of emotional ease and exploration tie into a culture in which the 'aesthetic life is the ethically good life' (Featherstone 1991: 48). On the other hand, Bell (1976: 83) maps similar developments, but comments that 'in the hedonistic life, there is a loss of will and fortitude'. When citizens become competitive with one another for luxuries, they lose the ability to share and sacrifice. While the development of the capitalist economy depends upon the continual expansion of needs and wants, it has helped to foster identities that are no longer capable of raising questions related to justice. The *jouissance* of contemporary consumption may allow for experimentation in sexual, aesthetic and cultural freedom, but collective consumer identities undermine the moral fabric of the community.

The contemporary author who has extended these arguments the furthest is Zygmunt Bauman. For Bauman (1998) we have moved from a producer to a consumer society. A producer society was defined through capitalism's requirement for an ever expanding supply of labour, collective provision, security through the welfare state, the disciplines of the work ethic and a collective concern for the poor. Under the rubric of consumer society, however, the duties of citizenship and the disciplines of work have become undermined by the desire of consumers to make individualized choices within the market place. Bauman (1998: 25) writes:

> Ideally, the consumer's satisfaction ought to be instant, and this is in a double sense. Consumer goods should bring satisfaction immediately, requiring no delay, no protracted learning of skills and no lengthy groundwork; but the satisfaction should end the moment the time needed for their consumption is up, and that time ought to be reduced to a bare minimum.

The consumer is easily excitable, quickly bored, has few substantial commitments and values individual choice above everything else. The consumer, in terms of citizenship, is guided by aesthetics rather than ethics, and is concerned less with political ideology than with an individualized 'right to enjoy, not a duty to suffer' (Bauman 1998: 31). The ability to be able to make different kinds of pleasurable choice then becomes the dominant principle, or what Castoriadis (1997) called 'social imaginary' among those who are not currently excluded from the labour market. The language and duties of citizenship, in this context, become overrun by the seductive rather than the disciplinary logics of consumer society.

Crucially, support for the welfare state becomes run down through the privatization of 'individual' insurance, a refusal to pay sufficient taxation and the progressive criminalization of the poor. The depoliticization of the vast majority of society, those living under the pleasurable engagements of consumption, has converted 'the poor' into society's new 'other'. Despite occasional 'carnivals of charity' (witnessed through mass mediated appeals), the poor become simultaneously airbrushed out of sight and demonized within our culture. In an age of flexible capitalism, the poor no longer act as a reserve army of labour and are better seen as the waste products of consumer society. We live in a world dominated by a huge consumer fun house that has little use for ideological debate or the most obvious losers of the economic system. The underclass in a society of post-ideological society is the new enemy to be kept outside of the places and spaces where the affluent enjoy themselves. Bauman reminds us that if we are to consider the question of politics within consumer societies, we can only do so if we acknowledge the link between a culture of pleasurable consumption and the progressive polarization of advanced capitalist societies. The relatively affluent are living within a society where needs are no longer fixed but have become increasingly plastic. The idea of workers labouring to meet preconstituted 'wants' and 'needs' no longer makes much sense in a society that endlessly simulates desires for new commodities and pleasurable forms of consumption. Consumption, argues Bauman (2001), can no longer be related to need but should be connected to the ability to act on impulse and to attain 'instant' gratification, and the maximization of consumption.

Similarly, Ritzer (1999) has argued that the development of new means of consumption (shopping malls, the Internet, the privatization of public space, catalogues etc.) has increased the number of opportunities to consume within modern society. This has led overdeveloped Western societies into a condition of hyperconsumption. Contemporary consumption is fuelled by increasing levels of personal debt, expansion of credit systems, declining levels of saving and the spread of American-style consumption patterns across the globe. The spread of sanitized and homogeneous practices of consumer behaviour is, however, masked by entertaining forms of distraction and simulation that have become progressively utilized to hide from consumers the ways in which they are being duped and exploited. Through spectacles, simulated events or celebrity endorsement, consumers are being entertained while they shop. This creates the sense of consumption as fun. Yet Ritzer argues that while consumers may resist such suggestions, the only real winners from this situation are the profit margins of global corporations.

The perceptions of Bauman and Ritzer bear a close family resemblance to a long tradition of theorizing about the exploitative and illusory nature of modern consumer societies. For example, both Adorno (1981) and Marcuse

(1968) argued that the culture industry fostered a 'happy consciousness' by converting everything, from art to baked beans, into a commodity. The age of manufactured individualism only confronted the 'something' that was lacking through art, convivial moments of intimacy or sensuous sexuality. Bauman and Ritzer, on the other hand, argue that a substantial politics cannot be recovered by a detour through the aesthetic, given its role in sustaining contemporary patterns of consumption. The novel, the beautiful, the libidinous and the different are not excluded by a system of mass culture but are increasingly drawn upon in the seduction and entertainment of consumers. As Bauman (1997) emphasizes, modern society is built not, as Adorno and Marcuse believed, upon normative regulation, but upon the dialectic of seduction and repression. While the relatively affluent are driven by a dialectic of semiotic design and unfulfilment, those who are unable to choose are progressively criminalized by calls for harsher sentences and punishments.

Bauman's bleak political vision, which is arguably an extension of some of Daniel Bell's arguments, offers little prospect of 'repoliticizing' consumer society other than through the recovery of more substantive ethical visions.

For Bauman (1999), and indeed many others, the citizen has become the consumer. Once the market and pleasures of consumption gain precedence over our shared abilities to act within the public sphere, we know that citizenship is in trouble. The market leaves each of us to pursue our own individualized version of the good life, whereas citizenship requires public forms of deliberation and shared concerns. Citizenship requires a republican ideal that puts active engagement and the common good at the heart of society. The pleasures of consumption, the declining power of nation-states, privatization of common resources and rituals, increased mobility, short-term contracts and market uncertainty all undermine the pursuit of a common citizenship. A new republicanism is, however, only possible once people are free from uncertainty and the threat of poverty. It is the recovery of social solidarity through a basic income (guaranteed to all irrespective of capacity to work) and new global republican institutions that stand the best chance of recovering the ethical life.

Bauman's aim is to reintroduce the possibility of other styles of living than one of hyperconsumption. Arguably, this only becomes possible in a society that has not just become fairer through the reduction of inequality, but has also become more stable and less uncertain and fearful. Such a society would need to introduce a substantial amount of social equality, rather than simply expanding the equality of opportunity. Citizenship would need to embrace substantive social rights (not merely cultural rights), promote the possibility of active citizenship and help to devise public places that enable people to rub shoulders with people who are unlike themselves. As David Miller (1997) has proposed, a society where citizens have few meeting points with each other will find it difficult to sustain solidarity across status and class divisions. A republican citizenship would require both the reduction of material inequality and more convivial common public places. The concern here is that those that can afford to do so will permanently withdraw from public places and institutions into more exclusive environments. Without more substantive features expecting citizens to consume less and deliberate more, consumerism will continue to dominate over citizenship.

There is a basic opposition between citizenship and consumerism that informs these perspectives. This opposition remains an important one, given the role it continues to play in warning citizens about the spread of corporate power, the divisive effects of commodification, and the environmental erosion caused by economic overdevelopment. For example, the increasing dominance and global power of brands such as Nike, McDonalds, Coca-Cola, Gap and others has begun to be politicized by anti-globalization protestors. According to Naomi Klein (2000), one of the movement's leading supporters, the aim of the protests that have stretched from the streets of London to Seattle, Paris and Zurich has been to construct a globally orientated citizenship. The main project of the protestors has been to claim back public space from the privatizing strategies of the brands. Seeking to politicize the working conditions of the 'unseen' and largely invisible workers of a number of corporations, the aim is to argue for more responsible and less indifferent forms of consumption. While many of those attending demonstrations would resist the idea that they belong to a unified 'movement', Klein (2001: 82) argues that there is a broadly shared reaction against 'the transformation of every activity and value into a commodity'. The threat of privatization and the loss of public space more generally connects a number of different social movements through televised protests and across the Internet. For Klein, the aim is to win back the possibility of a participatory democracy from corporate power and the liberalizing policies of McGovernment.

These are indeed important developments, challenging dominant conceptions of politics and providing a focal point for radical voices that are unlikely to find a place in mainstream political organizations. Yet I think there is also cause for concern here. Much of Naomi Klein's book reads as both a narrative warning against the power of dominant brands and an attack on the more pleasurable aspects of consumption. Such a strategy (unless carefully guarded against) could end up reducing consumption to economic imperatives, and repeating some of the mistakes of earlier forms of critical analysis. This should become more apparent as we discuss the connections between consumer culture and citizenship below.

Consumer culture as citizenship

In certain circles it has been precisely the 'demonizing' of consumer society that has led to the marginalization of progressive political forces. In Britain, a number of fresh perspectives formulated around the journal *Marxism Today* during the 1980s attempted to rethink the left's response to consumerism. These voices sought, in the language of the time, to reject a form of left moralism, and to engage with the ways in which consumer society had sought to create a new popular common sense. These viewpoints were tied to the analysis of a particular political terrain that saw the exclusion of left governments from political power throughout most of the 1980s. While this is not the place to review the success or failure of such 'rethinking', a number of more populist ways of viewing consumption became evident within this literature. Such perspectives, I argue, continue to have a relevance for the links between consumption and citizenship.

Particularly important here was the analysis by Stuart Hall (1988) of Thatcherism as a political and cultural hegemonic project. Thatcherism was of special interest due to the way in which it sought to construct a new common sense within civil society. For example, Hall tried to uncover the ways in which Thatcherism connected with and constructed a popular view that the market could be experienced as a domain of freedom. From this perspective, the state was represented as bureaucratic and repressive, whereas the market was the domain of choice and autonomy. While Hall has been criticized for overstating the ideological success of Thatcherism, his genius lay in the claim that such a view was not wholly illusory and that the left had much to learn from this position (Stevenson 2002).

Frank Mort (1989) argued in similar terms that a politics of consumption was as much about culture and language as economic policy. Consumption throughout the 1980s became associated with an array of popular images, including Yuppies and the affluent working class (popularized by comedian Harry Enfield's Loadsamoney). In this respect, Thatcherism had succeeded in translating 'policy into the popular aspirations' (Mort 1989: 164). The problem for left social democratic parties was that they were widely seen as the parties of production rather than consumption, and at worst were perceived as seeing the desire to consume as morally debilitating. The reorientation of capitalism around lifestyle niches and a heavier emphasis upon design actually interconnected with a number of new social movements articulating a politics around cultural difference and less stable social identities. The politics of consumption and the development of new social movements have many connecting points, which are not always appreciated by the kinds of moralizing prevalent within certain sections of the left. Social movements and consumer campaigns are mutually dependent upon the operation of powerful codes and the transmission of knowledge. The proliferation of consumer information, codes about responsibility and risk, and complex understandings of identity are the shared concerns of consumer cultures and a range of social movements.

How the rules of normality are established, what is considered 'other', who has the power to determine what everyone is talking about – these are shared concerns of consumer culture and social movements alike (Melucci 1985). Yet there are also dangers in pushing this argument too far. Many 'new' social movements are critical of the distribution of resources within society and have concerns that cannot be restricted to 'merely' cultural questions (Butler 1998). Such a reading would cancel many concerns evident within green, peace and 'Third World' movements about the long-term effects of capitalist growth and sustainability (Habermas 1981). These qualifications aside, new consumer environments and some of the new social movements do seem to share an emphasis upon spectacle, fun and pleasurable forms of identification.

Further, Mica Nava (1991) has argued that the political left have continued to ignore the progressive possibilities of a politics of consumerism. A common masculinist assumption that 'real' politics goes on within the government or the workplace has ignored new sites of activism within consumption. Nava, in this context, draws attention to the rise of ethical consumption, consumer boycotts and increased forms of ecological awareness amongst consumers. For example, in Britain we have witnessed consumer militancy in respect of Shell oil's desire to dump old oil rigs, Barclays bank's support of apartheid and, more recently, genetically modified foods (Vidal 1999).

Daniel Miller (1997), taking this argument further, has suggested that while politics is experienced as being hierarchical and bureaucratic, the practice of shopping can be an empowering experience. Both Nava and Miller argue that we see shopping as a daily election, whereby consumers, who wield considerable power, make daily ethical choices in terms of the goods they purchase and the way they inhabit public and private space. Indeed, implies Miller, a focus upon consumption, rather than citizenship, might under this reckoning reconnect questions of welfare and consumption. By this Miller does not mean abandoning citizenship (although its rights focus gives it a legalistic orientation) but instead favours a rejoining of consumption and welfare that sees them as equally important moral domains for the distribution of social goods. Such a switch would recognize the moral and ethical concerns involved within shopping, while refusing a certain masculine logic that sees it as a peripheral activity. It matters greatly if we can afford a balanced diet, how safe the food is in the supermarket and whether mobile phones cause cancer.

Some of these points are well made. It is undoubtedly the case that consumption is the place where politically marginalized groups (including gays, lesbians, young people, ethnic minorities and women) have sought to forge an identity. Put in terms of 'cultural' citizenship, consumption is one of the key places in the modern world where the 'right to be different' is pursued. Returning to Bauman's argument that consumer culture undermines citizenship, this is perhaps at its weakest in the recognition that consumption for many people is not experienced as either post-ideological or as atomized as he describes. The perspectives outlined above suggest that while the relatively affluent have been the main beneficiaries of the expansion of consumptive practices, such spaces and places have helped to inform 'new political agendas' that cannot be derived from a reformulated class politics. The 'right to consume' for many marginalized social groups has become linked to the struggle for recognition and difference. However, what is noticeable, particularly in retrospect, about the 'New Times' arguments is that they fail to raise substantive ethical and moral arguments in respect of equality and fairness. Perhaps unintentionally, however, these arguments are more easily associated with the flux of identity than with the need to close material social divisions. This is a major weakness in a society that has witnessed the exaggeration of wealth differences accompanying the spectacle of consumption. Accepting the legitimacy and complexity of popular pleasures while protesting against material and cultural exclusion seems like a line worth holding.

The cultural patterns of the discussions above are suggestive about the connection between citizenship and consumerism in a number of ways. First, 'political questions' are very much part of contemporary commercial cultures. Commercial and aesthetic cultures, in contemporary society, continue simultaneously to raise and to obstruct issues that can be related to the cultural nature of citizenship. Many marginalized groups have searched for an identity through a commercial culture, not only because other more 'political' avenues have been blocked, but because it has come to signify, increasingly within our culture, a domain of pleasurability and identification. This means that the politics of citizenship and questions of consumption cannot be opposed in any straightforward way. Paul Gilroy (1993) has argued that black music, for example, has been the key cultural location for the articulation of a sense of diasporic connection between Africa, America and Britain. This has operated in a number of ways, including the borrowing of musical styles and influences, protesting about injustice, the recording of struggles and, in certain rap songs, the display of misogyny. Through the fostering of a distinctively black aesthetic, Gilroy argues, music cultures have provided a uniquely 'connective culture' in a globalized civil society. The overlapping musical styles of what Gilroy (1993: 101) calls the black Atlantic resist notions of a pristine authenticity and a pluralized postmodernism to articulate a 'changing rather than an unchanging same'.

These features arguably pose critical questions to those who assume that consumption is a domain that is not already fraught with ambiguity and ethical complexity. However, and this brings me to my second point, it remains the case that while consumption may raise 'ethical' questions, it only does so by being connected to more formal citizenship criteria of rights, obligations and social exclusion. That is, we may become concerned about the effects consumerism is having upon the distribution of goods, how excluded groups are represented in tabloid newspapers or levels of ecological and environmental destruction, but this is only made possible by the fact that they have already been raised as political/moral issues. In other words, no matter how pleasurable and ethically complex, shopping cannot replace the dimensions of citizenship. While shoppers are invited to buy or boycott a particular product, citizens should seek to raise questions about the political context of production and consumption. Participatory notions of citizenship will seek to politicize and thereby transform the horizons of consumer-citizens through shared processes of deliberation. Citizenship – by giving voice to a diversity of concerns – seeks to modify the identities of those participating within a common dialogue (Mouffe 1993). This moves the focus of attention away from our relationship with sets of products, while seeking to politicize diverse global networks of production and consumption.

Questions of cultural capital

The problem with the discussion so far is that our analysis of culture has been preoccupied with either the production or the reception of commodity culture. Those who are concerned that the market will convert citizens into consumers have little to contribute on the reception of culture, whereas those who highlight the aesthetics of reception tend to neglect production-side questions (Lash 1993). By far the most sophisticated attempt to link these questions, while offering an understanding of culture and consumption that is connected to frameworks of power and domination, is offered by the French sociologist Pierre Bourdieu.

In the context of our discussion, Bourdieu's (1984) key insight is what he calls the 'arbitrariness' of culture. By this he means that there is no intrinsic reason why upper-class tastes, aesthetic preferences and cultural judgements should be taken as indicative of high culture. The love of abstract art, classical music and other cultural styles functions as a form of social distinction. What a society takes to be innovative, creative and culturally valuable is largely determined by the social structure. Hence, apparently disinterested practices like the appreciation of a fine wine, a visit to an art gallery or a preference for Stravinsky over Chopin are used to gain what Bourdieu calls cultural capital.

For Bourdieu, the social world is structured by different forms of capital, which are accumulated, gained and lost in a number of different social fields. While fields are the site of constant social struggle, they are also the places that distribute and determine access to different kinds of capital. The economists and orthodox Marxists are mistaken, in that they can only account for a narrow set of motivations that immediately lead to the pursuit of money and wealth (economic capital). Such a definition of capital ultimately colludes with artists and intellectuals who have sought to mystify their practices by presenting them as the pure pursuit of either art or knowledge. Indeed, Bourdieu's (1996b) work traces through the historical emergence of a bohemian view of art that opposed both the industrial bourgeoisie and so-called bourgeois art, while developing an aristocratic attitude towards consumption and sexuality. The development of 'art for art's sake' as the authentic value of artistic and cultural production helped to create a number of paradoxical attitudes towards the production and consumption of culture. First, the bohemian's suspicion of immediate market success meant that artistic success was secured through commercial failure. Further, the ideology of commercial disinterestedness favoured those who had inherited economic capital. In other words, economistic analysis fails to understand the 'profit', 'capital' and 'status' that were attributable to those who developed new aesthetic lifestyles.

Cultural capital in Bourdieu's (1986) analysis can exist within three forms. The first form of cultural capital exists within an embodied state, or what Bourdieu also describes as the *habitus*. The habitus is a set of cultural dispositions passed on through the family that become literally second nature. These embodied dispositions are a way of speaking, standing, walking, thinking and feeling. The habitus is largely structured through the opposition of different cultural characteristics found in different social classes. While the habitus can become transformed by entry into a different field or more generally through social mobility, it moulds the body in ways that are largely unconscious but relatively durable. Yet by virtue of the habitus, individuals become predisposed towards certain cultural preferences and tastes. Hence, it makes a good deal of sense to talk of consumer lifestyles in terms of both cultural and economic capital. Those who are able to define taste, vulgarity and discernment are able to impose these definitions on subordinate groups. For Bourdieu (1984) it was the new petit bourgeoisie (school teachers, artists, academics etc.) whose aesthetic lifestyles meant that they became the new arbiters of good taste. Taste is determined by those who are high in cultural, rather than economic, capital. The new petit bourgeoisie were able to distinguish themselves from industrialists (high in economic but low in cultural capital) and the working class (low in both economic and cultural capital) by seeking to expand the autonomy of the cultural field. Whereas the transmission of cultural capital through the body is the most efficient means, given its hereditary nature, it can also be reproduced through material objects. Cultural capital can exist in an objectified state through art collections, musical instruments, objects of art and jewellery.

Finally, we can talk of cultural capital in a third sense, the institutional confirming of educational qualifications. This confers on the holder a legally guaranteed amount of cultural respect and level of cultural competence. These three forms of cultural capital can of course all be converted into economic capital. In this sense, Bourdieu is able to talk of the symbolic as well as the material profits, due to its relative scarcity, from which its holders are able to benefit. In addition to economic and cultural capital, we can also talk of social capital. Social capital depends upon the networks and connections that an individual is able to maintain. In other words, economic capital is what you have, cultural capital is what you know and social capital is who you know. In this respect, social capital in part depends upon active forms of sociability that sustain relations of either friendship or acquaintance. However, despite these different types of capital, Bourdieu has consistently maintained that economic capital (in the final analysis) is at the root of the other forms of capital. The power and privilege that access different forms of capital reproduce class distinction. Hence, consumption and leisure and lifestyle patterns become important to the extent to which they link into economic, cultural and social capital.

More recently, Bourdieu and Darbel (1991) have sought to link these concerns to the cultural capital necessary to visit a museum or art gallery. These institutions were chosen because they are often (although not always) free at the point of access and emphasize a form of cultural self-exclusion. The study concludes that the best predictors of whether or not you are likely to attend a formal gallery or exhibition are family background and educational qualifications. Working-class people who lack the necessary cultural capital to make works of art meaningful are forced to make sense of them through more restricted repertoires of interpretation. Working-class visitors are 'condemned to see works of art in their phenomenal state, in other words as simple objects' (Bourdieu and Darbel 1991: 45). Those without the appropriate cultural capital complained of feeling out of place, were in constant fear of revealing their lack of knowledge and displayed most interest in art (like furniture) that had an obvious social function. This lack of affinity with the world of art was compounded by educational institutions that sought to transmit only a limited understanding of artistic works. Familiarity with a wide range of artistic and aesthetic practices was more often transmitted by the bourgeois family. For Bourdieu, a cultural democracy (or in our case cultural citizenship) can only be achieved by educational institutions seeking to make up for the lack of cultural capital available within the working-class family. Cultural citizenship, for

Bourdieu, cannot be sought by either celebrating a working-class populism or leaving artistic taste to the private discernment of individuals. Unless educational resources make some attempt to reverse the flow of cultural capital transmitted in the home, the end result will be enhanced forms of cultural inequality. Populist strategies that seek either to convert working-class culture into the curriculum or to create more opportunities for working-class children to visit galleries are unlikely to have much effect. The question is not crude populism as much as the transmission of aesthetic taste by habit, learning and exercise. Bourdieu and Darbel (1991) powerfully argue that the only way to short-circuit assumptions of working-class barbarism is to disrupt the idea that taste is naturally rather than socially reproduced. An inclusive cultural citizenship requires the intensification of the presence of the school within working-class people's cultural lives.

It might be objected that, if the dominant culture is 'arbitrary', why should dominant institutions seek to intensify rather than reform the cultures it socially reproduces? This is because, while the artistic avant-garde has historically pursued a strategy of distinction, it has also preserved a sense of cultural autonomy against the market place. While the idea of 'art for art's sake' is mystificatory, in that it hides the symbolic dividend of bohemian lifestyles, its mythology has preserved ideas of artistic creativity against the market place. The democratization of art cannot be pursued through its commercialization. The invasion of the market into the cultural domain will inevitably 'cheapen' the value of the work, and undermine the specialized knowledge and experience necessary to produce and experience the work of art (Crook 2000). Hence, Shusterman (1992) argues that while Bourdieu has exposed the hidden economy of the disinterested aesthetic of high culture, he remains so enchanted by its myth that he retains a hostility to popular art. This means that the creativity evident within popular forms, such as rap music, the working-class novel, diverse forms of youth culture or alternative art forms like Pop Art, is neglected by Bourdieu (Fowler 1997). The central question for cultural citizenship becomes how to promote social and cultural inclusion in a society where 'cultures' are organized hierarchically. Further, how might individuals and groups best be empowered in a situation where culture is the site of contestation?

These questions become particularly pressing once we consider the relationship between the market, popular culture and cultural policy. Here I argue for a cultural policy that pursues a strategy of equality, while continually seeking to deconstruct claims to cultural hierarchy and status. That is, Bourdieu is right to draw attention to the ways in which working-class people commonly exclude themselves from dominant cultural institutions, but mistaken in the way he remains sceptical of the aesthetic merit of many popular forms of cultural expression.

Paul Willis (1990: 15) has astutely observed in this context that young working-class people find themselves trapped between the exclusions of traditional artistic culture and the dehumanization of work. They respond to this by seeking forms of symbolic autonomy through the creative use of consumer culture. Willis's account seeks to emphasize the agency of young people in creating new meanings in terms of their participation within music, fashion, media and everyday forms of cultural expression. It is this everyday creativity and meaningfulness that Bourdieu's later writing passes over much too quickly. We shall see later that these arguments have particular implications for questions of cultural policy. Before addressing these issues, however, I briefly summarize the impact that questions of cultural policy are having upon notions of cultural citizenship more generally.

Cultural policy and questions of governance

The development of debates within cultural policy has been a welcome addition to a number of concerns mapped by cultural studies; European, North American and Australian governments in particular have sought to develop substantial cultural policies covering a range of practices. According to Tom O'Regan (2001), we might roughly talk of three ages of cultural policy. The first involved democratic initiatives, through arts councils and other publicly funded organizations, to bring the arts to the people. This approach largely characterized initiatives between the 1950s and 1960s, when a variety of cultural policies were developed to overcome social (mainly class-based) barriers to high culture. Since the 1970s there has been an increasing amount of questioning of what counts as 'art' or 'culture'. More inclusive definitions of 'cultural' experience and aesthetic forms of experimentation have sought to encompass more 'popular', community-orientated and multicultural definitions. Finally, these trends and directions have increasingly raised issues around diversity and identity. Here, cultural policy questions increasingly have to take into account the shifting terrain of popular taste and lifestyle. Such has been the impact of these developments that many commentators assume that postmodern cultures have eclipsed ideas of the 'high' and the 'popular'. Under postmodern definitions of culture both consumer and artistic cultures talk the language of strategic management, niche marketing, product differentiation and promotion. Within these definitions art has become democratized and commodified. These developments have seemingly brought to an end a long tradition of left-liberalism that sought to redistribute art and culture, rather than question what constituted it in the first place (Mulgan and Warpole 1986).

Particularly striking in the European context has been the development of city-based cultural policies. Since the 1980s local strategies have sought to diversify the economic base of the city and develop more cosmopolitan definitions of urban civil life. These trends, which build upon postmodern definitions of culture, have seen the decentralization of cultural policy and the development of more inclusive civic identities. In this context, the local state sought to promote a number of cultural identities as a means of both promoting new civic forms of identity and enhancing economic growth. For example, Simon Frith (1993) argues that in the 1980s there was a burst of state intervention in the production of popular music. This included attempts to enhance employment opportunities and grant access, knowledge and relevant technology to previously excluded groups of cultural producers. Yet there is growing concern that more inclusive cultural strategies are being progressively overshadowed by policies that more explicitly target urban regeneration. The neo-liberal need to maximize the economic potential of local cultural industries has meant that more inclusive strategies have become progressively sidelined (Bianchini 1993; Griffiths 1993). While a broadening of the definition of the 'cultural' had initially inclusive implications, attempts to combat social exclusion have increasingly given way to the needs of the market. For example, in the North American context, Sharon Zukin (1995) has reasonably argued that the rise of the symbolic or cultural city has primarily sought to establish the city as a safe place for cultural consumption, seeking to attract new business and corporate elites. As the city seeks to establish itself as a dynamic place of business, tourism and multiculturalism, it becomes progressively divided as its public places are commodified and under the constant watch of security cameras. Urban centres have become the playgrounds of the affluent classes (or those high in economic, cultural or symbolic capital), while also becoming places of surveillance and social division.

It is perhaps within this context that we should seek to judge Tony Bennett's (1992, 1998) arguments concerning the development of the idea of cultural policy within cultural studies. Bennett's main argument runs against both cultural Romanticism and culture as hegemony and symbolic struggle as the two traditions that have sought to detach cultural studies from policy studies. For the Romantics the aim has been to warn of the dangers suffered by culture once it becomes regulated by the forces of money and administration. The aim here has been to stress that authentic culture always escapes utilitarian forms of calculation and that culture is valuable precisely because it is useless. Alternatively, much of contemporary cultural studies has sought to uncover complex patterns of transgression and resistance on the part of consumers of popular culture. Bennett's aim is to shift from a Marxism that is overtly concerned with the colonization of aesthetics or semiotic warfare to a social democratic analysis that seeks to make cultural studies both more practical and more relevant (Miller 1998). This means that cultural studies should give up the practice of looking at either the ways in which artistic forms of culture are being eroded or the ways in which dominant cultures are resisted from below. In its place, Bennett proposes a view of cultural studies that offers a detailed knowledge of the workings of specific institutions, policies and practices. The intellectual becomes a technician who seeks to build up an in-depth under-standing of particular cultural practices. Cultural studies are less about the promotion of an aristocratic demeanour or the celebration of populist resistance than about the devising of specific techniques and strategies in order to achieve certain ends. By this, Bennett means that if we are concerned that museums are insufficiently multicultural or that television advertising promotes gender stereotypes, we need to work out specific strategies to pursue these ends. In short, we should view culture as a form of social regulation and governance.

At this point, Bennett's argument is indebted to Foucault's late writing on the concept of governmentality. For Foucault (1991), the concept of governmentality is intended to critique mainstream liberal ideas of citizenship. Whereas liberalism is concerned with institutions, ideas of contract and rights, Foucault investigates the ways in which the population becomes managed through a variety of techniques (Procacci 2001). Traditional understandings of citizenship are concerned too much with institutions and not enough with practices. For example, we may point to the ways in which the extension of social rights has increasingly brought the population under the normative gaze of the state. Foucault (1991) extends these reflections in his writing on governmentality by insisting that there is an art to the activity of governing. Foucault (1991: 93–4) best illustrates his concerns by asking what it might mean to govern a ship:

> It means clearly to take charge of the sailors, but also of the boat and its cargo; to take care of a ship means also to reckon with winds, rocks and storms; and it consists in that activity of establishing a relation between the sailors who are to be taken care of and the ship which is to be taken care of, and the cargo which is to be brought safely to port, and all the eventualities like winds, rocks, storms and so on; this is what characterises the government of a ship.

In other words, irrespective of whether the ship has a democratic constitution, is run by a drunken captain or has been captured by an enemy vessel, it will need to be efficiently run and managed. Within modernity, Foucault argues that the ultimate aim of government is the continuing and sustained welfare of the population. Government intervention through a variety of health campaigns, the regulation of disorderly activity, the monitoring of viruses and other mechanisms that by-pass traditional ideas of politics helps to constitute good government. In applying these ideas to cultural policy, Bennett argues that new programmes of cultural maintenance need to be devised to revise and reform existing industries. Our common culture needs to be minutely planned, administered and reformed if it is to serve the needs of a democratic and multicultural society.

Bennett's arguments, viewed generously, suggest that cultural studies need to become more responsible. Intellectuals are urged to come out of their ivory towers and engage in practical forms of analysis that could have measurable effects. There is, as Bennett identifies, a need for this kind of detailed policy-orientated work if cultural studies wish to have direct effects on the shape of our television industries, museums and local arts policies. However, there remain deep dangers and considerable evasions in such a strategy. Bennett's orientations in respect of cultural studies are overly critical of a number of different traditions that continue to ask relevant questions.

Here I focus briefly upon what the study and practice of cultural policy might continue to recover from cultural Romanticism and the study of hegemony and resistance. First, Bennett is critical of those, like Adorno, who would embark upon an unashamedly elitist strategy in which self-appointed cultural guardians utilize a policy framework to preserve high culture. Bennett (1998: 199) argues that, despite the attentions of a few 'retro-aesthetes' and cultural conservatives, we can now recognize that such dispositions represent 'merely a market segment'. Cultural policy should not only unashamedly treat culture as an industry, but also help to construct a variety of frameworks where we can assess different policies in terms of the different publics they might serve. The less intellectuals seek special licence for their own disposition towards culture, the better they are able to plan a coherent cultural policy. There is obviously much here that is objecting to the elitist positions taken by critics, like Adorno, who seek to preserve their tastes against those of others. Yet my concern is that this argument can be pushed too far.

If we return to Adorno's (1991) original essay on the subject of administration and culture, he voices a set of concerns about the relationship between the practice of administration and the dynamic complexity of culture that Bennett dismisses too easily. Adorno argues that under conditions of late capitalism 'culture' exists within an ambivalent relationship to questions of administration. The paradox is that 'culture' becomes damaged when we seek to plan and administer it, but that without institutional supports it quickly becomes marginalized. Adorno (1991: 101) famously identifies 'culture' as that which goes beyond questions of utility: it is its 'impractical nature' that makes it so special. A culture that was completely administered and planned would have driven out the individual impulse, crushed creativity and become largely uncritical. What Adorno is seeking to preserve is an avant-garde disposition towards culture that protects artistic practice as a field of aesthetic creativity. Within this, Adorno correctly perceives reactionary sentiments that would seek to restrict artistic freedom in the name of a crude populist democracy. Here, I think, we need to tread carefully. Bennett is of course correct that similar arguments have been used by cultural conservatives to maintain the superiority of Western art traditions. This poorly appreciates the sheer diversity of aesthetic practices and traditions that can be perceived within modern multi-cultural contexts. However, Romantic claims like Adorno's continue to have a point, in arguing that the vitality of a culture depends largely upon the autonomy, creativity and difference of its cultural producers. The idea that we could ever totally administer a culture remains a bureaucratic fantasy that is unlikely to find many supporters outside the offices of chief administrators. To argue that the development of cultural policies requires governance is one thing, but to suggest that cultures can (or indeed should) ever be subordinate to such logics is quite another. We might continue, to say that what Bennett offers is an overly instrumental understanding of culture. Any full understanding of this most contested of terms would need to emphasize that as members of over-lapping 'cultures' we are only ever conscious of a small part of their connecting elements. Given the different levels of interpretation, partly realized experiences and different semiotic networks, we are also some way short of a 'full under-standing' of even the most impoverished cultural life. This remains poorly appreciated by Bennett's technocratic language of 'regulation', 'effects' and 'management'.

Second, we might also argue that neo-Gramscian writing on hegemony (such as that of Stuart Hall, reviewed above) usually relies upon a wider under-standing of different sets of social relations from those offered by Bennett (Nixon 2000). Bennett emphasizes the managing and governing of culture, rather than the social and cultural context such processes inevitably work within. For example, Jim McGuigan (1996) has argued that for cultural policy to remain critical it needs to be informed by wider questions of political economy, democracy and class, which will play a large role in determining the field of struggle within which cultural policy operates. The Foucauldian attempt to recapture the micro-operation of knowledge and power obscures these necessary questions. While Foucault wishes to stress the ways in which subjects are governed, his analysis is of little use if we are trying to devise the principles of a democratic cultural policy. To this end, Bennett is unable to offer much help with regard to the normative values that should guide the operation of cultural policy. In the final section, I point to some of the ways in which we might begin to answer these questions.

A 'common' cultural citizenship

Here I aim to develop a normative model of cultural citizenship, and then seek to understand how it might help us with questions of cultural policy. My aim is to develop a framework for cultural policy that seeks to deconstruct ideas of high and low culture (that is, problematizing which cultures, artefacts and experiences require governing) within a context that both preserves difference against homogeneity and promotes a strategy of equality. My argumentative strategy has these key features: postmodern to the extent to which it questions distinctions between 'high' and 'popular' culture; egalitarian in that there is still a need to promote the widest of possible conditions of access to hierarchically organized cultures; and democratic in that we need to consider how to promote constructive forms of dialogue and participation across cultural divides. The idea here is that the commodification of culture has provided cultural policy with opportunities (the flourishing of a variety of lifestyles and the aestheticization of everyday life) and dangers (enforced patterns of social and cultural exclusion). Cultural policy as cultural citizenship needs to recognize that the ground it currently operates upon is historically determined (there seems little point in returning to the benign liberalism of the inter-war period) and that it will necessarily work within certain limits determined by the wider society.

The idea of a cultural policy based upon democratic citizenship is not a new one. The writings of Raymond Williams in many respects remain a considerable resource from which we can continue to mine many useful ideas. In particular, it is the idea of common culture to which I want to return. For many this will seem like an odd choice, given the increasing power of the cultural industry and the development of identity politics bringing enhanced forms of fragmentation. Surely it is better to give up on the idea of a common culture as a homogeneous and repressive ideology that would find few takers outside a few pipe smoking cultural conservatives. Yet if this is what Williams meant by a common culture, it would hardly be an idea worth revisiting. For Williams (1989b), a common culture had several aspects, but overall it was an instituted culture of dialogue, rather than agreement. To be able to talk of a common culture did not mean the possibility of reimagining a fragmented society as one of shared values and aspirations. The *common* element of Williams's argument concerns the ordinary ability of people to contribute, criticize and reinterpret aspects of their culture. Within this process, the meanings of 'high' or indeed 'popular' culture are not fixed in stone but require open criticism by members of the community. In particular, we need to pay attention to the material conditions and ideologies that aim to exclude different voices from full participation.

The second aspect of a *common* culture is the provision of institutions that transmit the knowledge, skills and resources that allow full participation. Here Williams seems to be saying that it is the most class-bound way of thinking that seeks to connect high culture with a privileged minority. Instead, works of literature (and other aspects of the culture) need to become openly interrogated through genuinely educated forms of dialogue. This is obviously different from saying that Shakespeare is for a minority, but also stops short from blandly saying he is for everyone. Instead, Williams is arguing that a community's self-realization depends upon 'adequate participation in the process of changing and developing meanings' (Williams 1989b: 35). This is not possible without mutually recognizing that everyone can participate, and seeking to secure the material and institutional means that might sustain such participation. In other words, contrary to Bourdieu, full participation does not come by simply providing working-class children with the adequate knowledge of the appropriate repertoires of art criticism. Williams (1989b: 36) goes considerably further than this, insisting 'that the culture of a people can only be what all its members are engaged in creating in the act of living'. For Williams, educational institutions need not only to familiarize working-class students with high forms of culture, but also to allow them to develop their own arguments and perspectives, which might well stop short of traditional forms of reverence. In these terms, Williams (1989b: 37) argues that perhaps a culture in common is a better description than the misleadingly titled common culture.

Despite the democratic bent of these ideas, we might still object that the pursuit of a culture in common remains an exclusive ideal. Here I briefly consider the argument that Williams poorly appreciates the symbolic creativity of popular culture, remaining more of a cultural conservative than he might seem; and that the forms of cultural difference that are likely to exist within a multicultural society have finished attempts to construct common cultures. These are both serious objections that are worthy of more extended treatment than I have space to explore here.

It remains the case that, despite Williams's sensitivity to questions of class, his own cultural ethos was that of a literary critic, rather than a fan of popular culture. This has led many, myself included, to argue that he has a tendency to be overly dismissive of the complexity of consumer culture (Stevenson 2002). If we were looking for a complex textual analysis of popular romances or soap operas, we would probably not call on Raymond Williams. Arguably, since Williams's time cultural studies have done much to extend our appreciation of the complex negotiations that are involved in the everyday consumption of consumer goods. Paul Willis (1998) has perhaps gone the furthest in claiming that the creative meaning-making of the excluded should be respected rather than reformed by cultural institutions. Here, Willis critically contrasts a dominant high culture of traditional artistic practices with a 'common culture' creatively made from everyday consumer culture. Willis argues that, despite arguments from people like Williams who sought to democratize high culture, it remains (and is likely to do so) fundamentally detached from the cultural experiences of the vast majority of the population. Instead, a democratic and egalitarian cultural policy should seek to empower young people to produce their own cultural forms. Whereas most cultural policy remains focused upon preserving the cultural and aesthetic choices of the educated middle classes, this needs to be radically reformulated. Willis, as I noted above, argues that working-class young people formulate their cultural experiences through an explicitly commercial culture. Hence, cultural policies need to be enacted that enable ordinary forms of symbolic creativity evident within a night at the pub, reading a lifestyle magazine or listening to a rap artist. The problem is not – as cultural elitists of the right and left would argue – that young people are consuming the 'wrong culture', but that they are restricted by a lack of access to consumer culture. Here Willis advocates the setting up of 'cultural exchanges' and 'cultural clubs', where symbolic material such as videos and CDs could be swapped and musical and recording material, as well as photographic equipment, made available for common usage. The key idea being pressed by Willis is not as much intercultural dialogue as a determination to provide people excluded from 'educated' culture with autonomy as cultural producers and consumers.

The problem with such proposals, according to Jim McGuigan (1997), is that they reproduce dominant ideas of consumer sovereignty, in that the market is the best provider of cultural goods and individuals are the best choosers. Willis's contribution to policy analysis fails to take account of the power of the market to privilege certain consumers over others, and to help to shape and determine certain tastes. While there is much to this criticism, I think Willis could be read as saying that policies are needed to empower young people who might become excluded from the market, so as to give them the confidence to become producers of cultural goods in their own right. These arguments, while populist, remain important, in that they deconstruct the assumed superiority of much high culture (is ballet really superior to rap?), and potentially give some young people access to a wider range of cultural repertoires, thereby expanding cultural literacy. Most music cultures are commercial cultures, and I am likely to become experimental in respect of my tastes if I am not overly prohibited from doing so by cost. However, if we refer back to Bourdieu's concern about different forms of capital, then we could equally argue that such a strategy could well compound social exclusion. Remember, it was Bourdieu's concern that a radical cultural policy should enable working-class people to 'appreciate' high art. Willis's proposals might be criticized because he simply assumes that, for most people, visiting art galleries, listening to classical music and reading modernist literature is out of bounds. Willis actively reproduces the idea of high and popular culture as inevitably disconnected, without any bridges between them. Whereas middle-class people may choose between the 'educated' and the 'popular', working-class people are more restricted in the range of repertoires they are able to access. We should be clear that this remains a restriction from full cultural citizenship. Here again, I would return to Williams's idea of a culture in common. Williams (1958) was rightly critical of the idea that high culture belonged to the educated middle classes. However, Willis reproduces this idea by reinforcing the prejudice that the lower orders are better served by the market and the middle classes by the art gallery. Williams's radicalism remains, in that he correctly perceived that such a situation could only be addressed by social and institutional change. The guiding feature of cultural policy for Williams is the ability to be able to promote dialogue across a number of cultural divides, and not the reproduction of class-based prejudices about the cultural capacities of the excluded. As Terry Eagleton (1990) has argued, the cultural preferences of excluded and marginalized populations may become reformulated if their general social conditions are transformed. While 'culture' may indeed be formed through processes of struggle and oppression, it does not mark its producer or consumer with an 'essential' identity.

Many of Raymond Williams's critics have been concerned that the idea of a common culture effectively silences subordinate voices. Williams's politics were mainly concerned with reconnecting questions of class with a literary artistic culture, rather than focusing on ethnicity, gender, multiculturalism and sexuality. Indeed, there is a growing literature that strongly suggests that Williams can be found wanting on most of these topics and concerns (Milner 2002). We might argue that the point is not to build a common culture, but to work out ways of empowering marginalized positions within the policy arena. However, Bhikhu Parekh (2000) has argued that a multicultural society needs a shared common culture fashioned out of diversity. In a multicultural society diverse cultures constantly encounter one another and change due to the presence of the other. As Parekh fully recognizes, unless we are content to live in a society of cultural apartheid and fragmentation, institutional conditions must be created to foster intercultural dialogue. While a 'common culture' cannot be engineered, the opportunities for a common dialogue need to be politically created. Just as Williams argued that the 'national culture' needs to be extended and criticized by working-class voices, so Parekh argues that similar privileges need to be extended to 'minorities'.

Within this process, both Williams and Parekh highlight the centrality of cultural and educational institutions. They are both critical of monocultural institutions that aim to impose a collective conformist culture. Yet for Williams the purpose of education was to provide citizens with the intellectual resources and self-confidence necessary for full cultural participation. This remains a pressing question in a society that has seen illiteracy rates rise in areas of high social exclusion. To achieve a common culture, citizens require basic skills so that they are able to write a letter to a newspaper, discriminate between different viewpoints and understand different kinds of artistic work. For Williams, these agendas were blocked by capitalism and cultural snobbery. Arguably, if basic literacy rates have fallen it is because society no longer requires their participation as workers, and the prejudice against people from poor class backgrounds remains as intense as ever. Alternatively, Parekh places emphasis upon the need to develop a genuinely multicultural system of education that aims to criticize the Eurocentric understandings that pervade the educational curriculum. A good education needs to be able to break with specifically 'national' and 'European' understandings of history, the arts and sciences, while building the experience of minorities into the common narrative of the community. Inspired by different questions, both Williams and Parekh place their faith in a common cosmopolitan dialogue in which new voices and experiences are brought into the centre of society's dominant self-understandings. The idea that questions of cultural policy have much to contribute in this regard is a position that they would both seek to endorse, while recognizing that such aims are restricted by wider questions of money and power.

Conclusion

We have seen that the attempt to promote a 'common' cultural citizenship in the context of consumer and public culture has provoked a number of complex questions. The attempt to foster more egalitarian and participatory cultures has to guard against not only the exclusionary logic of neo-liberalism, but also populist concerns that neglect the need to promote complex forms of cultural literacy. Citizenship strategies that aim for cultural equality need to avoid approaches that either reproduce the assumed superiority of traditional aesthetic pursuits or fail to provide the conditions for diverse forms of cultural respect. Similarly, attempts to encourage cultural difference and diversity will need to be careful not to foster autonomy at the expense of dialogue, but equally to resist the temptation to administer homogeneity. We also saw that, in the context of a pervasive consumer culture, we require new republican institutions that will enable citizens to resume identities other than that of the consumer. Yet we need to be careful in this context not merely to reproduce prejudices about other people's pleasures. We need to remind ourselves that we are never purely one thing, while seeking to promote a culture of dialogue and discernment, rather than agreement. If we can do this, we might develop a cultural citizenship genuinely alive to some of the central questions of our age.

Further reading

Bauman, Z. (1999) *In Search of Politics*. Cambridge: Polity Press.
Bennett, T. (1998) *Culture: A Reformer's Science*. London: Sage.
Bourdieu, P. and Darbel, A. (1991) *The Love of Art*. Cambridge: Polity Press.
Klein, N. (2000) *No Logo*. London: Flamingo.
Williams, R. (1965) *The Long Revolution*. Harmondsworth: Penguin.
Willis, P. (1990) *Common Culture: Symbolic Work at Play in the Everyday Cultures of the Young*. Milton Keynes: Open University Press.

CULTURAL CITIZENSHIP: A SHORT AGENDA FOR THE FUTURE

Cultural citizenship, as we have seen, is the contested desire to foster a communicative society. This, as I have repeatedly observed, can only be achieved by situating the normative questions of justice and difference within a rapidly changing global and information-based society. The need to create and revive a radical model of the public sphere has been at the heart of our concerns. More sustained opportunities to dialogue with one another at local, national and global levels can only be created through the simultaneous promotion of new institutions, opportunities to participate and a renewed emphasis upon dialogue. However, these ideals need to be promoted in full recognition that not everyone in a mediated culture will get their voice heard – the inevitability of exclusion – and that it is not possible to respond to every viewpoint within a global society. Cultural dimensions of citizenship should make us aware of the necessity of seeking to exclude 'ugly' citizens, but also of constantly reviewing these processes should we seek to nomalize the least powerful.

Perhaps the central question of an age that refuses central questions will become how to balance pleasure and responsibility in a cosmopolitan framework. We have seen how environmental degradation, economic globalization, ethnocentrism, consumerism, the mediated politics of human rights, the borders between technology, animals and humans, and social exclusion all ultimately pose questions of responsibility. We are currently being confronted with vexing questions as to how deep and how wide our responsibilities should reach. Citizenship-type questions include the well-being of our own and different species, future generations, and people and organisms that live in the far corners of our planet. Yet the alluring pleasures of contemporary lifestyles, modern cities, visual cultures and present levels of consumption often mean that such questions are difficult to face. Indeed, how pleasure (rather than duty) might be put back into citizenship is an issue for the future.

This question becomes evident if we consider individualization. Let me repeat: individualization can cut two ways. First, there is the individualization that delivers political freedom and autonomy, detaching subjectivities and horizons from exclusively national concerns. Cosmopolitan individualization asks how we might live more responsibly and what this means within a global context. It also asks how we might realize ourselves as human beings by living in a way that is true to ourselves. In a 'cultural society' this might mean living more creatively or seeking to develop our capacities in ways that become detached from the remorseless logic of more, bigger and better. Second, there is a form of individualization that is promoted by the market. This is not necessarily a culture of unbridled hedonism, but nevertheless views the good life through the purchase of consumer goods. The symbolic goods offered by the market are important sources of meaning and identity within modern societies and are often dismissed as ephemeral pleasures. Yet one of the key questions cultural citizenship needs to grapple with is how we might live both sustainably and pleasurably. That we have, as far as possible, to avoid opposing these terms should not detract us from acknowledging that they will inevitably come into conflict. There is a form of individualization that becomes defined by the neo-liberal argument that the market knows best. This can be viewed within contemporary lifestyles, where we value flexibility, 'individual' responsibility and the ability to choose above all else.

The reconnecting of individualization and the common questions of citizenship is not a task that will be undertaken easily. This, of course, does not mean that we should not try. The reconciliation of justice and difference, more complex understandings of culture and different kinds of normalization and social exclusion are all necessary within this venture. Bridging the ideological gap between the needs of the individual and that of the wider community requires a normative account of citizenship that links the personal with the public. The development of communicative institutions requires openness to new narratives and complex feelings, along with the emotional capacity to be able to live with the 'other'. Cultural citizenship aims to promote conversation where previously there was silence, suspicion, fragmentation or the voices of the powerful. We need to go beyond liberal demands for tolerance and instead edge towards more intercultural levels of communication. This requires us to become alive to the particularity of liberalism, our own personal identities and strategies that seek to normalize political viewpoints. Cultural citizenship can only promote dialogue in conditions where we have begun to realize the cultural complexity of different positions and viewpoints. This requires not only that we empower 'minorities' within public conversations, but that we also seek to understand the social processes that have historically promoted some views over others. The recovery of the 'other' and wider questions of justice remain essential to inclusive forms of citizenship. The key word here is respect, not tolerance. To repect the 'other' supposes a level of engagement that goes beyond mutual indifference. To recognize, dialogue with and welcome the 'other' entails human engagements beyond the cold exchange of reasons. Further, sensitivity towards those who are unable to participate directly (animals, plants, globally distant others, future generations etc.) but who are likely to be affected also needs to be taken into account. This remains a tall order. Indeed, it is likely to remain a considerable challenge to those citizens who are exclusively concerned with their own rights. Within such a society, the citizen would need to leave space for interpretative conflict, indecision, disagreement and contested understandings in ways that are poorly appreciated by liberalism's ideal of 'reasonable pluralism'.

This cannot be achieved without renewed attempts to foster active forms of identification with the values and virtues of citizenship involvement. Republican sentiments suitable for a global age would need to become part of a common education for citizenship. This would inevitably include the responsibilities of jury service, an awareness of global issues and problems, an understanding of intercultural questions, a broad appreciation of political institutions and a recognition of the power of the media of mass communication, among others. Further, this book has argued at length that a renewed stress upon 'culture' is central to these dimensions. Citizens need to become attuned to competing discourses and narratives that shape our understandings, from masculinity to the environment and from health to the politics of sexuality and race. In an age dominated by popular forms of culture, we need to find new ways of joining a politics of culture to cultural forms of politics.

Cultural citizenship is a politics of 'educated' dialogue, contested forms of understanding, respect and democratic public space. Arguably, many current social movements, from the anti-globalization protestors to proponents of multiculturalism, have the deepening and widening of democracy as one of their central aims. We need to be clear that there is no 'system' to overthrow and no revolutionary strategy adequate to these aims. The politics of cultural citizenship is more concerned with the generation of dialogue and the promotion of responsibility than with slogans. Yet, within a world dominated by neo-liberalism and a shrinking state, cultural citizenship remains utopian. The prospect of building new democratic and cultural engagements out of everyday life remains far removed from many of the 'realities' outlined in this book.

It is estimated that one billion people survive on less than a dollar a day, the Earth is threatened by extinction and 19,000 children die each day in the 'Third World', while US$1.5 trillion is moved around the world in currency speculation. It is only by developing more cosmopolitan dimensions of citizenship that we can even begin to address these questions. The growing demand that sociology, cultural studies and political theory investigate questions of ecology, globalization, animal rights, postmodern culture, transnational media organizations, masculinity, hetrosexism and racism, among other aspects, might seem small fry. Yet we have to start somewhere. My argument has been for sociologists and cultural theorists to become more concerned with normative questions, for cultural studies to seek a closer engagement with liberal agendas and for political theory to seek a more complex understanding of culture and identity. Such demands are unlikely to be popular with everyone working within these disciplines. However, I think there is much to be gained in more extended interdisciplinary dialogue and study. In the uncertain and less than radical times in which we live it is towards genuinely responsible, respectful and pleasurable forms of dialogue that this book has sought to move the reader.

GLOSSARY

Agency: the ability to be able to act within a social and cultural context while making a difference to the flow of events. Agency should not be thought of as the opposite of structure, but as dependent upon rules and resources generated by social structures. To have agency is defined by the ability to be able to intervene actively.

Citizenship: describes the common rights, responsibilities and symbols of membership that define the political community. Can also include practices of deliberation and public engagement that are drawn upon in deciding matters of public importance.

Citizens' jury: an assembly of ordinary citizens, experts and (sometimes) professional politicians who are called to give evidence and deliberate upon a specific concern, the results of which are usually made publicly available and fed into the policy process.

Civil society: usually refers to an intermediate zone between private life and the state, where relatively independent organizations are able to operate and circulate information relatively autonomously. This term is usually thought to offer a different understanding of culture and media from one that refers to control by the state or the market.

Commodification: refers to the extent to which media messages, symbolic goods and cultures have become products to be bought and sold on the market.

Cosmopolitanism: meaning the viewpoint of a citizen of the world. Can also refer to a set of perspectives that have sought to jettison viewpoints that are solely determined by the nation, or their geographical standing within the world. A cosmopolitan viewpoint would need to investigate carefully whether or not it was reaffirming prejudice towards the West or Western nations. Further, we can associate cosmopolitanism with the need to deconstruct boundaries and categories.

Culture: there are many different definitions of this term. It has been used to indicate the spread of civilized ideas and beliefs. This usage is no longer acceptable. Here it is used more neutrally to describe the symbols, meanings and practices that can be associated with living within a media-dominated society.

Cyborg: an organism, either in reality or within the imagination, that calls into question the boundaries between humans, animals and technology.

Difference: not to be confused with diversity. Ideas of difference refer not only to the multiplication of culture(s) but to the fact that they need to be performed, translated and interpreted in relations of power. The idea that cultures are more often the result of intermixing, dominance and complexity than of homogeneous purity.

Discourse: particular ways of talking, writing and thinking that can be organized into identifiable patterns of usage across time and space. Whether we are analysing a news broadcast or chat show we might be able to identify a number of different codes or ways of speaking that are more prevalent than others.

Globalization: describes a process in which the world's financial markets, political systems and cultural dimensions form increasingly intense relationships. There are a number of different consequences that may result from such processes. Some commentators view globalization mainly negatively, as markets are increasingly controlled by a handful of large corporations, resulting in the privatization of public space and the commodification of the public sphere. Others are less pessimistic, seeing the possible emergence of a new politics that aims for a more responsible world society based upon communication rather than domination.

Hegemony: implies a view that domination in society depends upon the winning of the active consent of the people. The mass media in this view either conceal or marginalize critical voices in order to reaffirm the status quo. However, within most accounts hegemony is always in process and employs military metaphors such as 'strategy' or 'war of position', implying the possibility of challenge and change.

Hybridity: a process whereby new cultural forms and identities come into being by combining different cultural elements. This term can be linked to globalization (the increasing movement of peoples and cultures) and/or media technological implosion, in which different technological elements combine to produce new hardware.

Identity: not something that is either natural or fixed, but something that evolves within a cultural context. Usually depends upon ideas of personal selfhood and other characteristics, including class, sex and gender, race and nation.

Individualization: the breakdown of tradition within modern society has meant that individuals have more consciously to plan their life strategies. The partial breakup of class cultures, fixed gender and sexual norms has meant that 'individuals' no longer live their lives as fate.

Information society: the argument that we have entered into a society different from that which came into being during the industrial revolution. Here information and knowledge become the key resources in determining economic success or failure. Further, such developments are also connected to the growth of the service sector and the enhanced role of culture in questions of social exclusion.

Internet: the worldwide system of computer-based interactive networks that support the growth in web pages, e-mail, interactive forms of communication and economic activity.

Liberalism: a political philosophy that emphasizes the capacity of individuals to make autonomous and informed decisions.

Marxism: a social theory that argues that the major ills of modern society can be attributed to its capitalist nature.

Neo-liberalism: a political viewpoint and social practice that places the needs of the market before other considerations.

'Other': a set of social and cultural characteristics that 'society' considers to be abnormal or undesirable and that has been partially excluded.

Mass culture: the idea that the increased bureaucratic and capitalist control over culture is producing a world of sameness, alienating technology, efficiency and commodification.

Multiculturalism: a social theory that seeks to understand how different cultures might best live together.

Network: a set of interconnected points within a circuit, which may involve actors (human, animals, technology) or organizations.

Omniopolis: the view that new media have not opened up a diversity of new realities, but led to a reduction in the field of vision. The media, in this respect, have imposed upon us a culture of speed and immediacy that has blunted the human senses.

Postmodernism: the ideas that features that were associated with modern society have come to an end. Currently, postmodern societies are witnessing the intermixing of the popular and educated forms of culture, the end of ideology and utopias (the death of socialism) and the idea that language mirrors rather than produces reality. Some versions of postmodernism believe that this spells the end of critical politics, whereas others welcome a cultural context that is more ambivalent and less certain.

Public sphere: the existence of a social space (whether face-to-face or mediated) where matters of public importance can be discussed to determine the public interest.

Risk society: the idea that within modernity we are living in the constant shadow of catastrophe. Yet we can never be certain as to how real or imagined these threats are to the planet and ourselves.

Reflexivity: the ability to be able to revise your actions in the light of new information. The argument is often made that information societies are becoming reflexive societies. That is, as the world becomes defined through information overload rather than information scarcity, it is argued, it also becomes increasingly reflexive. This means opening up questions on nature, gender, sexuality etc. that were repressed in previous historical eras.

Time–space compression: the idea that new technologies have made it possible to go travelling without leaving home. The arrival of real-time media experiences means that we are able to view an event irrespective of our geographical location and without any noticeable time delay. Within the economy this has introduced the possibility of 'just-in-time' forms of production, and within urban contexts the 24-hour city.

BIBLIOGRAPHY

Adam, B. (1996) Re-vision: the centrality of time for an ecological social science perspective, in S. Lash, B. Szerszynski and B. Wynne (eds) *Risk, Environment and Modernity*. London: Sage.

Adam, B. (1998) *Timescapes of Modernity: The Environment and Invisible Hazards*. London: Routledge.

Adam, B. and van Loon, J. (2000) Introduction: repositioning risk; the challenge for social theory, in B. Adam, U. Beck and J. van Loon (eds) *The Risk Society and Beyond*. London: Sage.

Adorno, T. (1981) *Prisms*. Cambridge: MIT Press.

Adorno, T. (1991) Culture and administration, in *The Culture Industry: Selected Essays on Mass Culture*. London: Routledge.

Agnew, J. C. (1994) Coming up for air: consumer culture in historical perspective, in J. Brewer and R. Porter (eds) *Consumption and the World of Goods*. London: Routledge.

Albrow, M. (1996) *The Global Age: State and Society Beyond Modernity*. Cambridge: Polity Press.

Alexander, J. (1992) The binary discourse of civil society, in L. Lamont and M. Fournier (eds) *Cultivating Difference*. Chicago: University of Chicago Press.

Alexander, J. C. and Jacobs, R. N. (1998) Mass communication, ritual and civil society, in T. Liebes and J. Curran (eds) *Media, Ritual and Identity*. London: Routledge.

Anderson, B. (1983) *Imagined Communities*. London: Verso.

Ang, I. (2000) Identity blues, in P. Gilroy, L. Grossberg and A. McRobbie (eds) *Without Guarantees: In Honour of Stuart Hall*. London: Verso.

Annesley, C. (2002) Reconfiguring women's social citizenship in Germany: the right to sozialhilfe; the responsibility to work, *German Politics*, 11(1): 81–96.

Appiah, K. A. (1998) Cosmopolitan patriots, in P. Cheah and R. Robbins (eds)

Cosmopolitics: Thinking and Feeling Beyond the Nation. Minneapolis: University of Minnesota Press.

Archibugi, A. (2000) Cosmopolitan democracy, *New Left Review*, 4: 137–50.

Barber, B. (2001) How to make society civil and democracy strong, in A. Giddens (ed.) *The Global Third Way Debate*. Cambridge: Polity Press.

Barry, B. (2000) *Culture and Equality*. Cambridge: Polity Press.

Barry, B. (2001) The muddles of multiculturalism, *New Left Review*, 8: 49–71.

Baudrillard, J. (1994) *The Illusion of the End*. Cambridge: Polity Press.

Baudrillard, J. (1998) *The Consumer Society: Myths and Structures*. London: Sage.

Bauman, Z. (1993) *Postmodern Ethics*. Oxford: Blackwell.

Bauman, Z. (1995) *Life in Fragments: Essays in Postmodern Morality*. Oxford: Blackwell.

Bauman, Z. (1997) *Post-modernity and Its Discontents*. London: Polity Press.

Bauman, Z. (1998) *Work, Consumerism and the New Poor*. Buckingham: Open University Press.

Bauman, Z. (1999) *In Search of Politics*. Cambridge: Polity Press.

Bauman, Z. (2000) *Liquid Modernity*. Cambridge: Polity Press.

Bauman, Z. (2001) Consuming life, *Journal of Consumer Culture*, 1(1): 9–29.

Beck, U. (1992) *Risk Society: Towards a New Modernity*. London: Sage.

Beck, U. (1995) *Ecological Politics in the Age of Risk*. Cambridge: Polity Press.

Beck, U. (1996) World risk society as cosmopolitan society? *Theory, Culture and Society*, 13(4): 1–32.

Beck, U. (1997) *The Reinvention of Politics: Rethinking Modernity in the Global Social Order*. Cambridge: Polity Press.

Beck, U. (1998) *Democracy without Enemies*. Cambridge: Polity Press.

Beck, U. (1999) *World Risk Society*. Cambridge: Polity Press.

Beck, U. (2000) The cosmopolitan perspective: sociology of the second age of modernity, *British Journal of Sociology*, 51(1): 79–105.

Beck, U. and Beck-Gernsheim, E. (1995) *The Normal Chaos of Love*. Cambridge: Polity Press.

Beck, U., Giddens, A. and Lash, S. (1994) *Reflexive Modernization: Politics, Tradition and Aesthetics in the Modern Social Order*. Cambridge: Polity Press.

Bell, D. (1976) *The Cultural Contradiction of Capitalism*. London: Heinemann.

Bellah, R., Madsen, R., Sullivan, N., Swider, A. and Tipton, S. M. (1996) *Habits of the Heart*. Berkeley: University of California Press.

Benhabib, S. (1996) Toward a deliberative model of democratic legitimacy, in S. Benhabib (ed.) *Democracy and Difference*. Princeton, NJ: Princeton University Press.

Benhabib, S. (1999) Citizens, residents and aliens in a changing world: political membership in the global era, *Social Research*, 66(3): 709–45.

Benjamin, J. (1998) *Shadow of the Other: Intersubjectivity and Gender in Psycho-analysis*. London: Routledge.

Bennett, T. (1992) Putting policy into cultural studies, in L. Grossberg, C. Nelson and P. A. Treichler (eds) *Cultural Studies*. London: Routledge.

Bennett, T. (1998) *Culture: A Reformer's Science*. London: Sage.

Benton, T. (1993) *Natural Relations: Ecology, Animal Rights and Social Justice*. London: Routledge.

Berman, M. (1997) Justice/just us: rap and social justice in America, in A. Merrifield and E. Swyngedouw (eds) *The Urbanization of Injustice*. New York: New York University Press.

Bernaver, J. and Mahon, M. (1994) The ethics of Michel Foucault, in G. Gutting (ed.) *The Cambridge Companion to Foucault*. Cambridge: Cambridge University Press.

Bhabha, H. (1992) *The Location of Culture*. London: Routledge.

Bhabha, H. (1994) *The Location of Culture*. London: Routledge.

Bhabha, H. (1995) Are you a man or a mouse?, in M. Berger, B. Wallis and S. Watson (eds) *Constructing Masculinity*. London: Routledge.

Bianchini, F. (1993) Remaking European cities: the role of cultural policies, in F. Bianchini and M. Parkinson (eds) *Cultural Policy and Urban Regeneration: The Western European Experience*. Manchester: Manchester University Press.

Billig, M. (1992) *Banal Nationalism*. London: Sage.

Bloomfield, J. and Bianchini, F. (2001) Cultural citizenship and urban governance, in N. Stevenson (ed.) *Culture and Citizenship*. London: Sage.

Bollas, C. (1992) *Being a Character*. London: Routledge.

Bollas, C. (1999) *The Mystery of Things*. London: Routledge.

Bourdieu, P. (1984) *Distinction*. London: Routledge.

Bourdieu, P. (1986) The forms of capital, in J. G. Richardson (ed.) *Handbook of Theory and Research for the Sociology of Education*. New York: Greenwood Press.

Bourdieu, P. (1996a) *On Television*. New York: New Press.

Bourdieu, P. (1996b) *The Rules of Art: Genesis and Structure of the Literary Field*. Cambridge: Polity Press.

Bourdieu, P. and Darbel, A. (1991) *The Love of Art*. Cambridge: Polity Press.

Bryld, M. and Lykke, N. (2000) *Cosmodolphins: Feminist Cultural Studies of Technology, Animals and the Sacred*. London: Zed Books.

Buchbinder, D. (1998) *Performance Anxieties: Re-producing Masculinity*. Sydney: Allen and Unwin.

Butler, J. (1990) *Gender Trouble: Feminism and the Subversion of Identity*. London: Routledge.

Butler, J. (1993) *Bodies that Matter: On the Discursive Limits of 'Sex'*. London: Routledge.

Butler, J. (1998) Merely cultural, *New Left Review*, 227: 33–44.

Byrne, D. (1999) *Social Exclusion*. Buckingham: Open University Press.

Caldeira, T. P. R. (1999) Fortified enclaves: the new urban segregation, in J. Holston (ed.) *Cities and Citizenship*. Durham, NC: Duke University Press.

Calhoun, C. (1994) Social theory and the politics of identity, in C. Calhoun (ed.) *Social Theory and the Politics of Identity*. Oxford: Blackwell.

Campbell, C. (1987) *The Romantic Ethic and the Spirit of Modern Consumerism*. Oxford: Blackwell.

Castells, M. (1996) *The Rise of the Network Society. The Information Age: Economy, Society and Culture, Volume 1*. Oxford: Blackwell.

Castells, M. (1997) *The Power of Identity. The Information Age: Economy, Society and Culture, Volume 2*. Oxford: Blackwell.

Castells, M. (1998) *End of Millennium. The Information Age: Economy, Society and Culture, Volume 3*. Oxford: Blackwell.

Castells, M. and Hall, P. (1994) *Technopoles of the World: The Making of Twenty-first Century Industrial Complexes*. London: Routledge.

Castoriadis, C. (1997) The imaginary: creation in the social-historical domain, in *World in Fragments: Writings on Politics, Society, Psychoanalysis and the Imagination*. Stanford, CA: Stanford University Press.

Champagne, P. (1999) The view from the media, in P. Bourdieu (ed.) *The Weight of the World: Social Suffering in Contemporary Society*. Cambridge: Polity Press.

Chicago Cultural Studies Group (1994) *Critical Multiculturalism*. Chicago.

Clark, N. (1997) Panic ecology: nature in the age of superconductivity, *Theory, Culture and Society*, 14(1): 77–96.

Clark, N. (1998) Nanoplanet: molecular engineering in the time of ecological crisis, *Time and Society*, 7(2): 353–68.

Cohen, L. and Arato, A. (1992) *Civil Society and Political Theory*. Cambridge, MA: MIT Press.

Cohen, S. (2001) *States of Denial: Knowing about Atrocities and Suffering*. Cambridge: Polity Press.

Crook, R. (2000) The mediated manufacture of an avant garde: Bourdieusian analysis of the field of contemporary art in London, 1997–9, in B. Fowler (ed.) *Reading Bourdieu on Society and Culture*. London: Routledge.

Crook, S., Pakulski, J. and Waters, M. (1992) *Postmodernization: Change in Advanced Society*. London: Sage.

Dahlgren, P. (1998) Enhancing the civic ideal in television journalism, in K. Brants, J. Hermes and L. van Zoonen (eds) *The Media in Question: Popular Cultures and Public Interests*. London: Sage.

Darier, E. (1999) Foucault against environmental ethics, in E. Darier (ed.) *Discourses of the Environment*. Oxford: Blackwell.

Davis, M. (1990) *City of Quartz: Excavating the Future in Los Angeles*. London: Verso.

Devereux, E. (1996) Good causes, God's poor and telethon television, *Media, Culture and Society*, 18: 47–68.

Dobson, A. (1994) *Green Political Thought*. London: Routledge.

Dobson, A. (1998) *Justice and the Environment: Conceptions of Environmental Sustainability and Dimensions of Social Justice*. Oxford: Oxford University Press.

Donald, J. (1997) This, here, now, in S. Westwood and J. Williams (eds) *Imaging Cities*. London: Routledge.

Donald, J. (1999) *Imaging the Modern City*. London: Athlone Press.

Douglas, M. (1992) *Risk and Blame: Essays in Cultural Theory*. London: Routledge.

Eagleton, T. (1990) *The Ideology of the Aesthetic*. Oxford: Blackwell.

Eagleton, T. (2000) *The Idea of Culture*. Oxford: Blackwell.

Elliott, A. (1992) *Social Theory and Psychoanalysis in Transition*. Oxford: Blackwell.

Elliott, A. (2001) *Concepts of the Self*. Cambridge: Polity Press.

Etzioni, A. (1997) *The New Golden Rule: Community and Morality in a Democratic Society*. London: Profile Books.

Falk, R. (1995a) The world order between inter-state law and the law of humanity: the role of civil society institutions, in D. Archibugi and D. Held (eds) *Cosmopolitan Democracy*. Cambridge: Polity Press.

Falk, R. (1995b) *On Humane Governance: Towards a New Global Politics*. Cambridge: Polity Press.

Falk, R. (2000a)The decline of citizenship in an era of globalization, *Citizenship Studies*, 4(1): 5–17.

Falk, R. (2000b) *Human Rights Horizons: The Pursuit of Justice in a Globalising World*. London: Routledge.

Faulks, K. (2000) *Citizenship*. London: Routledge.

Featherstone, M. (1991) *Consumer Culture and Postmodernism*. London: Sage.

Featherstone, M. (1999) Technologies of post-human development and the potential for global citizenship, in J. N. Pieterse (ed.) *Global Futures: Shaping Globalisation*. London: Zed Books.

Fiske, J. (1989) *Understanding Popular Culture*. London: Unwin Hyman.

Foucault, M. (1981) The *History of Sexuality: An Introduction*. London, Pelican.

Foucault, M. (1982) Afterword: the subject and power, in H. Dreyfus and P. Rabinow (eds) *Michel Foucault: Beyond Structuration and Hermeneutics*. Hemel Hempstead: Harvester Wheatsheaf.

Foucault, M. (1991) Governmentality, in G. Burchell, C. Gordon and P. Miller (eds) *The Foucault Effect*. London: Harvester Wheatsheaf.

Foucault, M. (1997) *Ethics, Subjectivity and Truth, Volume 1* (ed. P. Rabinow). London: Penguin.

Fowler, B. (1997) *Pierre Bourdieu and Cultural Theory: Critical Investigations*. London: Sage.

Franklin, S. (2000) Life itself: global nature and the genetic imaginary, in S. Franklin, C. Lury and J. Stacey (eds) *Global Nature, Global Culture*. London: Sage.

Fraser, N. (1995) False antitheses: a response to Seyla Benhabib and Judith Butler, in S. Benhabib, J. Butler, D. Cornell and N. Fraser (eds) *Feminist Contentions: A Philosophical Exchange*. London: Routledge.

Fraser, N. (1997) *Justice Interruptus*. London: Routledge.

Friedman, J. (1997) Global crises, the struggle for cultural identity and intellectual porkbarrelling: cosmopolitans versus the locals in an era of de-hegemonisation, in P. Werbner and T. Modood (eds) *Debating Cultural Hybridity*. London: Zed Books.

Frith, S. (1993) Popular music and the local state, in T. Bennett (ed.) *Rock and Popular Music: Politics, Policies, Institutions*. London: Routledge.

Frosch, S. (2000) Postmodernism and the adoption of identity, in A. Elliott and C. Spezzano (eds) *Psychoanalysis at Its Limits: Navigating the Postmodern Turn*. London: Free Association Books.

Frosch, S. (2001) Psychoanalysis, identity and citizenship, in N. Stevenson (ed.) *Culture and Citizenship*. London: Sage.

Fukuyama, F. (1989) *The End of History and the Last Man*. London: Hamish Hamilton.

Gadamer, H. (1996) *The Enigma of Health*. Cambridge: Polity Press.

Garnham, N. (1992) The media and the public sphere, in C. Calhoun (ed.) *Habermas and the Public Sphere*. Cambridge, MA: Massachussets Institute of Technology.

Gates, H. L. (1994) Goodbye, Columbus? Notes on the culture of criticism, in D. T. Goldberg (ed.) *MultiCulturalism: A Critical Reader*. Oxford: Blackwell.

Giddens, A. (1990) *The Consequences of Modernity*. Cambridge: Polity Press.

Giddens, A. (1991) *Modernity and Self Identity*. Cambridge: Polity Press.

Giddens, A. (1992) *The Transformation of Intimacy*. Cambridge: Polity Press.

Giddens, A. (1994) *Beyond Left and Right: The Future of Radical Politics*. Cambridge: Polity Press.

Giddens, A. (1999) *Runaway World: How Globalisation is Reshaping Our Lives*. London: Profile Books.

Gillespie, M. (2000) Transnational communications and diaspora communities, in S. Cottle (ed.) *Ethnic Minorities and the Media*. Buckingham: Open University Press.

Gilroy, P. (1993) *The Black Atlantic: Modernity and Double Consciousness*. London: Verso.

Gilroy, P. (2000) *Between Camps*. London: Penguin.

Giroux, H. (1992) *Border Crossings: Cultural Workers and the Politics of Education*. London: Routledge.

Giroux, H. (1994) Insurgent multiculturalism and the promise of pedagogy, in D. T. Goldberg (ed.) *MultiCulturalism: A Critical Reader*. Oxford: Blackwell.

Giroux, H. (1997) *Channel Surfing: Racism, the Media and the Destruction of Today's Youth*. London: Macmillan.

Giroux, H. (1999) *The Mouse that Roared: Disney and the End of Innocence*. Oxford: Rowman and Littlefield.

Gray, J. (2000) Wild globalisation, *Guardian*, 5 December: 23.

Griffiths, R. (1993) The politics of cultural policy in urban regeneration stategies, *Policy and Politics*, 21(1): 39–47.

Gross, L. (1995) Larry Gross talks with *Safe*'s Todd Haynes, *Filmmaker Magazine*, 3(4) (http://people.we.mediaone.net/rogerdeforest/haynes/text/haynin1.htm).

Grossberg, L. (1992) Is there a fan in the house? The affective sensibility of fandom, in L. Lewis (ed.) *Adoring Audience*. London: Routledge.

Habermas, J. (1979) *Communication and the Evolution of Society*. London: Heinemann.

Habermas, J. (1981) New social movements, *Telos*, 47: 33–7.

Habermas, J. (1989) *The Structural Transformation of the Public Sphere*. Cambridge: Polity Press.

Habermas, J. (1990) *Justification and Application: Remarks on Discourse Ethics*. Cambridge: Polity Press.

Habermas, J. (1993) *Moral Consciousness and Communicative Action*. Cambridge: Polity Press.

Habermas, J. (1994) Citizenship and national identity, in B. V. Steenbergen (ed.) *The Condition of Citizenship*. London: Sage.

Habermas, J. (1995) Reconciliation through the public use of reason: remarks on John Rawls's political liberalism, *Journal of Philsophy*, 92(3): 109–31.

Habermas, J. (1996) *Between Facts and Norms*. Cambridge: Polity Press.

Habermas, J. (1997) Kant's idea of perpetual peace, with the benefit of two hundred years' hindsight, in J. Bohmann and M. Lutz-Bachmann (eds) *Perpetual Peace: Essays on Kant's Cosmopolitan Ideal*. Cambridge, MA: MIT Press.

Habermas, J. (2001) *The Postnational Constellation: Political Essays* (trans. and ed. M. Pensky). Cambridge: Polity Press.

Hall, S. (1988) *The Hard Road to Renewal*. London: Verso.

Hall, S. (1992) Cultural identity and diaspora, in J. Rutherford (ed.) *Identity: Community, Culture, Difference*. London: Lawrence and Wishart.

Hall, S. (1996) Introduction: who needs identity?, in S. Hall and P. du Gay (eds) *Questions of Cultural Identity*. London: Sage.

Hall, S. (ed.) (1997) *Representation: Cultural Representation and Signifying Practices*. London: Sage.

Halliday, F. (1983) *The Making of the Second Cold War*. London: Verso.

Hallin, D. (1994) *We Keep America on Top of the World*. London: Routledge.

Halpern, D. (1995) *Saint Foucault: Towards a Gay Hagiography*. Oxford: Oxford University Press.

Hamelink, C. (1994) *The Politics of World Communication: A Human Rights Perspective*. London: Sage.

Hamelink, C. (1995) *World Communication: Disempowerment and Self-empowerment*. London: Zed Books.

Hannerz, U. (1992) *Cultural Complexity: Studies in the Social Organization of Meaning*. New York: Columbia University.

Hannerz, U. (1996) *Transnational Connections*. London: Routledge.

Hannerz, U. (1999) Reflections on varieties of culturespeak, *European Journal of Cultural Studies*, 2(3): 393–407.

Haraway, D. (1991) *Simians, Cyborgs, and Women: The Reinvention of Nature*. London: Free Association Books.

Haraway, D. (1997) *Modest Witness@Second Millennium. FemaleMan Meets OncoMouse*. London: Routledge.

Haraway, D. (2000) *How Like a Leaf: An Interview with Thyrza Nichols Goodeve*. London: Routledge.

Harvey, D. (1989) *The Condition of Postmodernity*. Oxford: Blackwell.

Hayward, T. (1994) *Ecological Thought: An Introduction*. Cambridge: Polity Press.

Held, D. (1995a) *Democracy and the Global Order: From the Modern State to Cosmopolitan Governance*. Cambridge: Polity Press.

Held, D. (1995b) Democracy and the international order, in D. Archibughi and D. Held (eds) *Cosmopolitan Democracy*. Cambridge: Polity Press.

Held, D., McGrew, A., Goldblatt, D. and Perraton, J. (eds) (1999) *Global Transformations: Politics, Economics and Culture*. Cambridge: Polity Press.

Herman, E. S. and McChesney, R. W. (1997) *The Global Media: The New Missionaries of Global Capitalism*. London: Cassell.

Hermes, J. (1997) Gender and media studies: no woman, no cry, in J. Corner, P. Schelisinger and R. Silverstone (eds) *International Media Research*. London: Routledge.

Hermes, J. (1998) Cultural citizenship, in K. Brants, J. Hermes and L. van Zoonen (eds) *The Media in Question: Popular Cultures and Public Interests*. London: Sage.

Hoggart, R. (1995) *The Way We Live Now*. London: Pimlico.

Holston, J. and Appadurai, A. (1999) Introduction: cities and citizenship, in J. Holston (ed.) *Cities and Citizenship*. Durham, NC: Duke University Press.

Honneth, A. (1995) *The Struggle for Recognition: The Moral Grammar of Social Conflicts*. Cambridge: Polity Press.

Honneth, A. (1997) Is universalism a moral trap? The presuppositions of a politics of human rights, in J. Bohmann and M. Lutz-Bachmann (eds) *Perpetual Peace: Essays on Kant's Cosmopolitan Ideal*. Cambridge, MA: MIT Press.

Ignatief, M. (1990) *The Milner Gray Lecture*. London: Chartered Society of Designers.

Ignatief, M. (2001) *Human Rights as Politics and Idolatry*. Princeton, NJ: Princeton University Press.

Irigaray, L. (2000) *Democracy Begins between Two*. London: Athlone Press.

Isin, E. F. (2002) *Being Political: Genealogies of Citizenship*. Minneapolis: University of Minnesota Press.

Isin, E. F. and Wood, P. (1999) *Citizenship and Identity*. London: Sage.

Jackson, P., Stevenson, N. and Brooks, K. (2001) *Making Sense of Men's Magazines*. Cambridge: Polity Press.

Jacobs, M. (1997) The quality of life: social goods and the politics of consumption, in M. Jacobs (ed.) *Greening the Millennium*. Oxford: Blackwell.

Julien, I. and Mercer, K. (1996) De margin and de centre, in D. Morley and K.-H. Chen (eds) *Stuart Hall: Critical Dialogue in Cultural Studies*. London. Routledge.

Jung, C. G. (1946) The fight with the shadow, in *Essays on Contemporary Events: Reflections on Nazi Germany*. London: Ark Paperbacks (1988).

Kant, I. (1970) Perpetual peace. A philosophical sketch, in H. Reiss (ed.) *Kant Political Writings*. Cambridge: Cambridge University Press.

Katz, C. (1998) Whose nature, whose culture?, in B. Braun and N. Castree (eds) *Remaking Reality: Nature at the Millennium*. London: Routledge.

Keane, J. (1989) *Democracy and Civil Society*. London: Verso.

Keane, J. (1991) *The Media and Democracy*. Cambridge: Polity Press.

Kellner, D. (1995) Intellectuals and new technologies, *Media, Culture and Society*, 17(3): 427–48.

Kenny, M. (2000) Socialism and the romantic 'self': the case of E. P. Thompson, *Journal of Political Ideologies*, 5(1): 105–27.

Klein, N. (2000) *No Logo*. London: Flamingo.

Klein, N. (2001) Reclaiming the commons, *New Left Review*, 9: 81–99.

Krisetva, J. (1992) *Strangers to Ourselves*. London: Harvester.

Kumar, K. (1993) Civil society: an inquiry into the usefulness of an historical term, *British Journal of Sociology*, 44(3): 375–95.

Kymlicka, W. (1995) *Multicultural Citizenship: A Liberal Theory of Minority Rights*. Oxford: Clarendon Press.

Kymlicka, W. and Norman, W. (1994) Return of the citizen, *Ethics*, 104: 352–81.

Laclau, E. and Mouffe, C. (1985) *Hegemony and Socialist Strategy*. London: Verso.

Lash, S. (1993) Pierre Bourdieu: cultural economy and social change, in C. Calhoun, E. LiPuma and M. Postone (eds) *Bourdieu: Critical Perspectives*. Oxford: Blackwell.

Lash, S. (1994) Reflexivity and its doubles: structure, aesthetics, community, in U. Beck, A. Giddens and S. Lash (eds) *Reflexive Modernization: Politics, Tradition and Aesthetics in the Modern Social Order*. Cambridge: Polity Press.

Lash, S. (2001) Technological forms of life, *Theory, Culture and Society*, 18(11): 105–20.

Lash, S. and Urry, J. (1994) *The Economy of Signs and Spaces*. London: Sage.

Leca, J. (1992) Questions of citizenship, in C. Mouffe (ed.) *Dimensions of Radical Democracy*. London: Verso.

Linklater, A. (1998) *The Transformation of Political Community*. Cambridge: Polity Press.

Lister, R. (1997) *Citizenship: Feminist Perspectives*. Basingstoke: Macmillan.

Lloyd, M. (1999) Performativity, parody, politics, in V. Bell (ed.) *Performativity and Belonging*. London: Sage.

Lunt, P. and Livingstone, S. (1994) *Talk on Television*. London: Routledge.

McCarthy, M. (2000) Wild flowers disappearing from the countryside, *The Independent*, 30 October.

McGuigan, J. (1996) *Culture and the Public Sphere*. London: Routledge.

McGuigan, J. (1997) Cultural populism revisited, in M. Ferguson and P. Golding (eds) *Cultural Studies in Question*. London: Sage.

McKibben, B. (1990) *The End of Nature*. London: Penguin.

McKie, R. (1999) Planet thrives on all kinds of everything, *Observer*, 13 June.

McNaughton, P. and Urry, J. (1995) Towards a sociology of nature, *Sociology*, 29(2): 203–20.

McNay, L. (1994) *Foucault: A Critical Introduction*. Cambridge: Polity Press.

Maffesoli, M. (1996) *The Time of Tribes: The Decline of Individualism in Mass Society*. London: Sage.

Marcuse, H. (1968) *Negations*. Boston: Beacon Press.

Marshall, T. H. (1992) *Citizenship and Social Class*. London: Pluto Press.

Martin-Barbero, J. (1993) *Communication, Culture and Hegemony: From the Media to Mediations*. London: Sage.

Massey, D. (1997) Space/power, identity/difference: tensions in the city, in America, in A. Merrifield and E. Swyngedouw (eds) *The Urbanization of Injustice*. New York: New York University Press.

Mattelart, A. (2001) Against global inevitability (http://www.wacc.org.uk/media/mattelart.htm).

Mead, G. H. (1934) *Mind, Self and Society: From the Standpoint of a Social Behaviourist*. Chicago: University of Chicago Press.

Melucci, A. (1985) The symbolic challenge of contemporary movements, *Social Research*, 52(4): 749–87.

Melucci, A. (1989) *Nomads of the Present: Social Movements and Individual Needs in Contemporary Culture*. London: Radius.

Melucci, A. (1996a) *The Playing Self: Person and Meaning in the Planetary Society*. Cambridge: Cambridge University Press.

Melucci, A. (1996b) *Challenging Codes: Collective Action in the Information Age*. Cambridge: Cambridge University Press.

Merchant, C. (1992) *Radical Ecology: The Search for a Liveable World*. London: Routledge.

Mestrovic, S. G. (1997) *Postemotional Society*. London: Sage.

Midgley, M. (1983) *Animals and Why They Matter*. Athens: University of Georgia Press.

Midgley, M. (1996) *Utopias, Dolphins and Computers: Problems of Philosophical Plumbing*. London: Routledge.

Miller, D. (1997) What kind of equality should the left pursue?, in J. Franklin (ed.) *Equality*. London: Institute for Public Policy.

Miller, T. (1998) *Technologies of Truth: Cultural Citizenship and the Popular Media*. Minneapolis: University of Minnesota Press.

Milner, A. (2002) *Re-Imaging Cultural Studies: The Promise of Cultural Materialism*. London: Sage.

Morley, D. (2000) *Home Territories: Media, Mobility and Identity*. London: Routledge.

Mort, F. (1989) The politics of consumption, in S. Hall and M. Jacques (eds) *New Times: The Changing Face of Politics in the 1990s*. London: Lawrence and Wishart.

Mosco, V. (1996) *The Political Economy of Communication*. London: Sage.

Mouffe, C. (1993) *The Return of the Political*. London: Verso.

Mouffe, C. (2000) *The Democratic Paradox*. London: Verso.

Mulgan, G. (1997) *Connexity: How to Live in a Connected World*. London: Chatto and Windus.

Mulgan, G. and Warpole, K. (1986) *Saturday Night or Sunday Morning: From Arts to Industry – New Forms of Cultural Policy*. London: Comedia.

Murdock, G. (1992) Citizens, consumers, and the public culture, in M. Skovmand and K. M. Schroder (eds) *Media Cultures*. London: Routledge.

Murdock, G. (1994) Money talks: broadcasting, finance and public culture, in S. Hood (ed.) *Behind the Screens: The Structure of British Television in the Nineties*. London: Lawrence and Wishart.

Murdock, G. (1999) Rights and representations: public discourse and cultural citizenship, in J. Gripsrud (ed.) *Television and Common Knowledge*. London: Routledge.

Nava, M. (1991) Consumerism reconsidered – buying and power, *Cultural Studies*, 5(2).

Newby, H. (1995) Citizenship in a green world: global commons and human stewardship, in M. Bulmer and A. M. Rees (eds) *Citizenship Today*. London: UCL Press.

Nixon, S. (2000) Intervening in popular culture: cultural politics and the art of translation, in P. Gilroy, L. Grossberg and A. McRobbie (eds) *Without Guarantees: In Honour of Stuart Hall*. London: Verso.

Norgaard, R. B. (1994) *Development Betrayed*. London: Routledge.

Nussbaum, M. C. (1996) Patriotism and cosmopolitanism, in J. Cohen (ed.) *For Love of Country*. Boston: Beacon Press.

Ogden, T. (1989) *The Primitive Edge of Experience*. London: Jason Aronson.

O'Regan, T. (2001) Cultural policy: rejuvenate or wither (professorial lecture) (http://www.gu.edu.au/centre/cmp/).

Pakulski, J. (1997) Cultural citizenship, *Citizenship Studies*, 1(1): 73–86.

Parekh, B. (1995) Liberalism and colonialism: a critique of Locke and Mill, in J. N. Pieterse and B. Parekh (eds) *The Decolonization of the Imagination: Culture, Knowledge and Power*. London: Zed Books.

Parekh, B. (2000) *Rethinking Multiculturalism: Cultural Diversity and Political Theory*. London: Macmillan.

Peters, J. D. (1999) *Speaking into the Air*. Chicago: University of Chicago Press.

Phillips, A. (1991) *Engendering Democracy*. Cambridge: Polity Press.

Pieterse, J. N. and Parekh, B. (1995) Shifting imaginaries: decolonisation, internal decolonisation, postcoloniality, in J. N. Pieterse and B. Parekh (eds) *The Decolonization of the Imagination: Culture, Knowledge and Power*. London: Zed Books.

Plummer, K. (1995) *Telling Sexual Stories: Power, Change and Social Worlds*. London: Routledge.

Plumwood, V. (1993) *Feminism and the Mastery of Nature*. London: Routledge.

Pred, A. (1998) The nature of denaturalized consumption and everyday life, in B. Braun and N. Castree (eds) *Remaking Reality: Nature at the Millennium*. London: Routledge.

Procacci, G. (2001) Governmentality and citizenship, in K. Nash and A. Scott (eds) *The Blackwell Companion to Political Sociology*. Oxford: Blackwell.

Rawls, J. (1996) *Political Liberalism*. Cambridge, MA: Harvard University Press.

Ritzer, G. (1999) *Enchanting a Disenchanted World: Revolutionizing the Means of Consumption*. London: Sage.

Robbins, B. (1998) Actually existing cosmopolitanism, in P. Pheng Cheah and B. Robbins (eds) *Cosmopolitics: Thinking and Feeling Beyound the Nation*. Minneapolis: University of Minnesota Press.

Robins, K. and Webster, F. (1999) *Times of the Technoculture: From the Information Society to the Virtual Life*. London: Routledge.

Robins, K. (1997) Cyberspace and the world we live in, in M. Featherstone and R. Burrows (eds) *Cyberspace/Cyberbodies/Cyberpunk: Cultures of Technological Embodiment*. London: Sage.

Roche, M. (1992) *Rethinking Citizenship: Welfare, Ideology and Change in Modern Society*. Cambridge: Polity Press.

Ropke, I. (1999) The dynamics of the willingness to consume, *Ecological Economics*, 28: 399–420.

Rosaldo, R. (1994) Cultural citizenship and educational democracy, *Cultural Anthropology*, 9(3): 402–11.

Rosaldo, R. (1999) Cultural citizenship, inequality and multiculturalism, in R. D. Torres,

L. F. Mirón and J. X. Inda (eds) *Race, Identity and Citizenship*. Oxford: Blackwell.

Rose, N. (2000) Governing cities, governing citizens, in E. F. Isin (ed.) *Democracy, Citizenship and the Global City*. London: Routledge.

Ross, A. (1994) *The Chicago Gangster Theory of Life: Nature's Debt to Society*. London: Verso.

Roszak, T. (1992) *The Voice of the Earth*. New York: Simon and Schuster.

Runnymede Trust (2000) *The Future of Multi-ethnic Britain: The Parekh Report*. London: Profile Books.

Rustin, M. (1991) *The Good Society and the Inner World*. London: Verso.

Rutherford, J. (ed.) (2000) *The Art of Life*. London: Routledge.

Sachs, W. (1999) *Planet Dialectics: Explorations in Environment and Development*. London: Zed Books.

Sachs, W. (2002) Fairness in a fragile world, *Resurgence*, 214: 6–9.

Said, E. (1999) *Out of Place*. London: Granta Books.

Salecl, R. (1998) *(Per)Versions of Love and Hate*. London: Verso.

Samuels, A. (1993) *The Political Psyche*. London: Routledge.

Sassen, S. (1998) *Globalization and Its Discontents*. New York: New Press.

Sandilands, C. (1999) Sex at the limits, in E. Darier (ed.) *Discourses of the Environment*. Oxford: Blackwell.

Schiller, H. (1996) *Information Inequality*. London: Routledge.

Schlesinger, P. (1991) *Media, State and Nation: Political Violence and Collective Identities*. London: Sage.

Sedgwick, E. K. (1995) Gosh, Boy George, you must be awfully secure in your masculinity, in M. Berger, B. Wallis and S. Watson (eds) *Constructing Masculinity*. London: Routledge.

Segal, L. (1999) *Why Feminism?* Cambridge: Polity Press.

Seidman, S. (1997) *Difference Troubles: Queering Social Theory and Sexual Politics*. Cambridge: Cambridge University Press.

Sennett, R. (1970) *The Uses of Disorder: Personal Identity and City Life*. London: Penguin.

Sennett, R. (1998) *The Corrosion of Character*. New York: W. W. Norton & Company.

Shattuc, J. (1996) *The Talking Cure*. London: Routledge.

Shusterman, R. M. (1992) *Pragmatist Aesthetics*. Oxford: Blackwell.

Silverstone, R. (1994) *Television and Everyday Life*. London: Routledge.

Smart, B. (1998) Foucault, Levinas and the subject of responsibility, in J. Moss (ed.) *The Later Foucault*. London: Sage.

Smith, A. D. (1995) *Nations and Nationalism in a Global Era*. Cambridge: Polity Press.

Solomos, J. (2001) Race, multiculturalism and difference, in N. Stevenson (ed.) *Culture and Citizenship*. London: Sage.

Soper, K. (1995) *What is Nature?* Oxford: Blackwell.

Soper, K. (2000) Future culture, *Radical Philosophy*, 102: 17–26.

Sparks, C. (1998) Is there a global public sphere?, in K. T. Daya (ed.) *Electronic Empires: Global Media and Local Resistance*. London: Arnold.

Sreberny, A. (1998) Feminist internationalism: imagining and building global civil society, in K. T. Daya (ed.) *Electronic Empires: Global Media and Local Resistance*. London: Arnold.

Sreberny, A. (2000) Media and diasporic consciousness: an exploration among Iranians in London, in S. Cottle (ed.) *Ethnic Minorities and the Media*. Buckingham: Open University Press.

Stallabras, J. (1996) *Gargantura: Manufactured Mass Culture*. London: Verso.

Stevenson, N. (1995) *Understanding Media Cultures: Social Theory and Mass Communication*. London: Sage.

Stevenson, N. (1999) *The Transformation of the Media: Globalisation, Morality and Ethics*. London: Longman.

Stevenson, N. (ed.) (2001) *Culture and Citizenship*. London: Sage.

Stevenson, N. (2002) *Understanding Media Cultures: Social Theory and Mass Communication*, 2nd edn. London: Sage.

Steward, F. (1991) Citizens of planet Earth, in G. Andrews (ed) *Citizenship*. London: Lawrence and Wishart.

Szerszynski, B. (1997) The varieties of ecological piety, *Worldviews: Environment, Culture, Religion*, 1: 37–55.

Taylor, C. (1992) *Multiculturalism and the Politics of Recognition*. Princeton, NJ: Princeton University Press.

Tester, K. (1991) *Animals and Society: The Humanity of Animal Rights*. London: Verso.

Tester, K. (1995) Moral solidarity and the technological reproduction of images, *Media, Culture and Society*, 17: 469–82.

Tester, K. (1997) *Moral Culture*. London: Sage.

Tester, K. (1999) The moral consequentiality of television, *European Journal of Social Theory*, 2(4): 469–83.

Tester, K. (2001) *Compassion, Morality and the Media*. Buckingham: Open University Press.

Thompson, E. P. (1982) *Zero Option*. London: Merlin Press.

Thompson, E. P. (1985) *The Heavy Dancers*. London: Merlin.

Thompson, E. P. (1990) The end of the Cold War, *New Left Review*, 182: 139–46.

Thompson, J. B. (1990) *Ideology and Modern Culture*. Cambridge: Polity Press.

Thompson, J. B. (1994) Social theory and the media, in D. Crowley and D. Mitchell (eds) *Communication Theory Today*. Cambridge: Polity Press.

Thompson, J. B. (1995) *The Media and Modernity: A Social Theory of the Media*. Cambridge: Polity Press.

Touraine, A. (2000) *Can We Live Together?* Cambridge: Polity Press.

Trainer, T. (1991) The technological fix, in A. Dobson (ed.) *The Green Reader*. London: Routledge.

Tucker, V. (1999) The myth of development: a critique of a Eurocentric discourse, in R. Munck and D. O'Hearn (eds) *Critical Development Theory*. London: Zed Books.

Turner, B. S. (1994) Postmodern culture/modern citizens, in V. B. Steenbergen (ed.) *The Condition of Citizenship*. London: Routledge.

Turner, B. S. (1997) Citizenship studies: a general theory, *Citizenship Studies*, 1(1): 5–18.

Turner, B. S. (2000) Cosmopolitan virtue: loyalty and the city, in E. F. Isin (ed.) *Democracy, Citizenship and the Global City*. London: Routledge.

Turner, B. S. and Rojek, C. (2001) *Society and Culture: Principles of Scarcity and Solidarity*. London: Sage.

Urry, J. (1995) *Consuming Places*. London: Routledge.

Urry, J. (2000a) *Sociology Beyond Societies: Mobilities for the Twenty-first Century*. London: Routledge.

Urry, J. (2000b) Global flows and global citizenship, in E. F. Isin (ed.) *Democracy, Citizenship and the Global City*. London: Routledge.

Van Dijk, J. (1999) *The Network Society*. London: Routledge.

Van Steenbergen. B. (1994) Towards an ecological citizen, in *The Condition of Citizenship*. London: Sage.

Verdery, K. (1993) Wither nation and nationalism, *Daedalus*, 122(3): 37–46.

Vidal, J. (1999) Power to the people, *Guardian*, 7 June.

Virilio, P. (1997) *Open Sky*. London: Verso.

Virilio, P. (2000a) *The Information Bomb*. London: Verso.

Virilio, P. (2000b) *Polar Inertia*. London: Sage.

Virilio, P. (2000c) *Strategy of Deception*. London: Verso.

Wacquant, L. J. D. (1999) America as social dystopia: the politics of urban dis-integration of the French uses of the American model, in P. Bourdieu (ed.) *The Weight of the World: Social Suffering in Contemporary Society*. Cambridge: Polity Press.

Waldron, J. (1999) Minority cultures and the cosmopolitan alternative, in W. Kymlicka (ed.) *Minority Cultures*. Oxford: Blackwell.

Walby, S. (1997) *Gender Transformations*. London: Routledge.

Walzer, M. (1992) The civil society argument, in C. Mouffe (ed.) *Dimensions of Radical Democracy*. London: Verso.

Warkentin, C. and Mingst, K. (2000) International institutions, the state, and global civil society in the age of the world wide web, *Global Governance*, 6: 237–57.

Warnke, G. (1993) *Justice and Interpretation*. Cambridge, MA: MIT Press.

Weber, M. (1932) *The Protestant Ethic and the Spirit of Capatalism*. London: Allen & Unwin.

Webster, F. (1995) *Theories of the Information Society*. London: Routledge.

Weymouth, A. and Lamizet, B. (eds) (1997) *Markets and Myths: Forces for Change in the European Media*. London: Longman.

Williams, R. (1958) *Culture and Society*. London: Penguin.

Williams, R. (1962) *Communications*. London: Penguin.

Williams, R. (1965) *The Long Revolution*. Harmondsworth: Penguin.

Williams, R. (1980) Problems of materialism, in *Problems in Materialism and Culture*. London: Verso.

Williams, R. (1985) *The Country and the City*. London: Hogarth Press.

Williams, R. (1989a) Culture is ordinary, in *Resources of Hope*. London: Verso.

Williams, R. (1989b) The idea of a common culture, in *Resources of Hope*. London: Verso.

Williams, R. (1989c) Socialism and ecology, in *Resources of Hope*. London: Verso.

Williams, R. H. (1982) *Dream Worlds: Mass Consumption in Late Nineteenth Century France*. Berkeley, CA: University of California Press.

Willis, P. (1990) *Common Culture: Symbolic Work at Play in the Everyday Cultures of the Young*. Milton Keynes: Open University Press.

Willis, P. (1998) Notes on common culture: towards a cultural policy for grounded aesthetics, *International Journal of Cultural Policy*, 4(2): 413–30.

Wilson, E. (1991) *The Sphinx in the City*. Los Angeles: University of California Press.

Wynne, B. (1996) May the sheep safely graze? A reflexive view of the expert–lay knowledge divide, in S. Lash, B. Szerszynski and B. Wynne (eds) *Risk, Environment and Modernity*. London: Sage.

Yearley, S. (2000) Environmental issues and the compression of the globe, in D. Held, A. McGrew, D. Goldblatt and J. Perraton (eds) *Global Transformations: Politics, Economics and Culture*. Cambridge: Polity Press.

Young, I. M. (1989) Polity and group difference: a critique of the ideal of universal citizenship, *Ethics*, 99: 250–74.

Young, I. M. (1990) The ideal of community and the politics of difference, in L. Nicholson (ed.) *Feminism/Postmodernism*. London: Routledge.

Young, I. M. (1996) Communication and the other: beyond deliberative democracy, in S. Benhabib (ed.) *Democracy and Difference*. Princeton, NJ: Princeton University Press.

Young, M. and Cullen, L. (1996) *A Good Death: Conversations with East Londoners*. London: Routledge.

Young, R. J. C. (1995) *Colonial Desire: Hybridity in Theory, Culture and Race*. London: Routledge.

Yuval-Davis, N. (1997) *Gender and Nation*. London: Sage.

Zukin, S. (1995) *The Culture of Cities*. Oxford: Blackwell.

INDEX

MEDIA, RISK AND SCIENCE

Stuart Allan

- How is science represented by the media?
- Who defines what counts as a risk, threat or hazard, and why?
- In what ways do media images of science shape public perceptions?
- What can cultural and media studies tell us about current scientific controversies?

Media, Risk and Science is an exciting exploration into an array of important issues, providing a much needed framework for understanding key debates on how the media represent science and risk. In a highly effective way, Stuart Allan weaves together insights from multiple strands of research across diverse disciplines. Among the themes he examines are: the role of science in science fiction, such as *Star Trek*; the problem of 'pseudo-science' in *The X-Files*; and how science is displayed in science museums. Science journalism receives particular attention, with the processes by which science is made 'newsworthy' unravelled for careful scrutiny. The book also includes individual chapters devoted to how the media portray environmental risks, HIV-AIDS, food scares (such as BSE or 'mad cow disease' and GM foods) and human cloning. The result is a highly topical text that will be invaluable for students and scholars in cultural and media studies, science studies, journalism, sociology and politics.

Contents

Series editor's foreword – Introduction: media, risk and science – Science fictions – Science in popular culture – Science journalism – Media, risk and the environment – Bodies at risk: news coverage of AIDS – Food scares: mad cows and GM foods – Figures of the human: robots, androids, cyborgs and clones – Glossary – References – Index.

256pp   0 335 20662 X (Paperback)   0 335 20663 8 (Hardback)

openup

ideas and understanding
in social science

www.**openup**.co.uk

 **Browse, search and order online**

 **Download detailed title information and sample chapters***

*for selected titles

www.**openup**.co.uk